100 THINGS
76ers FANS
SHOULD KNOW & DO
BEFORE THEY DIE

Gordon Jones and Eric Stark

TRIUMPH
B O O K S

Library of Congress Cataloging-in-Publication Data

Jones, Gordon, 1957–
    100 things 76ers fans should know & do before they die / Gordon Jones and Eric Stark.
        pages cm
    ISBN 978-1-60078-825-3
    1. Philadelphia 76ers (Basketball team)—Miscellanea. I. Stark, Eric, 1972– II. Title. III. Title: One hundred things Seventy-sixers fans should know and do before they die.
    GV885.52.P45J65 2014
    796.323'640974811—dc23
                                          2014020079

This book is available in quantity at special discounts for your group or organization. For further information, contact:
    Triumph Books LLC
    814 North Franklin Street
    Chicago, Illinois 60610
    (312) 337-0747
    www.triumphbooks.com

Printed in U.S.A.
ISBN: 978-1-60078-825-3
Design by Patricia Frey
Photos courtesy of AP Images unless otherwise indicated

To the late Phil Jasner. A giant.
—Gordon Jones

To my proofreader and wife, Cindy, and son, Jesse.
Also, to Chad Hurst, whose father, Paul, took me to
my first Sixers training camp when I was 10 years old.
That's when the love/hate relationship began.
—Eric Stark

Contents

Foreword

My last act as general manager of the Philadelphia 76ers was to ask the Cleveland Cavaliers for $800,000.

It was June 16, 1986. We held the first pick in the NBA Draft, but for various reasons had decided to part not only with that but with center Moses Malone, the driving force behind our championship run just three years earlier.

After much discussion two separate deals were struck: Moses to the Washington Bullets for Jeff Ruland and Cliff Robinson, and the No. 1 choice to the Cavaliers for forward Roy Hinson. Our owner, Harold Katz, wanted something more out of the latter deal, so I dialed Ed Gregory, a scout who served as our contact since the Cavs didn't have a general manager at that moment, and asked for $800,000.

When I told Harold that news, his response was priceless: "Why didn't you get a million?"

It would be a fateful day in Sixers history, as injuries prevented Hinson, Ruland, and Robinson from having much impact in Philadelphia, while the Cavaliers used the top choice on North Carolina center Brad Daugherty, who was an effective player for the next eight years.

The following day I flew to Orlando, having previously decided to join in that city's effort to lure an NBA expansion franchise—an endeavor that led to the birth of the Magic in 1989—leaving behind nearly a million memories from my 13 years as GM in Philadelphia.

Many of them are recounted in this book, as are those of many others. In these pages authors Gordie Jones and Eric Stark write about the following:

- The depths of despair the Sixers reached in 1972–73, when they went 9–73; the soaring heights we reached in 1982–83; and all the frustrating in-betweens.

- The stars who have worn a Sixers uniform over the years, including Dolph Schayes, Wilt Chamberlain, Julius Erving, Moses Malone, Billy Cunningham, Charles Barkley, and Allen Iverson.
- The coaches, such as Billy and Alex Hannum, who both won championships, and Larry Brown, who came close.
- The special moments, like Wilt's 100-point game, Dr. J's levitation in the 1980 Finals, and Allen Iverson's crossover against Michael Jordan.
- The unique personalities, including Darryl Dawkins, World B. Free, and (at the other extreme) Bobby Jones.

It's all here. And I was blessed to be part of so much of it, having spent a year as the team's business manager in 1968–69, then returning in 1974 to serve as general manager.

I was born in Philadelphia in 1940, and grew up in Wilmington, Delaware. Later I was a minor league catcher in the Phillies system, though a scout named Wes Livengood was prescient when he wrote this about me then: "Has a bright future in a front office."

I started out as the business manager of the Miami Marlins, then a minor league club, and later became the GM for the Spartanburg Phillies. One day in 1968 I had a message to call Jack Ramsay, then the Sixers' general manager. When I reached him, he told me he planned to get back into coaching, and asked if I would be interested in taking on a front-office role with the team.

I was. So began a new chapter in my life, one that would ultimately leave me with a million memories. You can read about them here.

—Pat Williams
Orlando, Florida
March 10, 2014

1 Fo', Five, Fo'

Engraved on one side of the 76ers' 1982–83 championship rings are the words "Fo', Five, Fo'," an unwieldy (yet historically accurate) variation on Moses Malone's pre-playoff prediction of three four-game sweeps.

With memories dimmed by the passage of time, there is some dispute about exactly when and where the Sixers center uttered those truncated words. Some even question whether he said them at all. "My vote is, if he didn't, he should have," retired *Philadelphia Inquirer* columnist Bill Lyon once said.

But Malone insisted he did, and several reporters confirmed as much. It was never intended to be a battle cry or bold prediction, but the team almost made good on his claim, sandwiching sweeps of the Knicks and Lakers around a five-game defeat of Milwaukee in the Eastern Conference finals.

"We had played so many games during the regular season, and I just felt, why play 21 more in the playoffs?" Malone said. "Just win 12 more and go home to rest up for the next year. I spoke to a group of writers, and I was serious. It was no joke, because I felt we could go fo', fo', fo' and have a big ending."

As assistant Matty Guokas said, "It wasn't brash. It was just his way of saying, 'We won 60. If we do what we normally do, we should go right through it.'"

"He said it in a very matter-of-fact way—no big deal in his tone of voice or speaking style," said Roy S. Johnson, who then worked for the *New York Times*. "Moses just believed it and laid it out there."

Coach Billy Cunningham nonetheless remembers Malone mouthing those words in the trainer's room of the Spectrum, raising the possibility that he said them twice. And a radio reporter named Don Henderson swears Malone made his prediction after a practice at St. Joseph's University, while strength-and-conditioning coach John Kilbourne said he did so from the driver's seat of his GMC Jimmy.

Jack McCaffery, a sportswriter then working for the *Trenton Times*, believes it happened in the Spectrum locker room on the eve of the playoffs.

"My recollection is, it was some sort of pre-playoff media event," McCaffery said. "There were a lot of people in the room at the time.... My recollection is, he said it's going to be a long process. We have to win four, then another four, then four again."

Henderson was just as sure that it happened in the same way—but at the locker room at St. Joe's. And Kilbourne's version is the most theatrical of all. He recalled a group of reporters following Malone out to the parking lot at St. Joe's, when *Inquirer* beat writer George Shirk asked Moses how he thought the playoffs would go.

Malone, who by this point was behind the wheel of his Jimmy, rolled down the driver's side window, spouted, "Fo', fo', fo'," rolled the window back up, and drove off.

Shirk, who was also there, did not recall that exchange.

Billy Cunningham is just as insistent about the trainer's room scenario. And Phil Jasner, the late *Daily News* beat writer, recalled Cunningham's bemused expression as he emerged from the room wondering what Malone might have meant.

Whatever the case, the impact of Moses' words was widespread. The Lakers' Michael Cooper said he hated the fact that Malone made such a bold prediction. Others, like Milwaukee's Paul Pressey, secretly admired it. "Just like Muhammad Ali, Moses put it right out there in everyone's face," Pressey said, "and almost backed it up."

But it wasn't intended to be anything other than a statement of fact. "Moses wasn't real cocky," said Bobby Jones, the team's sixth man. "He was telling you what he thought. Moses was never one to exaggerate or blow things out of proportion."

The statement nonetheless took on a life of its own. "It turned into Babe Ruth pointing into the bleachers and hitting a home run there," forward Marc Iavaroni said.

Julius Erving

Former 76ers general manager Pat Williams is a gifted storyteller, having written dozens of books and, in his guise as motivational speaker, given hundreds of speeches. And one of his favorite tales is about when Julius Erving came to town.

Erving had already become a legend in the old American Basketball Association, yet it was a league that operated far below the radar. TV coverage was rare. Crowds were sparse. Much of what was known about the league was passed along through word of mouth, and so it was with Erving. Could the man known as Dr. J really fly as high and score as creatively as rumored? Why, yes. Yes, he could.

The ABA merged with the NBA in 1976, and the New York Nets, Erving's employer, had cash problems (not uncommon for an ABA team). Not only did Nets owner Roy Boe need to scrape together $3 million for his team to become one of four ABA squads to join the NBA, he was also at odds with Dr. J, who claimed Boe had promised to renegotiate his contract if the two leagues ever merged.

A holdout ensued, and Williams contacted the Nets' general manager, ex-Sixer Billy Melchionni, to declare the Sixers' interest in him, should things ever deteriorate to the point that New

York might be willing to trade. Two weeks into Dr. J's holdout, Melchionni called to say it would take $3 million to pry Erving away. There was also the prospect of paying him $450,000 for each of six seasons under a renegotiated contract, no small sum in that day and age.

Williams paid a visit to the Sixers' new owner, Fitz Dixon. Dixon, who died in 2006 at age 82, was by all accounts a wonderful and generous man. Born into wealth—his mother was a Widener, a family that built a transportation empire—he nonetheless taught and coached at his alma mater, Episcopal Academy. He gave to charitable causes. And at one time or another he had a stake in all of Philadelphia's sports franchises.

But he was still learning basketball in 1976, which led to the following conversation that fateful day:

Pat: "Fitz, there is a player available from the other league. [Dramatic pause.] And his name is Julius Erving."

Fitz: "Now tell me, Pat, who is he?"

Pat: "He's kind of the Babe Ruth of basketball."

Sold.

Erving not only gave the franchise 11 seasons of spectacular play but also an identity. He was the team's focal point, leader, and primary drawing card. And he was an ambassador not only for the club but the entire sport.

Only later would the clouds emerge. Only after he was done playing would there be revelations of infidelity; he fathered professional tennis player Alexandra Stevenson in 1980 with journalist Samantha Stevenson, which led in part, years afterward, to the dissolution of his marriage. Only later would he lose a son, who appeared to be overcoming a drug-addled past, only to drown when he accidentally drove his car into a retention pond near the family's Florida home. Only later would it be revealed that he sold some $3.5 million worth of memorabilia, leading to speculation that he had financial problems (which he denied).

Eventually there would be evidence that Julius Erving wasn't everything he was thought to be. During his playing days, sportscaster Al Meltzer once said, Dr. J seemed to possess "the perfect combination of talent and poise—a once-in-a-lifetime package." He appeared "more comfortable in his own skin than any other superstar" as former *Philadelphia Daily News* columnist Ray Didinger once put it. "He took the business of being an ambassador of basketball seriously," Didinger said.

"He could walk through a crowd of 1,000 people and make everybody feel he cared about them," said Mark McNamara, who played for the Sixers in 1982–83 and again from 1987 to 1988. "It was amazing."

Williams had seen that for himself dozens of times, but never more vividly than one summer's day in Schroon Lake, New York. Erving had flown overnight from Denver to help out at a basketball camp, and despite sweltering heat he spent the entire day working with youngsters, offering encouragement and signing autographs. Williams was moved to tears upon returning to his hotel room that night.

Another time the late Phil Jasner, who for years covered the Sixers for the *Philadelphia Daily News*, watched as Erving made his way to baggage claim in the Dallas–Ft. Worth airport. Dozens of high school cheerleaders, in town for a competition, noticed him immediately and begged for his autograph. He said he would be happy to do so, but only if they agreed to perform their routines. They quickly obliged, and he sat down on a suitcase and signed for every last one of them.

He was no less gracious with the reporters who crowded around his locker every day, and remarkably cordial to those with whom he worked most closely. Consider two plane flights, years apart. The first came in 1976, shortly after he arrived in Philadelphia. Matt Guokas Jr., later a Sixers assistant coach, was just starting out as a broadcaster. His first chance to introduce himself to Dr. J came when he sat down next to him on a flight out of Kansas City, after a game in which Erving had played poorly.

Erving was paying his bills, but put his checkbook aside and settled into a conversation. He somehow remembered crossing paths with Guokas years earlier, when the Nets faced the Chicago Bulls, for whom Guokas had played. Guokas was immediately impressed with how gracious he was, "where most players would be mad."

"He acted," Guokas said, "the same way as if he'd scored 35 points. He had the ability to keep himself under control and be nice to people. That stuck with me the whole 11 years."

The other flight came in 1982. This time Erving invited rookie forward Russ Schoene to sit alongside him. And for starters he told Schoene that in some ways he reminded Doc of himself.

"That kind of blew me away," Schoene recalled. "Quite honestly, I don't remember the next five minutes of what he said. It was like, *What? How in the world could I ever remind him of himself?* It was pretty uplifting. It gave me a spring in my step."

Erving did the same for opponents. When Billy McKinney broke into the league with Kansas City in 1978, Erving went out of his way to welcome him to the league during warm-ups before a game against the Sixers. And Mark Eaton, Utah's 7'4" center, marveled at Erving's "statesmanlike demeanor."

He was, Eaton said, "the ultimate gentleman"—to a point, anyway. Once the game started, Eaton said, Dr. J would "go out and dunk on my head."

Eaton certainly wasn't alone in that regard. Erving was an All-Star every year he played in Philadelphia, an All-NBA choice seven times, and the 1980–81 MVP. But his disappointments were no less profound. The Sixers lost in the Finals in '77, '80, and '82, and after the last failure Erving found himself weeping in the locker room of the Fabulous Forum in Los Angeles, where the Lakers closed out the Sixers in Game 6.

Moses Malone arrived the following season, bringing with him the keys to the vault. The Sixers stormed to 65 regular-season victories and swept 12 of 13 playoff games, nearly fulfilling Malone's "fo', fo', fo'" prediction.

Game 4 of the 1983 Finals unfolded in storybook fashion, with the Sixers rallying from deficits of 14 at halftime and 11 after three quarters. Erving scored seven critical points in the closing minutes, including the three-point play that put his team ahead to stay with 59 seconds left and a clinching jumper over Magic Johnson moments later.

"I didn't find that shot," Erving told reporters afterward. "It found me."

Looking back, sportswriter Jack McCaffery observed, the entire team seemed to take on Erving's late-game persona for an entire season. "Late in the game, he seemed to have a different face," McCaffery said. "He went into another personality. He didn't have to say he wanted the ball; he gave a walk and a little sneer, which meant: 'Give me the ball. I'm going to find a way for us to win.'… He went from someone who was enjoying the game to almost anger. The '83 year was an entire year of that, an entire year of Doc's look."

The success didn't last. The Sixers remained a strong team the last four years Erving played for them, and he remained a viable (if diminishing) player. He retired after the 1986–87 season, and was accorded a farewell tour of the league, as well as a parade through the streets of Philadelphia.

It had been clear long before that that Pat Williams' called shot on "the Babe Ruth of basketball" had sailed well over the fence.

Wilt

His is a complicated legacy. Even now, 41 years after his retirement and some 15 years after his death, it is hard to comprehend Wilton Norman Chamberlain. One hundred points in a game? An average of 50 for an entire season? More than 31,000 points and 23,000 rebounds in 14 NBA seasons? How do you wrap your mind around all that?

And while you're trying, how do you figure the numbers at the other end of the spectrum? Just two championships? And 51 percent free-throw shooting for his career?

He was a larger-than-life figure, so often cut down to size. And still is, really. It is now universally accepted that Michael Jordan was the greatest player of all time, without discussion. (Or none, at least, until LeBron James gets a little more seasoned.) Wilt, the first of the one-name superstars, is seldom mentioned, even though he revolutionized the game, rewrote the record book, and still has his name scrawled all over it.

"Nobody loves Goliath," he once said. But that's not completely true, for despite his legion of detractors—those with short memories, and those who gleefully point out that he could take the measure of Bill Russell's vaunted Celtics just once in eight playoff meetings—he has just as many people in his corner, eager to preserve and protect his memory.

"There's only one Big Fella," Fred Carter said. "Everybody else was just tall. When it comes to basketball, Wilt was the Colossus of Rhodes."

Carter is, like Wilt, a Philadelphian, and during his eight-year career played against Chamberlain. (Carter also played for the

Sixers, notably on that 9–73 team in 1972–73, and coached the club in the '90s.)

"Wilt I swear by," Carter said. "I hear guys say that Shaq's the most dominant player to ever play, and I say, 'Father, forgive them; they know not what they say.' That's basketball blasphemy."

Carter's is a view shared by another Philadelphian, Wali Jones, one of Chamberlain's teammates on the Sixers' 1966–67 championship team. "The greatest basketball player ever is Wilt Chamberlain," Jones said in an interview for this book. "The greatest winner of all time is Bill Russell. One of the greatest players to play the game: Michael Jordan."

Jones and Wilt were close. Like any Wilt supporter, Jones puts a lot of stock in those huge numbers Chamberlain put up early in his career, with the Philadelphia / San Francisco Warriors. The 100-point game against the Knicks in March 1962, in (of all places) Hershey, Pennsylvania. The 50.4 points-per-game average, that very same year. Averages of at least 33.5 in each of his first seven years.

A Sixer for just three and a half seasons (from the middle of 1964–65 until the end of 1967–68), he was, in the words of 1966–67 teammate Billy Cunningham, "the most special player I've ever had the opportunity to be around."

"He never got the credit," Cunningham said. "He was always Goliath, even when we played. He's supposed to do that. You know, *you're over seven feet tall. Look at how strong.* People have the ability to downplay or find a way to downplay scoring 100 points in a game, or averaging whatever amount of rebounds he did, or averaging over 50 points a game. There's always a 'but' next to Wilt Chamberlain. All you need to do is open a record book."

Cunningham finds it "mind-boggling" that Chamberlain averaged 48.5 minutes a game during that 1961–62 season—that is, he averaged (because of overtimes) more minutes than there are in a regulation game. "Think about that," Cunningham said. "And he was flying coach, and we had to take the first flight out the next morning after a game. You didn't have charter planes. You didn't have all the things that are going on today for an athlete to make things a little easier and help them play at a higher level."

He amazed on an almost nightly basis, but the play that stands out to Cunningham and another member of that great 1966–67 team, Matt Guokas, is a shot by the Bullets' Gus Johnson that he blocked one night in Baltimore. Johnson was a muscular, athletic forward, a tough guy in the Charles Barkley mold. He collected a loose ball in the open court, and in Cunningham's telling only Chamberlain was back on defense. (That is also Carter's memory; he was with the Bullets at the time.) In Guokas' recollection, Wilt—once a track star at Philadelphia's Overbrook High—ran him down from behind. ("He had a good 10-yard advantage on him," Guokas said.)

Either way, Johnson rose for one of his signature windmill dunks, only to see Chamberlain deny him with such authority that Johnson was left with a dislocated shoulder. Everyone's mouths were agape, Guokas said.

It wouldn't be the last time, either. "Even though he had not won any championships [before 1966–67]—he had not been on any championship teams, let's put it that way—he was certainly a championship-caliber player," Guokas said.

Wilt's personality was as outsized as his physique. Guokas, a rookie in 1966–67, said Chamberlain could dominate a room, but that he also liked to blend in with the team, to have his share of fun. He was "a great needler, and could take it back the other way, to a degree," Guokas said. "Just incredibly well read and aware of the world around him. And if he didn't know something, he would yell loud enough that he convinced you he had the answer."

But usually he knew a great deal. Certainly he knew his stats, even as a game was going on. More than once, Guokas recalled,

Wilt would be handed a box score at halftime by the Sixers' legendary public-relations guy, Harvey Pollack, and say that he had been shorted a rebound. And Wilt would be examining this data while chowing down on a steak and apple pie—at halftime! "He had a pancreas problem," Guokas said—and indeed, Chamberlain had suffered a bout of pancreatitis a few years earlier, while playing in San Francisco. "Whatever medication and supplements he was on, his own feeling was, he had to continue to eat to deal with it. He'd eat about half a steak—you could tell it had already been chewed on pretty good—and about a half an apple pie, at halftime. From the beginning of the game to the end of the game, [he would drink] a good quart of 7-Up."

Wilt's obsession with individual accomplishments—even Wali Jones admitted he was "particular" about them—has helped fuel his detractors. If he had been a little less focused on such matters, the argument goes, his teams would have been more successful. And indeed it is true that the two seasons he was asked to scale back his scoring—1966–67 and 1971–72 (while with the Lakers)—his teams not only won titles but boasted two of the best records of all time—68–13 and 69–13, respectively.

The only compelling counterargument (though one frequently refuted) is that Chamberlain usually did not have as strong a supporting cast as Russell, his primary antagonist and winner of 11 titles. That made it that much sweeter when Chamberlain did finally scale the summit.

"To have a championship come to Philadelphia for Wilt—I really wanted that thing off his shoulders," Jones said. "I was really young [in only his third season], but I didn't realize how he wanted it so bad.... I wanted to win—not only for myself, but I wanted to win for him, because they said he was never a winner, because of Bill Russell."

Wilt would not win another in Philadelphia, nor any other before Russell retired. And if that failure remains a big part of his legacy, his supporters have tried to paint a fuller, more forgiving picture of the man.

In 2004 a three-ton, 18-foot-tall statue of Wilt was unveiled outside the Sixers' home arena, one that shows him swooping to the basket, but also stooping to help others. And that latter side is the Wilt who often escaped notice, in no small part because he fostered his reputation as a hedonist—notably by claiming in his 1991 auto-biography that he bedded some 20,000 women during his career.

But it is this less familiar depiction that his supporters wanted to see endure—and not just through the statue. There's also a learning center in North Philadelphia and an athletic club in Los Angeles (one that served as a springboard for Jackie Joyner-Kersee and others). There were generous contributions to charities like Operation Smile, which provides plastic surgery to children in Third World countries born with cleft palates and other facial deformities.

Cunningham, cochairman of the Wilt Chamberlain Memorial Fund, said the day of the unveiling that Wilt donated "at least $10 million" to those in need before his death or through his will. More than that are the random acts of kindness. Paul Arizin, who played with Chamberlain on the Philadelphia Warriors, said Wilt befriended his son Michael when the younger Arizin was just a boy.

Years later Michael's daughter Stephanie was stricken with an inoperable brain tumor. Her one wish was to get the autograph of every member of the NBA's 50th anniversary team, which gathered at the 1997 All-Star Game in Cleveland. Wilt made it happen, pushing Stephanie's wheelchair around and coaxing all the players to sign—even guys who don't normally do so, like Russell.

There are those who have argued that maybe Wilt was too nice, that it was Russell's ruthlessness that set him apart from his rival. Case in point: Russell told *Sports Illustrated*'s Frank Deford in 1999 that if he had been faced with a hobbled Willis Reed in Game 7 of the NBA Finals, as Chamberlain was when his Lakers squared off against Reed's Knicks in 1970, Russell would have demanded the ball again and again. But Wilt seemed unable, or perhaps unwilling, to take advantage. And the Lakers lost.

As Cunningham said the day of the unveiling, Wilt was "too gentle." He wanted people to love him, and many did. But as with so many things Wiltian, it was never enough.

4 Charles Barkley

As during his playing days, Charles Barkley continues to thunder along, now with microphone in hand as opposed to a basketball. He is paid to deliver opinions, and deliver them he does, even if on occasion he treats facts as he once did puny point guards whenever they dared get in his way during one of his patented court-length rushes—as something to be shunted aside, disregarded. But nobody really seems to care, for it's all part of the show, all part of his reinvention.

As great as his life's first act was—and let us never forget what a truly unique player he was—there is much to like about his second act. We are reminded of that when he pops up on Turner Sports' NBA coverage, usually in the network's studio in Atlanta. Also in other ways, too.

"Hey—y'all still got them rats in here? Them rats as big as cats?"

That was Barkley one night in January 2013, standing in a hallway in the bowels of the Wells Fargo Center and loudly needling a nearby Sixers official before providing color commentary for TNT's broadcast of a game against the Spurs. He does such work on occasion these days; he said it is a welcome departure from his studio appearances, for which he won a second Emmy in 2013.

And on this occasion he had taken his act to an arena in which he had never actually performed as a home player (he was likely thinking of the Spectrum when he mentioned the rats), but where he had played his final road game, in December 1999, blowing out a quadriceps tendon as a bloated Houston Rocket.

In short order he visited Jeff Millman, the team's longtime assistant equipment manager, in the laundry room; said hello to John Brong, who has guarded the door of the Sixers' locker room, in one building or another, for 36 years ("Looking good, man," Barkley said.); huddled with Harvey Pollack, the ageless statistician ("You've done a lot of great things in your life."); ribbed general manager Tony DiLeo while passing along best wishes to his wife ("Anna, right? How long she been stuck with you?"); posed for a photo with Ryan Lumpkin, a ball boy and son of director of basketball administration Allen Lumpkin ("Stay in those books, man."); and commiserated with *Inquirer* columnist Bob Ford ("I hope I don't die. I can steal this money for a long time.").

Again one was left to ponder the difference between the boorish Barkley of years past—the one who infamously (and accidentally) spit on a little girl and was known for brawling with overserved barflies—and this guy, who seemed so...so...likable. Again one was left to recall something his good friend Dave Coskey, the former Sixers publicist, always said about Barkley: While many athletes are bad guys who want the public to believe they are good guys, the Chuck Wagon is a good guy who wants everyone to believe he is a bad guy.

Far more of the good guy is in evidence these days than the bad boy. If his misdeeds once detracted from his accomplishments, the script has now flipped. Now people are more inclined, because of his essential decency, to cut him a break when he goes astray. "There's not a nicer person on this planet than Charles Barkley," former Sixers president Pat Croce said in the fall of 2012, as he sat in the office of his Villanova home. "He's a special person."

Barkley turned 50 in February 2013, three days after his good friend Michael Jordan. TV specials were scheduled to commemorate Barkley's milestone, but it did not quite inspire the lovefest that heralded Jordan's half-century. *Sports Illustrated* devoted most of an issue to His Airness, and ESPN.com's Wright Thompson—as gifted a writer as you will find—crafted a compelling profile, one

One of the 76ers' best-ever draft picks, the man who would become "Sir Charles," is seen here with NBA commissioner David Stern in 1984.

that duly noted how restless Jordan has become since he retired for the third and (perhaps) final time in 2003.

In the story there was the suggestion that Jordan, majority owner of the Charlotte Bobcats (now Hornets) might want to play again—yes, even at 50—for nothing else gives him quite so much fulfillment as being on the court. It is something he had also said during his Hall of Fame induction speech in 2009. Clearly the itch is still there.

You will hear no such talk from Barkley, and not just because he was so terribly out of shape for so long; only in recent years has he lost 60 pounds, with the help of Weight Watchers (for which he has done some promotional work). There was some mention, a few years back, that he wouldn't mind playing alongside Jordan when he made his ill-fated comeback with the Doug Collins–coached Washington Wizards, but that never materialized. More recently there was talk of Charles playing two-on-two with Kenny Smith, one of his studio partners at Turner, against the likes of ESPN analysts Magic Johnson and Jalen Rose. Nothing came of that, either.

Barkley seems settled, content, aware of where he is in his life. It stands in sharp contrast to Jordan, and is perhaps the one and only time Barkley has gotten a leg up on him. The court jester overshadowing the king. Imagine that.

Barkley, who maintains a summer home in Philadelphia (he winters in Arizona, the better to bludgeon golf courses in another state), was accorded a standing ovation during a first-quarter timeout of that Sixers-Spurs game, memories of his eight years with the Sixers having been refreshed by a highlight video shown on the scoreboard. He played 16 seasons in all—Phoenix and Houston were his other stops—making 11 All-Star teams (not to mention the Hall of Fame) while becoming only the third man in NBA history to collect more than 20,000 points, 10,000 rebounds, and 4,000 assists. The others are Wilt Chamberlain and Kareem

Abdul-Jabbar, both of whom stood over seven feet tall. Barkley was listed at 6'6" but actually stood a shade under 6'5".

"He's a Hall of Fame player, so people have to appreciate it, but he's special among that group," said Jim Lynam, who coached Barkley during part of his Sixers tenure. "That's how talented he was. And the word right there along with it is 'unique.' On Noah's Ark, two of everything. Well, I've got news for you—that partner fell off the edge of the boat. There's one of him. *One.*"

Lynam was always in Barkley's corner, defending him when he veered off the tracks ("Charles is Charles," the coach would say, as a way of sidestepping particularly thorny questions) and building his offense around him. The joke among veteran beat writers is that those Sixers ran one play: "Turn Cholly." But Lynam also challenged him, stoked his competitive fire. Mike Gminski, who played center for Lynam and with Barkley from 1988 to 1991, recalled that the team was in San Antonio, and at the end of a game-day shootaround Lynam bet Barkley $100 he could score on him.

According to Gminski, Barkley took that action in a nanosecond. Lynam, talking smack, took the ball at the top of the circle. "And Charlie's all worked up," said Gminski, who now lives in Charlotte and broadcasts ACC games. "Jimmy throws him a little head fake, and Charlie goes flying up in the air, trying to block it. Jimmy takes a couple dribbles, lays the ball in, starts laughing, and walks off the floor."

Lynam, who now does TV work for Comcast SportsNet, would not confirm this story, though he did add, with the smallest of grins, "That I could get a basket without a great deal of difficulty on Barkley, I can confirm that." Barkley did confirm it in March 2013, but quickly changed the subject, saying how much he enjoyed playing for Lynam.

They won an Atlantic Division title together in 1989–90, but things quickly went south. And in June 1992 Lynam, by then the Sixers' general manager (and working at the behest of owner

Harold Katz), sent Barkley to Phoenix for Jeff Hornacek, Andrew Lang, and Tim Perry. That came after Barkley, in his final season with the Sixers, was brought up on an assault charge after striking a man outside a tavern in Milwaukee—a charge for which he was later acquitted. And it came well after he accidentally spit on eight-year-old Lauren Rose while aiming at a heckler during a game in the New Jersey Meadowlands in March 1991. He paid the $10,000 fine, apologized to the girl, and befriended her and her family—the worst and best of Barkley, side by side.

Looking back, he has one overriding regret about his time in Philadelphia: "I should have got out of there two years sooner, because the seventh and eighth years were a waste of my time.... The Sixers were not a good organization at that time."

But he stopped short of saying he was trying to orchestrate a trade. "No, I didn't try to get out," he said. "It was frustrating, just hearing the rumors. My last three years, all I heard was [trade] rumors, every single day.... We went to the Sixers at the end of the [1991–92] season and said, 'I like Philadelphia; it's a great city. The fans treated me great. I'm not coming back here, ever, to play.' Thank goodness they traded me over that summer. It would have gotten ugly, because I wasn't coming back there."

There are those close to the organization who remember it quite differently, those who say he frequently made it known he wanted out. What he does know is that he was "a much better player" with the Sixers than he was in Phoenix, even though he was named NBA MVP in 1992–93, his first season with the Suns, and led them to the Finals. There they lost, naturally, to Jordan's Bulls.

"When I was MVP, I probably had five better years in Philadelphia than I did in Phoenix," Barkley said. "I just had more help in Phoenix."

Even now he wonders how his career might have played out had the Sixers stood pat in the 1986 draft and used the first overall pick on North Carolina center Brad Daugherty, rather than trading that choice to Cleveland while at the same time shipping Moses Malone to Washington. Those deals brought Roy Hinson, Jeff Ruland, and Cliff Robinson in return, none of whom made a significant impact. Even now Barkley has been known to joke about the time he was told the Sixers acquired Shaq, only to learn to his chagrin that it was Charles Shackleford, not Shaquille O'Neal.

Coskey is certain that the team's struggles fueled Barkley's discontent, and led to some of his escapades. The Sixers' chief publicist from 1986 to 1988 and an executive from 1996 to 2001, he now serves as president of Longport Media in South Jersey. He and Barkley grew close during Coskey's first stint with the team, and remain so; Charles is even godfather to the youngest of Coskey's three sons.

"Charles," Coskey said, "hit me as a person who would do anything in the world for you. He's still that way. It's a shame not everybody gets to see that side of him." Certainly Coskey has seen it often enough. There was the time a 76-year-old Trenton woman, Mary Walsh, called a Philadelphia radio station and ripped Barkley. He responded by inviting her to a game—the Sixers sent a car and everything—and presenting her with a dozen roses as she sat courtside.

And there was the time, much more recently, when Coskey asked Barkley to do the introduction for the highlight video for his middle son's high school basketball team. Coskey gave him some of the players' names, figuring Charles' commentary would spice up the team's year-end banquet.

Barkley went the extra mile, though, recruiting his fellow studio hosts at TNT to record a full-fledged video about a team they had never seen. "You had adults [at the banquet] falling on the floor laughing," Coskey said. "It was Charles being Charles. It did not take a great amount of time, but it took some time to do that. I'm not sure he realizes the lasting impression he has. There were

200 people at a banquet, and they all walked out Charles Barkley fans. "That's the guy Coskey has always known. And it's the one the rest of us are seeing more and more often these days.

5 Allen Iverson

Once more Allen Iverson stood on the court in the Sixers' home arena and heard thunderous cheers. Once more he cupped his hand to his ear and begged the fans to raise the volume even more. Once more they obliged.

But in reality, the echoes of Iverson's heyday were few on the night of March 30, 2013. The Sixers invited him back to take a bow before a game against the Charlotte Bobcats. Bobbleheads were given away in his likeness, and he appeared wearing a throwback Phillies jacket and cap, along with sunglasses, a white T-shirt, and baggy jeans. Diamonds sparkled in both ears. Several thick gold chains hung from his neck.

By all accounts his life was in tatters. His NBA millions were gone. His marriage had dissolved. His prospects appeared bleak. A former Sixers teammate, Roshown McLeod, was quoted as saying Iverson had hit "rock bottom" in a story that appeared in the *Washington Post* some three weeks after Iverson's homecoming. Iverson's former coach with the team, Larry Brown, told the author of the piece, Kent Babb, that he was worried about the guy who had earned an MVP award and three of his four scoring titles during Brown's six years with the Sixers.

Other friends were no less concerned. "Whatever demons that it is he's fighting, he has to deal with those first, before you can address anything else," Aaron McKie said in an interview for this book late in the 2012–13 season. "You can try to get all the help in the world, but you've got to be willing to help yourself."

McKie, a Sixers assistant at that point, had been one of Iverson's teammates in Philadelphia, and still considers him a friend. He has tried to keep in touch with him through the years (which has not always been easy), and had spoken with him the night of his return. "When we talk, I always just ask him, 'How are you doing?'" McKie said. "We don't even get into all the issues or anything. 'How are you doing? You OK?'"

Not well, it would appear. Multiple accounts, including Babb's, indicated he had burned through the $150 million in salary he earned during his 14 pro seasons. Babb also quoted testimony from 2012 divorce proceedings involving Iverson and his wife, Tawanna—testimony that indicated Iverson drank excessively, spent lavishly, and had little interest in raising his five children.

"I think he's making strides," McKie told this author, "but I think the most important thing is making sure he establishes a relationship with his kids, because at the end of the day, I don't care what they're saying about finances or what they say about him individually, that will tear your heart out.... You could have all the money in the world, but if the kids ain't right because that relationship ain't right, it don't mean nothing."

Iverson had never been known to toe the line, even in the best of times. He wasn't big on sharing the ball when he was the Sixers' centerpiece. Nor did he care much about practice (as he asserted, memorably, during a 2002 news conference). And he feuded with coaches (most notably Brown). But if his rebelliousness was viewed as abhorrent in front offices, it was often seen as appealing by paying customers. "Iverson probably sold more season tickets than Wilt [Chamberlain] and Julius [Erving]," Orlando Magic senior vice president Pat Williams, the Sixers' general manager from 1974 to 1986, said. "There was a great love affair with him. He was everybody's rascal, Peck's Bad Boy. He was always in trouble with the teacher. He stirred people's emotions. Nobody was ever neutral with him."

When his talents waned, few teams seemed inclined to deal with all those peripheral issues. He last played in the NBA during the 2009–10 season, when the Sixers foolishly brought him back for a 25-game swan song. Afterward he played briefly in Turkey and spent time with a team in China. There was also an offer from Dallas early in the 2012–13 season to play for the Mavericks' team in the NBA Developmental League. But Iverson turned that down and officially announced his retirement in October 2013.

Those who know him best were convinced that in 2012–13 he was still good enough to play in the NBA, even at the age of 37. It was more a question of whether he was willing to go along with a given team's program, and accept a reduced role.

"Allen had that reputation of a bad boy," McKie said months before his friend's retirement, "so that's going to stay with him. I don't think any of that will change.… I just think people say, 'Well, I really don't want that baggage. I really don't want to deal with that.' Any time you sign Allen Iverson, I think for the most part you know what you're getting. I don't think any of that will ever change. Example: If he would have come in here that Saturday when we played Charlotte with a suit on and a tie, I think that would have shocked a lot of people. I think they would have said, 'Well, maybe this guy's changed. He's different.'"

That didn't happen. The end had come.

But in the beginning, he was a lightning bolt, a whirlwind. Only he made those Sixers teams for which he toiled early in his career watchable. He never shied away from a shot, never backed away from a challenge, never seemed to be going at anything less than warp speed.

One other thing, too: at six feet and 165 pounds, he seemed as tough a player as any in the league. "Tougher," said former Sixers president Pat Croce, who took Iverson first overall in the 1996 draft. "Tougher than anyone in the NBA."

Croce, a martial arts enthusiast and once the team's strength-and-conditioning coach, could appreciate that as much as anyone. And Iverson's grit played just as well in the locker room. He was a guy, said former Sixers center Todd MacCulloch, who "really led by example by how hard he played. He really played every game like it could be his last, and sacrificed his body. Was never afraid to go to the hole and fall hard. He was definitely a special player, and fun to be on the court with."

He was also a guy who placed few limits on himself. At a game-day shootaround one time, MacCulloch recalls Iverson coming up to him and saying, "I feel pretty good, Todd. Think I'm gonna go for 48 tonight."

MacCulloch, a bright, engaging guy, didn't skip a beat. "Think I'm gonna go from four *to* eight tonight," he deadpanned.

Former Sixers forward George Lynch called Iverson "a great teammate" and said he too enjoyed playing with him. "He just didn't like to practice," said Lynch, who in 2013-14 served as an assistant to Brown at SMU. "I understand that; some guys don't want to go through the little details. And he didn't need to. He was a great enough player. You just put the ball in his hands and let him play. Coach Brown was trying to get details for the players like [me], Eric Snow, and Aaron McKie, who weren't as talented as Allen. Allen could take 30 days off and still be in better shape than most guys today in the league."

The problem, Croce said, was that Iverson tended to take too much time off. Yes, he led the Sixers to the Finals in 2000–01 (the year he was named MVP) and continued to play at a high level for years after that. But his off-court habits were bound to catch up with him. "You can't, in the off-season, not do anything," Croce said. "God's talent is eventually going to diminish. As a physical conditioning coach prior to being a CEO, my biggest disappointment with A.I. is that he didn't stress conditioning and work on his weaknesses in the off-season. He'd still be playing [if he had]. No different than Ray Allen or Kobe Bryant—he'd still be playing."

But he was not, and seemed unlikely to do so again. Iverson grants few interviews, and the night of his homecoming spoke only with a reporter from Comcast, the arena's parent company. He said he was putting his future "in God's hands."

"I've accomplished a lot in the NBA, and if the road ends here, then it does," he added. "And I'm not bitter about it. I don't feel no type of way. I just understand that He helped me accomplish a lot of things in the NBA. I've done so many things that people thought that I couldn't do.... But at some point, it comes to an end. And regardless of however it comes—regardless if it's retirement, injury, or whatever—at some point, it comes to an end."

A few months later, the handwriting was on the wall. The end had arrived for Allen Iverson, whether he was ready for it or not.

Moses Malone

Some 2 million souls lined the route when the Sixers paraded down Broad Street to celebrate their NBA championship in June 1983. That included 30 construction workers who happened to be on their lunch hour when the flatbed truck carrying the players rolled past. Upon seeing Moses Malone, the tireless center who keyed the title run, the workers raised their lunch pails in salute. Clayton Sheldon, the team's assistant director of group sales, witnessed that gesture and thought it fitting: a bunch of blue-collar workers were paying tribute to one of their own, to the ultimate hard-hat player.

Everyone seemed to realize Moses was the missing piece to the Sixers' puzzle when they acquired him in a trade with Houston the previous September, after signing him to a free-agent offer sheet that would pay him $13.2 million over six years—a lavish sum in that day and age. He had won two MVP awards and three rebounding titles in six seasons with the Rockets, but he was never better than he was in 1982–83 (and indeed would never be quite so good again).

Again he grabbed more boards than anyone else. Again he was the MVP, as well as the MVP of the NBA Finals, in which the Sixers swept the shorthanded Lakers. And the Sixers had the physical presence they had lacked since the days of Wilt Chamberlain. It was, Boston Celtics forward Cedric Maxwell said, "a before-and-after thing." The two men who had manned the post immediately before Malone, Caldwell Jones and Darryl Dawkins, both had their strengths. Jones was a versatile defender, and Dawkins teased everyone with his talent. But Moses pounded people every night.

He once summed up his approach as follows: "I turn, and I go to the rack." And it was true: He seemed to pursue every rebound, especially off his own team's misses. It was often claimed, in fact, that there were times Malone missed on purpose so that he might pad his already-prodigious offensive-rebounding stats. He has always denied that, and either way his relentlessness was without equal.

"Moses wasn't the greatest athlete in the league," said Mike Dunleavy, who played alongside him in Houston. "He didn't have huge hands, and he wasn't a great leaper. But he worked so hard. His effort was off the charts, proving if you try your hardest all the time, there's no telling where you might end up. You'll surprise yourself sometimes."

Moses, who would ultimately end up in the Hall of Fame, started out in a tough neighborhood in Petersburg, Virginia, called the Heights. His father was out of the picture; his mother, Mary, worked two jobs to make ends meet. Moses honed his game at a local playground, often during solitary late-night sessions, and was the driving force of a high school team that swept 50 straight games while winning a state title each of his last two seasons.

Recruiters camped out in Petersburg for months on end, and Moses made 24 college visits. He wound up committing to Maryland, but when he dominated a summer league in Washington, DC, it seemed less and less likely he would ever play for the Terps. Meanwhile, ABA teams were out to make him the first player to jump directly from high school to the pros. Mary wasn't big on the idea, but when the ABA's Utah Stars offered him $3 million over seven years, there was no turning back.

He was great right away, averaging 18.8 points and 14.6 rebounds in his first season, and his teammates took to calling him "Superkid." A radio guy, noting Malone's truncated speech pattern, was less kind; he called him "Mumbles."

The ABA folded after Moses' second season, and in short order he went from Portland to Buffalo (for a first-round draft pick) to Houston (for *two* first-round draft picks). And it was with the Rockets that he really established himself. One of his coaches there, Del Harris, discovered the folly of some long-held notions about Moses. First, he was more athletic than anyone believed; Harris saw him touch his forehead to the rim on a bet. Second, he was no dummy. When Malone toured the Dominican Republic with a group of players, he exchanged the local currency for American money at a better rate than Harris and his teammates.

Harris then asked him why he had done it so quickly.

"I don't want no money that doesn't have George Washington's picture on it," Moses said.

The Sixers gave him a big pile of money that was so emblazoned, and in exchange he gave them remarkable consistency that first season in Philadelphia. He opened with a 21-point,

Moses Malone jams on the Lakers in the 1983 NBA Finals en route to the championship.

17-rebound effort against the Knicks. Five games in, he played 56 of a possible 58 minutes while collecting 28 points and 19 boards in a double-overtime victory over the archrival Celtics.

In mid-December he collected 29 and 14, respectively, in a victory over the Lakers in Los Angeles. Particularly telling were three stick-backs down the stretch. "Broke their backs," coach Billy Cunningham told reporters afterward. He broke the will of Kareem Abdul-Jabbar, too; the Lakers' star center settled for 15 points and two rebounds.

"I'm always the most optimistic guy in our locker room," Jack McMahon, the late assistant coach, told Phil Jasner, the *Philadelphia Daily News*' late beat guy, "and seeing this performance makes me believe we're right there again, with a chance to win the whole thing. I know I always feel that way, but this time I feel a little better than I usually do. I mean, I've seen Kareem so many times, and we've never had anybody who could neutralize him. Now we do."

Malone became like a metronome, supplying a steady back-beat: 24 and 20 in Seattle, at the end of a long road trip…23 and 10 in a rout of Dallas, after returning from the bedside of his mother, who had suffered a mild stroke…24 and 12 in the second victory in as many nights over the rugged Bullets. Beating them, Moses told reporters, was "like trying to kill two bulls, then having to fight the matador, too."

Sixers radio/TV voice Neil Funk, who would later call Chicago Bulls games, said Malone's relentlessness was on par with only one other player he had seen: Michael Jordan. Others were similarly awed.

"Moses doesn't get tired," Mark Whicker, then a columnist with the *Daily News*, wrote after a December 21 victory over Boston, "but he's a carrier."

Malone was sidetracked only slightly by tendinitis in both knees late in the regular season. He put up 38 points and 17 rebounds in the Sixers' first playoff game, a victory over the Knicks, and was right back at it again.

"Y'all make it sound like I'm dyin' here," he told reporters after that one. "I told you, everything's gonna be all right."

That underscores one other misconception about Moses: that he was a lousy quote. While he didn't give many long interviews (though he did submit to a question-and-answer session after the 1982–83 season with *Playboy* magazine, which reportedly paid him $40,000 for the privilege), he had a way of boiling things down to their essence. That was most vividly shown by his "fo', fo', fo'" prediction before the playoffs, of course.

Around his teammates, it was different. "Everybody loved Moses," said Mitchell (J.J.) Anderson, a rookie forward who spent the early stages of the 1982–83 season with the team. Another rookie that year, Marc Iavaroni, said Malone was "the team entertainer." He called yet another first-year player, center Mark McNamara, "Tank" after the comic-strip character. He joked that the rented Dodge Colt driven by John Kilbourne, the strength-and-conditioning coach was "a Matchbox car." And he gave star guard Andrew Toney constant grief about his wardrobe.

He also engaged in spirited half-court games with the rookies, and shooting contests with Kilbourne, with the loser—Kilbourne, of course—buying lunch. And never mind that Kilbourne earned one-tenth the salary Malone did.

But when reporters showed up, Moses shut it down. *Daily News* columnist Ray Didinger found out about that late in the championship season, when he was assigned to write a feature story about Malone. Malone wouldn't agree to an interview, even when Cunningham, team owner Harold Katz, and Moses' agent, Lee Fentress, intervened on Didinger's behalf. Nor would Moses talk when Didinger accompanied the team on a road trip, hoping to grab a minute or two with him, here and there.

Finally Didinger came home and wrote the story, relying only on secondary sources. It was entitled "Moses Makes His Private Life Most Valuable." It also earned Didinger a statewide writing award. "I guess that tells you interviews are overrated," Didinger said, years later.

The day of the championship parade, Didinger wracked his brain about what to write. Every angle, it seemed, had long been exhausted by then. Then he thought about a Jason Miller play he had seen called *That Championship Season*, about a high school basketball team's 20th reunion—a play later turned into a motion picture.

What, Didinger wondered, would the Sixers be doing 20 years down the road? McMahon decided Julius Erving would be President of the United States. Kilbourne figured Bobby Jones would be a missionary. Al Domenico, the mischievous trainer, guessed that point guard Maurice Cheeks would be head of a baking company—"all chocolate chip cookies."

And Moses?

"In 20 years?" McNamara told Didinger. "He'll still be leading the NBA in rebounding."

7 Dolph Schayes

Dolph Schayes, who played almost his entire career with the Sixers' forerunner, the Syracuse Nationals, is a name on a stat sheet—and a Hall of Fame plaque. He is an image on a grainy piece of black-and-white video. It is difficult to define his career a half-century after he hung up his high-top Chucks, though some of his contemporaries have tried over the years to do so.

The comparison they usually draw is to none other than Larry Bird. The late Carl Braun and Tom Gola did so in Terry Pluto's 1992 book *Tall Tales*. Braun, who played for the Knicks and Celtics from 1947 to 1962, said that like Bird, Schayes could shoot it from deep. Gola, who played for the Warriors and Knicks from 1955 to 1966, said both were earthbound rebounders and "self-made players." And while Bird was the superior passer of the two, Gola told Pluto that the 6'8" Schayes wasn't exactly deficient in that department.

An 84-year-old Schayes said in early 2013 that the comparison was "one of the greatest compliments" he could ever receive because he "idolized" Bird. "The love of the game just came out of his pores as he was playing," Schayes added. "I appreciated it."

And while he was apt to question any similarities, he didn't dismiss them entirely. He said that much like Bird, he was in constant motion on the court. And he agreed that neither of them could jump. Former teammate Al Bianchi told Pluto that Schayes couldn't even dunk. That wasn't true, Schayes said; it was just that dunking was considered "show-offy" in that era—that he could jam but only did so "a half a dozen times" in his entire career.

"If I can compare to Larry Bird," Schayes said, "I would say he and I had good anticipation. In other words, when the ball came off the boards, we knew where it was going to go. We always knew where a ball was. In basketball, you have to find the ball all the time. You have to know where it is, all the time. And I think that comes by just playing the game. I played an awful lot in schoolyards and in high school and *Y*s. You develop a sixth sense. You play with focus."

Schayes, who scored 18,438 points while playing from 1949 to 1964, was single-minded about the game even as a youngster growing up in New York City. He can remember lying on his bed, ball in hand, and just flicking it toward the ceiling, again and again.

"You have to shoot and you get a touch with the fingertips," he said. "I probably would have been a good safecracker."

Out on the playground, he played a lot of three-on-three. And rather than honing his post moves like most players his size, he developed what he called "the pure game": an ability to hit outside shots and running one-handers—with either hand. "And that really helped me tremendously in the pro game," he said, "because most of the guys at 6'8" didn't have the moves and the quickness that I had, or the outside shot. So I was able to take advantage of the pure game by taking big guys outside and driving by them."

He starred at New York University, where he also earned an engineering degree and a job offer from Boeing. He chose instead to sign with the Nationals. He became the first player to score 15,000 points—"not in one game," he cracked—and the first player to grab 1,000 rebounds in a season. He also made 12 All-Star teams in his 15 seasons. All while playing, again, "pure basketball."

While there is no question in his mind that the players of today are superior in ability and athleticism, he's not convinced the game—now so dependent on pick-and-rolls and isolation plays—is better than it was in his day. "We moved the ball a lot, and that's what basketball, I think, is all about," he said. "Basketball is shooting the ball and moving well."

Appointed player-coach in 1963–64, the year the Nats moved to Philadelphia and became the Sixers, he stepped down as a player after 25 games—"stupidly," he said. He rues the fact that he deprived himself of a chance to reach the 20,000-point plateau.

He pointed out that he did set a dubious record while playing—most career personal fouls (a mark since eclipsed). But he jokingly noted that that might have helped him years later, when the league was looking to appoint a director of referees. "They said, 'Why don't we get Dolph, because he really knows what a foul looks like.'"

Before assuming those duties, he had coached the Sixers for three years in all, his tenure marked by playoff failures in Boston, including the 1965 Eastern Finals, which were capped by John Havlicek's steal at the end of the Celtics' one-point victory in Game 7. Again Schayes second-guesses himself, saying he was guilty of "one of the worst play calls in the history of the game"—i.e., trying to set up a shot for Hal Greer, the inbounder, rather than something for Wilt Chamberlain, who was dominating the game. But Schayes believes to this day the Celtics would have fouled Chamberlain, a notoriously poor free-throw shooter. Still, it remains an everlasting regret.

"But at least I made Havlicek very famous, didn't I?" he asked.

He didn't do badly for himself, either.

8 Hal Greer

Author Bill Simmons named former Sixers guard Hal Greer the 46th-best player of all time in his 2009 work *The Book of Basketball*, while at the same time noting that it was difficult to define Greer's 15-year career. There were no revealing anecdotes, no flashy quotes—just a hail of mid-range jump shots that led to some spectacular career numbers.

About the most interesting thing Simmons could unearth was the fact that Greer was so proficient with his jumper that he even used it on free throws, which he nailed at an 80 percent clip in his career. It's also notable that Greer was involved in a play that defined the Sixers' frustrations in the 1960s—i.e., "Havlicek Stole the Ball"—and that he was one of the key cogs on the 1966–67 championship team, voted the greatest club of the NBA's first 35 years.

But for the most part, the numbers are the thing with Greer. The 21,586 career points, No. 32 on the all-time list. The 10 All-Star appearances. The 1,122 games, more than anyone else in franchise history. His inclusion among the 50 greatest players of all time. The fact that he had his college and pro uniform numbers— No. 16 at Marshall, No. 15 with the Sixers—retired.

"Consistency," he once said, according to his NBA.com biography. "For me, that was the thing. I would like to be remembered as a great, consistent player."

There's no denying him that. The guy played just about every game, and made shot after shot—so many that he's in the Hall of Fame. So many that he is widely viewed as one of the greatest guards of his era, dwarfed only by Jerry West and Oscar Robertson. (Those contemporaries explain why he was never an All-NBA first-teamer. He was a second-teamer no fewer than seven times.)

Former Sixers executive Pat Williams described him as a "tough little bulldog" in a 2012 interview with the *Wilmington News Journal.* "Bulldog" was in fact his nickname, former teammate Al Bianchi once told author Terry Pluto, "because he had that kind of expression on his face and it never changed."

Matt Guokas, drafted by the Sixers in 1966 and part of the team for four seasons, marveled at Greer's durability in an interview for this book, and the way he played off point guard Larry Costello. "As a young player, the thing you learned from those types of guys was that they're not going to have it every night," Guokas said. "They're tired. The season is wearing on you. You're getting a little older. But they found ways to go out there and perform, and get… the job done. They were just pros."

But they also knew how to pace themselves. Guokas recalls that he and fellow rookie Billy Melchionni were pulled aside by coach Alex Hannum three days into their first training camp, in Margate, New Jersey. They were tired and sore, but Hannum said they were actually lucky.

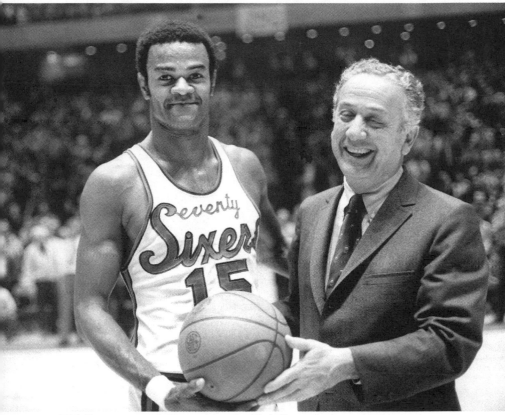

Hal Greer poses with Sixers owner Irv Kosloff to commemorate Greer's achievement of becoming the sixth player in the NBA to eclipse 20,000 career points.

"Back in the day," he said, "Hal and Costy would have beaten you guys up by now." Because veterans were always laying down the law on the court, forever wary of rookies stealing their minutes. It was that way with Guy Rodgers and Al Attles, whom Hannum coached in San Francisco, and used to be that way with Costello and Greer.

But they were settled by then, established. The rookies would pose no threat to them. And as Guokas watched Greer, he learned that the Bulldog would also stand his ground at the defensive end.

"He wasn't just an offensive player," Guokas said. "He stuck his nose in there defensively. Quick feet, quick hands."

"Hal Greer always came to play," his former teammate and coach, Dolph Schayes, once told NBA.com. "He came to practice the same way, to every team function the same way. Every bus and plane and train, he was on time. Hal Greer punched the clock. Hal Greer brought the lunch pail."

But the jumper was his bread and butter. Williams thought he might be the best middle-distance shooter of all time, and there are few dissenters on that score.

Greer, now 78 and living in Scottsdale, Arizona, suffered a stroke in 2006 that affected his right side. He no longer makes many public appearances. Nor does he do interviews, though as his wife, Mayme, told the *Morgantown Dominion-Post* in 2011, "He wasn't much of a talker before anyway."

Chet Walker, another Hall of Famer and a member that great 1966–67 team, said in the 2012 book *NBA List Jam!* that Greer was "difficult to get to know because he was introverted and insecure in some ways. I guess you would call him a little antisocial." At the same time Walker listed him among the teammates who most impacted his life—and, naturally, mentioned what a great mid-range shooter he was.

Greer, a native of Huntington, West Virginia, was the first African American to earn a scholarship to Marshall, his hometown school. He averaged more than 19 points and 10 rebounds in his career there and was a second-round pick of the Syracuse Nationals, the Sixers' predecessor, in 1958. He had already established himself by the time the team moved to Philadelphia in 1963, having made his first All-Star appearance three years earlier.

But for all he and his teammates accomplished, they kept bumping their heads against a glass ceiling constructed by the Celtics. The Sixers came close in the 1965 Eastern Division Finals, extending Boston to a seventh game in the fabled Garden. And there was Greer, attempting to inbound the ball from underneath his own basket with his team trailing 110–109 with five seconds left.

Schayes, then the coach, would be widely second-guessed for his play call. Fearing that the Celtics would foul Wilt Chamberlain, he wanted Greer to pass to Chet Walker. Greer was then supposed to come off a screen by Johnny Kerr and receive a return pass, so that he could shoot his patented jumper.

"I wanted Greer to be the shooter—[he was] the best shooter we had, a great shooter," Schayes said in an interview for this book. "But nobody would suspect Greer would shoot it; he's taking it out of bounds.... I figured that was our best-percentage shot."

But Havlicek tipped Greer's pass to teammate Sam Jones, as Celtics broadcaster Johnny Most croaked out his three-packs-a-day call.

The Celtics won the title that year, and again in 1965–66, their eighth straight. The Sixers finally broke through in 1966–67, going 68–13, knocking off Boston in the playoffs and then beating the San Francisco Warriors for the title. Greer averaged 27.7 points per game during the playoffs, best on the team and his highest average in any postseason during his career.

Again, it was all about the numbers with him. Always the numbers.

He gave the smallest of glimpses into his psyche in a 1989 *Philadelphia Inquirer* story about his daughter Cherie, who was then playing high school basketball. As always, the subject turned to shooting.

"The scorers get the money," he said. "Everybody can't shoot."

He could. It's as fine a legacy as any.

Chet Walker

Turns out that Chet Walker's nickname—Chet the Jet—was something of a misnomer.

"You were slow, Chet," a smiling Billy Cunningham told Walker while introducing him for his induction into the Naismith Memorial Basketball Hall of Fame in September 2012.

Not so slow that Walker, a crafty forward, didn't score 18,831 points in 13 NBA seasons. Or that he wasn't the third-leading scorer (behind Wilt Chamberlain and Hal Greer) on the 76ers' 1966–67 championship team.

Walker, who spent his rookie year with the Syracuse Nationals and the next six in Philadelphia when the Nats relocated, became the fourth player from that 1966-67 club to reach the Hall of Fame. Chamberlain had been selected in 1979, Greer in '82, and Cunningham—"the greatest sixth man ever to play in the NBA," as Walker told the crowd the night of his induction—made it in '86.

But Walker belonged right alongside them. "You knew what he was going to do, and you couldn't stop the man," Cunningham said as he stood on stage to present Walker that night. And by that Cunningham meant that Walker could take his defender wherever he wanted—that he could either shoot over him or take him to the hole. And if he was fouled, he was deadly, making about 80 percent of his attempts at the line during his career, and well over that in his last several seasons.

But he was never in a hurry. "I was more rhythm than fast," Walker, 72 at the time of his induction, told the *Philadelphia Inquirer*'s Frank Fitzpatrick.

He had been a star at Bradley University, winning a pair of NIT titles there at a time when the tournament was still at the height of its prestige. He averaged just more than 12 points a game as a rookie, but according to Wayne Lynch's book *Season of the 76ers*, coach Alex Hannum wanted Walker to be more assertive at the offensive end.

The next year, coached by Dolph Schayes after Hannum left to take a job with the Warriors, Walker improved his average by five points a night, and he was on his way. He would ultimately make seven All-Star teams during his career, and in that 1966–67 season—a season that saw the Sixers go 68–13 and end Boston's run of eight straight titles—he scored a shade more than 19 points a night, his best average in his time in Philadelphia.

But after the 1968–69 season Jack Ramsay, by then the Sixers' coach and general manager, was bent on trading Walker to Chicago. And when the Bulls called and asked about hiring Sixers business manager Pat Williams to be their new GM, Ramsay was happy to let him go, even though Williams had two years left on his contract.

The only stipulation was that Williams get the Walker deal done. Which he did, the very same day of his introductory news conference. "I'm sure in Chicago people were thinking, *This guy's an absolute whirlwind*," Williams recalled with a laugh in 2012.

The only problem was, Walker didn't want to leave the Sixers for a Chicago team that had won 33 games the previous year. There was even talk that he might retire, so Williams and coach Dick Motta hustled to Philadelphia in hopes of persuading him otherwise.

They went to his apartment and pounded on the door. No answer. "We couldn't get him to open the door," Williams said.

The next day Williams and Motta began making inroads. They would in time sign Walker to a three-year contract extension, one that was worth $165,000, according to Williams—big money in those days. And, Williams said, "He absolutely put our team on the map."

Walker was the go-to guy, the guy who always got the ball at the end of tight games. And with players like Jerry Sloan, Norm Van Lier, and Bob Love, he was part of teams that were consistently strong, teams that did not win any titles but often made it difficult for those that did.

Walker also became something of a pioneer, twice suing the NBA and paving the way for free agency. As he told the crowd the night of his Hall of Fame induction, the league was very different before that occurred.

"Everything," he said, "was second class."

But once Walker and his fellow players won their legal battles, everything changed. It meant, he said, "that players could now make more money and if they felt like it they could take their talents to Cleveland."

He chuckled, then pointed to Miami Heat star LeBron James, seated in the crowd. Two years earlier James had announced on a TV special that he was taking his talents from Cleveland to South Beach.

James smiled. Chet the Jet, it seemed, had pulled a fast one on him.

10 Wali Jones

Wali Jones' approach remains that of the point guard he once was. He is still out front, still eager to run the show, just as he was when he filled that role on the Sixers' 1966–67 NBA championship team. Recalling those days in a December 2012 interview, he said, "It's a lot of responsibility, but I've always been a quarterback."

That did not change as the years passed and he left the game behind. Across time he reached out to kids and teachers. He sought to combat gangs and promote education. And even as he reached his seventies, that hadn't changed. Any discussion of his life includes his work with a plethora of charitable organizations, notably Shoot for the Stars, which he founded during his 20-year run as the Miami Heat's community affairs liaison.

It was through that program that he sought (and still seeks) to reach kids on a grassroots level, to teach them about the importance of hitting the books and being leaders, of being out front and assuming ownership of their lives and their schools. "I'm really about education," he said.

And he believes it is one thing for him to parachute into a school—followed by a platoon of athletes and former athletes and hauling all manner of officially licensed souvenirs—and spout his message, quite another for the students themselves to take up the cause. "When legends speak, people listen," he said, "but when kids speak, people listen."

His other efforts have been wide-ranging. Through Silence the Violence, he sought to counter inner-city gangs, and was honored by Bill Clinton in 1999 with the President's Medal as a result. Through Books and Basketball, he traveled the Caribbean, holding clinics and handing out books. He also does a clinic every year in Philadelphia, and travels to other cities, doing what he can.

His activism took root, he said, in 1969. Amid that turbulent time—a time when racial equality was at the forefront of many issues simmering in the U.S.—Jones traveled with several other athletes to Washington, DC, to see how they could make a difference in their cities. It led to the formation of programs such as Each One Teach One in New York City and Concerned Athletes in Action.

His life's course was set. After his 12-year playing career ended in 1976, he spent seven years with the Sixers as a scout, then seven more working for the United State Department of Education, at the Center for Educational Development in San Antonio. It was while he was there that he formulated his plan for Shoot for the Stars and shared it with former Sixers teammate Billy Cunningham, by then a part owner of the Miami Heat.

Cunningham—who, Jones said, is "like a brother" to him—liked what he saw, and brought him on board.

Their first collaboration had been no less productive. They both arrived in Philadelphia in 1965, Cunningham as the Sixers' first-round draft pick and Jones—a native son who had played at Overbrook High and Villanova—via a trade from Baltimore. Both would be key members of a title team the following year. Cunningham was the sixth man, relieving starting forwards Chet Walker and Luke Jackson (and playing alongside Wilt Chamberlain). Jones began the year in a three-guard rotation with Larry Costello and Hal Greer.

When Costello was lost for the season to a torn Achilles in January 1967, Jones stepped in as a starter, with nary a drop-off. That team went 68–13 ("We could have won 71," Jones said). And in the playoffs he averaged 17.5 points a game, including 27 in Game 6 of the Finals, when the Sixers closed out the San Francisco Warriors.

"When you get on the court, I don't care whether it's Sam [Jones] or Jerry West or Oscar [Robertson]. You feel you're just as good as them," Jones said. "That's the way I was taught. You're not intimidated by anybody. Nobody's better than you. You have just as much skill. The main thing is this: I wanted each NBA player I competed against to respect my game."

He sought respect off the court, too, which wasn't easy for an African American in that time. He remembered how his dad, Walter, struggled to make a living as an interior decorator. He saw how things were when he visited his brother Bob at North Carolina A&T—how blacks were not served in certain restaurants, how they could not use certain water fountains, how they were forced to sit in the balcony at movie theaters. And as a Baltimore Bullets rookie he was not allowed to stay in the team hotel when the Bullets traveled to New Orleans for an exhibition game.

Those experiences shaped him, and certainly informed his decision to convert to Islam—which resulted, among other things, in him changing his first name from "Wally" to "Wali." His switch came in the same era when Lew Alcindor converted, becoming Kareem Abdul-Jabbar, and others followed suit. And it wasn't always well received. "I had unfortunate letters," Jones said. "You have different people that were rather negative to you."

But he stuck to his guns, stuck to his beliefs. He did so when, in 1971, he held out while seeking a new contract from the Sixers, resulting in his suspension by the team, the filing of an antitrust suit on his behalf, and eventually his trade to Milwaukee. He spent two years there, another with Utah in the ABA, and in time finished up where he started, with the Sixers, in 1975–76.

And after his playing career ended he remained out front— forever a point guard, forever a quarterback.

Bobby Jones

Bobby Jones—chalky, gaunt, and hollow-cheeked—never looked like much. It looked, in fact, like he couldn't withstand a stiff breeze, much less a good power forward.

But he always seemed to be the last man standing.

Nor did he ever have to say much. Because everybody knew what he stood for. Everybody knew the depth of his faith, the strength of his character. "I used to tease him all the time: 'Have a beer, Bobby,'" said Darryl Dawkins, his devilish former teammate. "He'd say, 'No, I don't do that.' He always said he was living for the Kingdom."

It was Dawkins who took to calling Jones "White Lightning," because he was, in Dawkins' view, the "baddest white dude in the NBA." Every night he ran the floor tirelessly, defended relentlessly, and crashed into scorers' tables when necessary—all while on medication to keep his epilepsy in check. Jones played with such fury for reasons both spiritual and secular. He believed there was no better way to honor the Lord than to approach his profession in that fashion. He also believed he wouldn't be able to keep up if he didn't.

"I always felt like I had limitations on offense," he said in the fall of 2012, "and I felt like I had to make up for that with an intensity level on defense and on offense."

He was coaching middle-school kids by then, back in his hometown of Charlotte, North Carolina. He has been working with kids ever since his retirement in 1986. It seemed a natural progression, something everybody could have pictured him doing when his playing days were done. He begged to differ, though, saying he didn't envision himself coaching any more than he had envisioned himself playing in the NBA in his younger years. Both just sort of happened.

The defensive linchpin of the Sixers' 1982–83 championship team, he was part of the league's All-Defensive team in all but the last of his eight years in Philadelphia. Those who played against him underestimated him at their own peril, as he was 6'9", supremely athletic, and competitive to the nth degree. Former Indiana Pacers forward Clark Kellogg, now a respected broadcaster, once said that despite all appearances Jones was "hard-nosed."

"Anybody who plays at the level he played at, despite the soft-spoken demeanor, is a hard guy," Kellogg said. "There's a hardness to him…a toughness…a focus…a tenacity. It just doesn't manifest itself in the ways it does in other people. But you can't deny it."

Jones began playing as a kid only because his dad and older brother, both of whom played at the University of Oklahoma, goaded him into joining them on the family's tiny backyard court. He would later remember it as "an awkward time" for him; he was not very coordinated and didn't believe he had much of a future in the game.

"As a middle schooler I would see NBA games on TV and think that was the farthest thing I could ever do in my life," he said. "Seven or eight years later, I was in the league."

His dad worked with him, and both of them began to see that he wasn't nearly as gawky as either of them believed. And other factors came into play. Because the right side of the family's court had been washed away by rain, he developed his left-handed shot, something that later became one of his trademarks.

He was a star at South Mecklenburg High School, then at the University of North Carolina, where his propensity for getting rid of the ball quickly—again, because he was never very good at dribbling—fit perfectly in the Tar Heels' share-the-wealth system. He was also a first-rate finisher, leading the Atlantic Coast Conference in shooting percentage all three years he played for UNC and shooting 61 percent for his career. And when coach Dean Smith asked his players to point to teammates who assisted on their baskets, he was fastidious about that, too—to the point that he once pointed to guard George Karl, even though Jones missed a layup.

That led Smith to institute the Bobby Jones Rule, where Heels were asked to point, even after misses. "It's a team game," Jones said years later. "You don't score by yourself. Even if I missed a layup, I would thank someone for the pass. It wasn't his fault I missed. It was just a show of appreciation."

Before his senior year at UNC, he proposed marriage to his girlfriend, Tess. She balked, saying she wasn't sure she could ever wed someone who wasn't "a committed Christian." He wrestled with that, first thinking of Christians as weak before coming to the conclusion that that wasn't the case. It was a realization that informed him from that point forward.

It was also at North Carolina that he had his first epileptic seizure. He had another while a member of the Denver Nuggets, early in his professional career—that one particularly scary, since he hit his head on a butcher-block table he and Tess had in their kitchen, opening a gash—and was prescribed phenobarbital to arrest it. He was taking another medication for a heart arrhythmia, and in combination the drugs rendered him sluggish.

It led the Nuggets to make the fateful decision to trade Bobby to the Sixers in 1978, in exchange for George McGinnis. The heart condition immediately cleared up—likely because Jones was no longer playing at high altitude—and he spent eight years with the Sixers. If the fans didn't quite know what to make of him at first (for he was nowhere near the scorer McGinnis had been), they quickly warmed to him because of his no-holds-barred style.

"He didn't know how to lose," former *Philadelphia Inquirer* sportswriter George Shirk said. "It was so against the grain of what he was. He would have his left leg right at every opponent's jaw when he went in for a layup. He was a fearsome player in that he knew how to position his body. He was 6'9", and it was all knee coming at you. You got in the way of that at your own peril."

Jones was a starter in his first season with the Sixers, before second coach Billy Cunningham decided to go with a bigger lineup featuring Dawkins and Caldwell Jones. Cunningham figured that would be a tough sell with Bobby, but Jones agreed to it after a discussion that lasted "about 30 seconds," as Cunningham once said.

Jones quickly became one of the league's foremost subs and in 1982–83 was named the inaugural Sixth Man of the Year. "When I think of Bobby, I think of how brave he was," Mark McNamara, a backup center on that team, once said. "He felt a low-grade malaise, and he just rose above it. He went out and played like a brave warrior.... He was one of the key factors. He was one of those guys who made you say, 'Without him, I don't know [if a title is possible].'"

12 Maurice Cheeks

Maurice Cheeks, the best pure point guard ever employed by the 76ers, used to do this thing. This thing where he would coil in front of the luckless soul he was guarding on the perimeter. And as the guy attempted to lob a pass over Cheeks' head to a teammate nearer to the basket, Maurice would spring into the air, as a cat would toward a ball of string. It was a fast-twitch kind of thing, subtle yet impressive—the ball two, three feet out of the passer's hands, but now suddenly in possession of the Sixers.

And Cheeks did this other thing. This thing where he would sneak up behind an opposing center or forward and swipe the ball before the big galoot knew what had happened. He did this so often to Milwaukee center Bob Lanier (a guy whose size 22 feet made it appear he could step on a mite like Cheeks and squash him) that even years later Lanier would refer to him as "that damn Maurice Cheeks," and it was hard to tell if Lanier was speaking out of grudging admiration or genuine annoyance.

Cheeks did these other things, too. Things like swish open jump shots whenever the defense tilted toward his explosive backcourt partner, Andrew Toney, or retreated into the laps of Moses Malone and Julius Erving in the low post. Things like drop in layups on the fast break, after which he would often wind up splayed on the court's apron, arms and legs every which way. Sometimes it was because he was trying to draw a whistle, but just as often some Celtic or Laker or Buck or Hawk had sent him flying.

For 11 years he did his thing (or things) for the Sixers, and played 15 years in the NBA in all. His career was elegant and understated, and for a long time people said he was "underrated." It actually became ridiculous after a while, how often they said it, because the more they did so, the less true it became. The guy made four All-Star teams, four All-Defensive teams, played in three NBA Finals, and punctuated the Sixers' 1982–83 title with a joyous exclamation point of a dunk, uncharacteristic for a guy who seldom let his feelings leak out. And he has been a Hall of Fame finalist multiple times.

Underrated? No. Overlooked? Well, yeah, that argument could be made. Erving and Malone were all-timers. So too was Charles Barkley, one of Cheeks' later teammates. Toney was an ill-fated star, bound for Springfield until his body betrayed him. And let's not forget Bobby Jones, who was great in his own right. But Maurice Cheeks? Who thought about him?

That had been the case as long as anybody could remember. Go back to 1974, when the coach at West Texas State, Ron Ekker, was recruiting a big guy at Chicago's DuSable High School named William Dise. Only in passing did Ekker learn of Cheeks, Dise's teammate.

In Ekker's version of the story, DuSable coach Bob Bonner put him on to Cheeks, and he checked him out and offered a scholarship. In Dise's telling, the big forward agreed to come to West Texas State (now West Texas A&M) but asked if he might bring his point guard along. As he put it in a 2005 interview with this author, "If you have someone who butters your bread, you keep him around."

At any rate, both Cheeks and Dise wound up in Canyon, Texas—and hated it. One can only imagine the culture shock felt by two big-city African American kids when they wound up in a town of 9,000 in the middle of nowhere. Dise departed after a year, and in that first season, Cheeks threatened to leave, like, every other

Cheeks goes for a jumper in a 1982 contest against the Milwaukee Bucks.

week. Ekker was ready to let him go, too. Then Maurice's mom laid down the law: he would stay, and that was that.

Cheeks became a three-time All-Missouri Valley Conference selection but escaped the notice of most pro scouts in that pre-Internet era (though not Sixers sleuth Jack McMahon, who had seen him and liked him). So Laurie Telfair, who grew close to Maurice after he befriended her younger daughter, Michele, organized some ballot-box stuffing for the Pizza Hut Classic, a Las Vegas–based postseason All-Star Game (now defunct) whose performers were chosen by fan vote. And in the end, Canyon rigged the election in a fashion that would have done Chicago proud. Cheeks drew some 400,000 votes.

Then he went out and with supersized Afro flapping in the breeze dismantled Marquette All-American Butch Lee. That concerned the Sixers, who had secretly worked Cheeks out and planned to draft him. Now they were crossing their fingers, hoping he hadn't blown his cover by performing so well in such a high-profile setting.

But as it turned out, he was still there for them in the second round, an incredible bargain. Years later, when Cheeks was on the eve of his first season as the Sixers' head coach, someone asked him what he might have been if all that good fortune hadn't come his way. "Maybe a schoolteacher," he said. "Maybe a lawyer, architect, I don't know."

Or maybe something less. He grew up in the Robert Taylor Homes, a notorious housing project on the Windy City's South Side that was once called "the place where hope goes to die." Had Cheeks not gotten out—or if Dise and Telfair hadn't intervened on his behalf along the way—it's entirely possible that his story would have had a different ending. "There's a lot of ifs that go around this world, and that happened to be my 'if' that turned out for me," Cheeks said that day in 2005, as he relaxed in the coach's office in the Wells Fargo Center. "Those two things that happened in my life put me where I am today."

"The point of Maurice's story," Telfair said, "is that we wanted to step up and make good things happen for him. He's a good person. The other thing is, he's been able to take the opportunities and use them."

He had been done dirty by the Sixers when they traded him to San Antonio in 1989, learning of the deal not from a team official but a TV reporter. But he later spent seven years in Philadelphia as an assistant coach and in 2005 returned as the head man, after holding the same job in Portland for three-plus years. He would last another three years and change with the Sixers before being fired early in the 2008–09 season, then resurface as an assistant in Oklahoma City to Scott Brooks, his former backup in Philly. It is a position Cheeks held until June 2013, when he was hired as the Detroit Pistons' head coach (a position he held for less than a season). "I've always been more in the backseat—kinda, sorta," he said. "Always have been. It's always worked for me."

It was easy to forget about him back there. But then he would emerge, and start doing things—things that might have gone overlooked then, but remain fixed in memory now.

13 Mike Gminski

By January 2013, Mike Gminski was on the verge of a divorce, and had long been "estranged"—his word—from his parents. Yet he was buoyed by his burgeoning broadcasting career, by his relationship with his teenage son, which he vowed to make better than the one he had with his own father, and by memories of his 14-year playing career.

He spent parts of four seasons as the Sixers' starting center—they were, he said, "the best years of my professional career." He played for a coach, Jim Lynam, whom he revered. He played alongside Charles Barkley and Rick Mahorn, whom he came to regard as brothers. He was part of an Atlantic Division championship team in 1989–90. And if things ended badly in Philadelphia—his production fell off markedly early in the following season, resulting in a trade to the Charlotte Hornets—things seem to have come full circle.

"I still tell people I miss Philly, and I still wish I was there," said Gminski, who now lives in Charlotte. "It's funny—all the people that were killing me on WIP [a sports-talk radio station] at the end of my career now come up and tell me I'm the third-best center, behind Moses and Wilt. It's the one thing about the Philly fans— they will rehabilitate you after a period of time."

He is proud of the numbers he put up during his NBA run— averages of 11.7 points and 6.9 rebounds—as well as his sheer longevity. He disproved the long-held notion that Duke big men could not succeed in pro basketball, and proved that a late bloomer from a small Connecticut town (Monroe) could hit it big; Gminski didn't start playing organized basketball until the eighth grade, and then spent only three years in high school.

While he looks back fondly on his time with the Sixers, he came to Philadelphia reluctantly, in a January 1988 trade with New Jersey. He had been quite content with the Nets, with whom he spent his first seven and a half NBA seasons. He had established himself as a player, and he and his then-wife Stacy had put down roots in the New York metropolitan area—Stacy while working as a vice president for the brokerage firm Smith Barney.

The trade, Gminski said, was "traumatic." And it's not as if Barkley rolled out the welcome mat for him. Not in the first few practices, anyway.

"He tested me," Gminski said.

Barkley yapped at Gminski, tried to get under his skin. Gminski thought it not unlike the way Michael Jordan treated new teammates, and chirped right back at him.

"He just wanted to see if I was going to roll over to him or stand my ground and just be me," he said. "And I stood my ground, and I think he respected me from then on. I think if I would have caved and just tried to suck up to him that things probably wouldn't have gone as well."

They became good friends. And against all odds, Gminski grew close with Mahorn when he arrived in a trade with Minnesota in the fall of 1989. Mahorn, a bad man when he played for Washington and a fully fledged Bad Boy for the two-time champion Pistons, always operated within the rule book's gray areas (and then some), drawing opponents' ire in the process. Gminski was no exception.

"I hated him so bad for eight years, it wasn't even funny," he said. "If he were drowning, I would have stomped on his head and put him underwater."

But no sooner did Mahorn arrive in town than he invited Gminski to lunch, just to calm the waters. They were teammates now, Mahorn told him, and he would always have Gminski's back. And he did.

Barkley, Mahorn, and Gminski were the foundation of Philly's 53-victory team in 1989–90. The guards, Johnny Dawkins and Hersey Hawkins, were solid. The bench, featuring Derek Smith, Ron Anderson, and Scott Brooks, was deep. They were also an unusually close team.

"When we went into a city, eight, nine, 10 guys would go out to dinner," Gminski said. "That really didn't happen [in] a lot of places back then. And I think that was a large part of our success."

Lynam, Gminski's favorite pro coach "by far," orchestrated things perfectly. Blessed with unusual people skills, he would circulate among his players before practice each day, Styrofoam coffee cup in hand, and bounce ideas off them. It was his way of including everyone, of making sure they felt fully engaged.

There would be no happy ending for the 1989–90 Sixers, as Jordan's Bulls took them out in five games in the second round of the playoffs. And the team that had gelled so well was broken up with stunning suddenness. Gminski was among the first to go, traded to Charlotte in January 1991. His scoring average had slipped from a career-high 17.2 in 1988–89 to 13.7 in 1989–90 to 9.1 in the early stages of 1990-91, but he will always believe the bigger factor was his salary increase, from roughly $650,000 in 1988–89 to $1.7 million the following year.

"[Team owner] Harold Katz loved me at $600,000 a year," he said. "He hated me at $1.7 [million].… It was just sticker shock."

Gminski spent a few more years in the league, then became a successful broadcaster—first doing Hornets games, then gravitating to ACC ball when the Hornets relocated to New Orleans. His relationship with his parents—particularly his dad, Joe, whom the younger Gminski once described as "the ultimate Little League parent"—dissolved for reasons he doesn't wish to divulge. Same for his marriage to Stacy, whom he had known since his days at Duke.

But Mike still had his son, Noah, who despite standing 6'6" had taken up lacrosse, and was quite good at it. "I tell him I love him every day, more than once," Mike said. "That's something I never heard from my father. I try to take a gentler hand with him."

The elder Gminski continues to treasure the relationships he has with guys like Mahorn and Barkley. When Barkley had his No. 34 retired by the Sixers, and again when he was inducted into the Basketball Hall of Fame, he invited Moses Malone—who, he said, was the father he never had—as well as his two former teammates Mahorn and Gminski, calling them the brothers he never had.

"I don't know that I've ever been more touched by anything than that, for him to say that in a public forum," Gminski said. "To this day, like my Duke guys, we're a team."

14 Hersey Hawkins

It's unclear what Woody Allen said, or even if he did. Did he really say 90 percent of life is just showing up? Eighty? Less? A Google search is little help in the matter, but the saying (and attribution) persists, not to mention the sentiment. And whether Hersey Hawkins is a fan of Woody or not, he would certainly agree, at least as it pertains to the NBA: it's all about showing up.

The travel is hard, the games harder, the aches and pains constant. "There's plenty of days and nights where you're not feeling it, or your ankle's sprained or whatever, that you sort of have to suck it up and play," he said. "I think that's probably what I'm most proud of, that I really played pretty much every night and gave all I had. There weren't any nights where after the game I'd sit in the locker room or go home and think I didn't play as hard as I could [have]."

He played 13 years, the first five of them with the Sixers. In six of those seasons, he played all 82 games. In two others he missed one, and there were two more in which he missed no more than three. Not until his last three seasons did he sit out any appreciable action.

It all added up to a career in which he averaged 14.7 points—not Hall of Fame–worthy but very solid—and, according to Basketball-Reference.com, earned him more than $30 million. And certainly there were some hurdles to clear, the first coming in the playoffs at the end of his rookie year (1988–89).

He had seemingly settled in by then, having long since passed the inevitable test from Charles Barkley, who upon Hawkins' arrival the previous summer asked to see his "big penny"—that is, the bronze medal he earned at the 1988 Summer Olympics.

(Barkley, who earned gold with the Dream Team four years later, mentions it "even to this day," Hawkins said with a laugh.)

Their friendship established, Hawkins became the perimeter sniper the Sixers had lacked at shooting guard since Andrew Toney's heyday, scoring at a 15-point-per-game clip that first year and making the All-Rookie team.

Then the playoffs arrived, and he disappeared. In a three-game sweep by the Knicks he put up 24 shots. He made exactly three. Coach Jim Lynam had no choice but to replace Hawkins with veteran Gerald Henderson for long stretches. It was that bad.

He admits now to being "shell-shocked" by the physical nature of playoffs basketball, that he had no idea it would be so different from regular-season play. "There was never a time in my career where I wasn't looking to shoot the ball or was afraid to shoot it," he said, "but that was a time I had lost so much confidence that I really didn't want to shoot the ball. It was brutal.... When you're paid to go out there and score and take some pressure off Charles and the inside guys and you're not doing your job, it's the worst feeling."

It was so bad that that summer he volunteered to join the rookies and free agents in summer-league play in Los Angeles, a highly unusual move for a high draft pick coming off a solid rookie season. But he was desperate to regain his confidence, and that of the team's brain trust. "When you come off the kind of playoff series I had," he said, "I think you'll do anything to get back in good graces."

There were only a few similar bumps in the ensuing seasons. Hawkins can recall having a scoreless first half against Detroit one time in a game in the Spectrum—probably his second season, when the Sixers won the Atlantic Division. Barkley performed an intervention of sorts as the players were retreating to the locker room at halftime. "And," Hawkins said, "he grabs me by my collar and just rips into me: 'Hawk, you're too effin' good to have zero points at halftime.' And he's just killing me…. I'm in shock, because no one grabs anybody by the collar. I think I went off and had 20 the second half."

Hawkins took the gesture as it was intended. "I owe a lot of my success to him," he said. "Just letting me know, 'Hey, you have the talent to go out there and succeed. You just play hard.' That was something that's invaluable."

Hawkins had grown up in Chicago, nearly giving up the game at Westinghouse High School "out of pure laziness"—he couldn't stand getting out of bed for the team's early morning practices. "My mom sort of made me stay on the team," he said. "She pretty much told me that I wasn't quitting: 'Like it or not, you're on the team.' Thank God she made me stay."

He wound up at Bradley but nearly departed after his sophomore season, when the school went on probation and coach Dick Versace was fired. Villanova was Hawkins' likely destination, because Wildcats coach Rollie Massimino was a friend of Versace's. "It was pretty much a done deal that I was transferring," he said. He reconsidered after sitting down with the new Bradley coach, Stan Albeck, and hearing all that he had planned for him.

It turned out to be quite a lot: Hawkins put up 27 points per game as a junior, and 36 as a senior, the latter leading the nation and resulting in his selection as College Player of the Year. There were setbacks ahead, not the least of which was settling for the big penny, but over the long haul there was much for him to savor.

In fact, the thing he savors most is that there was a long haul.

15 Guarding the Greats: Bobby Jones on Julius Erving

It is the ultimate before and after: The Julius Erving who played in the ABA had big hair and a big, flamboyant game (not to mention a cool nickname—Dr. J). He would fly through the air waving that red, white, and blue basketball in one huge paw, and do things nobody had ever seen before.

The Julius Erving who migrated to the NBA in 1976 wore his hair shorter—he called it his "corporate" 'do—and was a bit more understated. Not completely, mind you, for there were still times when he let the old Doc come out and play, as when he went baseline on the Lakers in the 1980 Finals, or swooped out of the rafters to dunk on Los Angeles' Michael Cooper in the '83 regular season. But it wasn't quite the same. *He* wasn't quite the same.

His last gasp in the ABA was a how-did-he-do-that cry of wonder, an individual tour de force in a six-game victory by his New York Nets over the Denver Nuggets in the upstart league's last championship series. (After that the league would fold up shop, with the Nets, Nuggets, Indiana Pacers, and San Antonio Spurs joining the NBA, and the ABA's other players dispersed throughout the old league.)

Erving's performance in that series—he averaged 37.7 points, 14.2 rebounds, and six assists—came at the expense of Nuggets forward Bobby Jones, one of the finest defensive forwards of his day and later Erving's teammate with the Sixers (as well as a close friend).

All these years later, Jones remembers Erving burying an 18-foot jumper over him to win Game 1—"I was hanging all over him," he said—and the Nets rallying from a huge deficit to win the clincher. (Quite so: New York, down 80–58 in the third quarter of Game 6, came back to win it 112–106.)

Jones, curiously, seemed almost fascinated by Erving's display. "I really enjoy watching him," he told *Sports Illustrated* at the time, "because every time he does one of those moves I know it's something I may never see again."

Reminded of that in April 2013, he chuckled. He talked about being "in a very unique position," in that he not only checked Erving but had as a Nuggets teammate David Thompson, a spectacular offensive player in his own right. In his mind those two, along with Michael Jordan, were as uniquely skilled as anyone he ever saw.

In that long-ago *SI* story, Jones said there wasn't much he could do against Erving. In the first game of that series, he said, he tried to make the Doctor go baseline, and he went right by him. Jones then tried to force him middle, but Erving made jumpers or blew past him in that direction.

Jones did manage to cut off Erving's baseline drive in the closing seconds of Game 1, only to see Erving rise up for his decisive jumper. "[I] barely missed getting a piece of the ball," Jones recalled. "But he swished it. Just a great shot…. I think I played the play really well. I knew what he was going to do, and I still couldn't stop him."

Erving scored 45 in that one, 48 in Game 2, and no fewer than 31 in any of the other four games. Jones said he tried to front him in an attempt to deny him the ball, only to see the other Nets lob it over the top, knowing that the Doctor, with his leaping ability, was sure to get it. There were also times when Erving foiled Jones' attempts at denial by bringing the ball up himself.

Double-teaming? That was tough, too, because Erving was such a good passer. "With his hang time and his ball control with his hands, he could make a lot of passes that a lot of guys couldn't make," Jones said. "It would be like somebody throwing a volleyball."

Jones would continue to guard Erving his first two years in the NBA, while still a Nugget. But after he was traded to the Sixers in 1978, they seldom squared off in practice, since the team didn't scrimmage all that much.

They remained teammates for eight years, until Jones retired in '86, one year before Erving. Asked to single out something that amazed him most about Erving, Jones pointed not to his friend's play but to the way he treated his teammates.

"You hear a lot about superstars, [how] they put pressure on younger guys to come up to their level," he said. "Julius was such an encourager. That's what stood out in my mind, I think, the entire time I was with him: He wasn't arrogant. He didn't consider himself better than anybody. He worked as hard as anybody, if not harder. Didn't put anybody down for the mistakes that they made. That's easy to do at that level, when the game's on the line or something's on the line. He knows he can do it, but you're in a position where you have to do it and you don't, it takes strength of character to say, 'We're in this together. We win together, we lose together.' I think that was probably, to me, his greatest quality."

Most everyone saw the best of Julius Erving in the ABA. Bobby Jones, it appears, saw the best of him much longer than that.

16 Guarding the Greats: Nate Thurmond on Wilt Chamberlain

On the eve of training camp in 1963, most of the San Francisco Warriors had settled into their hotel in San Jose. Everybody but Wilt Chamberlain. Not to worry, though—the Big Fella was coming. That's what everybody kept saying—the Big Fella was coming.

Rookie Nate Thurmond could appreciate the nickname, as that's what everybody had called him all his life. At 6'11" and 225 pounds, he was a sturdily built guy, destined to play 14 years and land in the Hall of Fame. Naturally he knew all about Wilt and his many feats, but he had never seen him in the flesh.

Finally, as Thurmond gathered with his new teammates in the room of veteran guard Al Attles, he heard a loud banging on the door. It was the Big Fella, of course, and finally Thurmond could fully appreciate just how massive Wilt was. Listed at 7'1" and 275 pounds, he was surely closer to 290 at that point. He bent to enter the room and then, well, unfolded.

"All I'm thinking is, *Tomorrow morning I have to practice against him*," Thurmond recalled in March 2013. "And I was weighing 228. I thought I was pretty good-sized.... The first practice, I was almost afraid to touch him. Here's a guy I had heard about who scored 100 points in a game. I didn't want to make him mad, so I probably didn't put as much force on him as I did once I got to know he was not a mean guy."

That was the thing about Wilt: he was a gentle giant, probably too gentle for his own good on the court. "If he had been a guy like Shaq, who would throw a few elbows and bull his way in," Thurmond said, "he could have scored 60 a game."

Wilt's nature informed the way Thurmond defended him when they became opponents midway through Thurmond's second season, after Chamberlain was traded to the Sixers. The first order of business was to play him not for the power move but for his fadeaway jump shot, which he launched from the right side of the lane.

"The best thing in getting him off his spot was not letting him get on his spot," Thurmond said. "In other words, I'd beat him down the court and I'd set up where he liked to set up. I would try to make him get me off the spot."

There was no question about Wilt's strength. Thurmond was among those who regarded Chamberlain as being almost "superhuman." On one of those rare occasions when he was angered during a game, Chamberlain picked up an opponent under the armpits—Thurmond doesn't remember the player's name, only that he was "a good-sized guy"—and moved him several feet.

But mostly, Thurmond said, "Wilt didn't like to use his strength." So Thurmond tried to beat him to the spot, force him farther out than he preferred. He was wary of Wilt's countermove—a spin into the lane for a dunk—and tried to limit his fast-break and offensive-rebounding opportunities. And certainly if Wilt did put Thurmond in a compromising position, he could always foul him, given Chamberlain's struggles at the free-throw line.

Thurmond's memory is that he fared rather well against Wilt. "He never got 50 on me," he said. "I don't know about 40. I made him shoot more shots than he normally would to get what he got. Sometimes he was in the high 30s, whatever, but he didn't go crazy on me."

There's little question in Thurmond's mind that he gained a full understanding of Wilt's arsenal while they were teammates. But Thurmond took his defensive duties seriously no matter the opponent—so much so that he jotted down notes about every center he faced in a notebook, then reviewed those notes before facing that opponent the next time.

In his mind, his toughest cover was Kareem Abdul-Jabbar, who made his debut in 1969, when Thurmond was in his seventh season. "That hook shot—not too many shots were better than that," he said.

But the Big Fella wasn't far behind. He seldom took a backseat to anybody.

17 Guarding the Greats: Malik Rose on Charles Barkley

Charles Barkley was just trying to do Malik Rose a good turn, as Rose had once done him. Granted, Barkley's charity only went so far. But the first time they met on the court as NBA players—Rose as a rookie second-round draft pick of the Charlotte Hornets and Barkley as a grizzled 13-year veteran with the Houston Rockets—the older man was willing to extend a helping hand.

They had known each other dating back to the time when Rose, a Philly kid from Overbrook High, worked in the kitchen at the Sixers' summer camp in East Stroudsburg, Pennsylvania. One day Barkley and teammate Rick Mahorn showed up to speak to the campers, but when lunchtime rolled around the two players judged the meal to be unpalatable. Rose—who had always idolized Barkley and would indeed grow to become a similarly sized player—was dispatched to prepare a batch of peanut butter–and-jelly sandwiches. "And I bring them out to them," Rose, now the color analyst on Sixers television broadcasts, recalled in early 2013, "and they devour those things."

Fast forward a half dozen years. Rose had starred at Overbrook, then Drexel. Barkley had moved on from the Sixers to Phoenix, and then Houston. And there was Rose, entering a preseason game for the Hornets.

"When I check in, he's like, 'Hey, you're the Sixer camp kid,'" Rose said. "He remembered me, which put me not on cloud nine [but] on cloud 99."

Barkley went to work against the rookie, backing him down toward the basket. He chattered as he went, but was not demeaning in any way. Rather, he was instructive.

"The whole time I'm guarding him," Rose said, "he's like, 'No, you don't want to do this. If you do this, I'm going to go this way on you.' And he scores on me. Then the next time: 'Now that I've scored on you, you don't want to let me go this way, because I'll do this.'… He's schooling me while he's…schooling me. He's giving me pointers like 'Keep your hands up this way. Keep your foot this way.' And all the while he's scoring on me. So it was a memorable first time I played Barkley."

Rose's career, which would span 13 years and four teams, overlapped with Barkley's for four seasons. He came to understand that the best way to defend a player of Barkley's caliber was to meet him as far out on the court as possible—"at the top of the key, or at the latest the foul line," Rose said—shadow him everywhere and make him earn everything he gets. But the task was never all that easy.

"Barkley," Rose said, "was one of the toughest [to play], just because he could do so many things."

Get up on him, and Barkley was quick enough to drive to the rim. Lay off him, and he would hit his jumper. The best any defender could do was limit Barkley's options as he set up in his preferred spot on the left block.

"With Barkley you couldn't let him feel your body," Rose said, "because if he felt your body, he could either move you out of the way or he could roll off you. So I stayed on his right hand, all the while keeping my distance, so he couldn't feel my body. And that kind of gave me a little bit of an edge."

As much as could be expected, anyway. Barkley was always going to get his points.

"You don't get discouraged, because he's one of the 50 all-time greatest in NBA history," Rose said. "It's almost like an honor. I didn't like getting scored on, and half the time I got scored on I got subbed out. I had no room for mistakes…. But if Barkley scored on me or Shaq [O'Neal] or [Dirk] Nowitzki or Rasheed Wallace— whoever—it was like, you're guarding the best player on that team. He's going to score every now and then. But if you stop him, then it's a huge feather in your cap."

18 Guarding the Greats: Matt Harpring on Allen Iverson

Orlando Magic coach Chuck Daly came to rookie Matt Harpring before a first-round playoff series in 1999 and told him he had one job: frustrate Allen Iverson.

Frustrate Iverson? Really? Frustrate a guy Harpring would come to regard as "the ultimate competitor"—as a player who never seemed to tire, never seemed to grow discouraged, never seemed to stop attacking? Yes, Iverson would miss shots. He would miss a lot of them. But he never hesitated to take the next one. That quality would not always make him an ideal teammate, as Harpring would learn when he played for the Sixers three years later. But it made him a nightmare to defend.

The Magic were the Eastern Conference's third seed in 1999, having gone 33–17 during the lockout-shortened regular season. The Sixers had gone 28–22 and were seeded sixth. But Harpring, now a Utah Jazz TV analyst, said in early 2013 that Philly was "the one team in the league we did not want to play," since the Sixers had beaten the Magic twice in three regular-season meetings.

They won the best-of-five series as well, in four games, as Iverson averaged 28.3 points. That would seem to indicate that Harpring failed in his attempts to frustrate the Sixers star, but Iverson himself was complimentary of Harpring's defensive work afterward, and Philadelphia coach Larry Brown went so far as to tell the Magic rookie that he wouldn't mind coaching him someday— as indeed he would when Harpring arrived in Philadelphia via trade in August 2001.

What Brown saw—what everybody saw—was Harpring bumping Iverson off the ball, trying to make him go where he didn't want to go. He insists he wasn't dirty, but he was physical. And when Iverson did catch it, Harpring shaded his right hand, wary of "that great left-to-right crossover—the killer cross."

"You had to shade one way," Harpring said, "and you always shaded for him to cross back over and go to his right hand."

While doing that, Harpring, who at 6'7" was seven inches taller than Iverson's listed height, backed off a step, the thinking being that it was always better to make Iverson shoot a jumper over an extended hand than allow him to invade the lane. He was, Harpring said, "probably the best layup shooter" he had ever seen, a guy who could finish over bigger defenders, and despite contact.

"More people laid him out on the floor than I've seen anyone else," Harpring said. "He could take a hard pounding, and he'd bounce right back up.... He was not a guy that got intimidated. I'm sure he didn't like it, but he never let it affect him either."

Iverson scored 30 points, albeit while shooting 12-for-29, in Philadelphia's Game 1 victory, then was limited to 13, on 4-for-15 shooting, as Orlando won Game 2. But he exploded for 33 and 37 points as the Sixers won the last two games, shooting 14-for-28 and 14-for-27, respectively.

As Iverson went about his work, he was never one to say much, according to Harpring. "He's not a trash-talker," he said. "He will [do so] if you say something to him, but he's not really one to go after you and start talking."

Harpring spent the 2001–02 season playing alongside Iverson, averaging 11.8 points. He came to appreciate Iverson's competitiveness, while learning to live with the fact that he was going to dominate the ball. "I enjoyed playing with a guy that just cared so much," Harpring said. "Yeah, I mean it's frustrating when you don't get the ball. You know Allen's going to shoot it 30 times a game, and you're out there open sometimes. All those things kind of went through me when I played. But on the other side of it, he won us some big games, and without him we wouldn't have won some of those games."

Harpring moved on to Utah the next season—"basketball heaven," he called it—averaging a career-best 17.6 points on a free-flowing offense featuring John Stockton and Karl Malone. In all he played the last seven of his 11 seasons there.

And if he was not always overjoyed about Iverson being "the first, second, and third option" in Philadelphia, as he put it, he developed a deep, abiding respect for him.

"He's a popcorn popper's player," Harpring said. "When the popcorn was popping, he was ready. It didn't matter what he did, 12 hours beforehand or [in] practice or whatever. When that ball went up, that guy was ready to play. He was focused in, never wanted to come out of the game. Played through pain. Played hurt. And I just enjoyed it. I love when guys put their heart and soul into things."

19 Guarding the Greats: Danny Schayes on Moses Malone

When it came to defending Moses Malone, size didn't matter. Even Mark Eaton, who stood 7'4" and weighed 275 pounds in his heyday with the Utah Jazz (some six inches taller and 20 pounds heavier than the 6'10", 255-pound Malone), said he "hated" facing him.

And when defending Malone, fundamentals mattered only to a point. Danny Schayes, who played for seven teams over 18 years (1981–99) and considered himself a technically sound defender, nonetheless knew Moses, who spent five of his 20 NBA seasons with the Sixers, presented an enormous challenge.

The key was matching Malone's ferocity and focus. Understanding how the game was going to be called, and if (or, at least, how much) the calls were going to favor him. And then just hanging in there, because as Schayes said, playing Moses was like playing the Tasmanian Devil: "He was coming at you all the time."

Other post players of that era, such as Kareem Abdul-Jabbar and Hakeem Olajuwon, were almost elegant in their approach; Moses was not. Others, such as Kevin McHale and Patrick Ewing, had precise footwork and patented moves; Moses did not. "Moses had an ugly shot," Schayes said, "and he dribbled inefficiently…. But he was just everywhere. He was relentless. And he was effective as hell, doing whatever he was doing. That made him a tough guard. He was unpredictable."

That being the case, Schayes, son of longtime Syracuse Nationals star Dolph Schayes, always knew it was going to require a "big-effort game" against Malone. He promised himself he would always try to match Malone's intensity—no easy task—that he would always try to stand up to him and keep him off the offensive glass.

But there were no guarantees. The officiating was, in Schayes' mind, the biggest wild card. "You wouldn't know if you would get three touch fouls or he's slamming into you," he said. "He always got way better calls than I got."

During a game in 1982–83—the season Moses led the Sixers to a title—Schayes can remember Malone grabbing him around the neck and throwing him to the floor. And that *Schayes* was the one called for the foul.

Moses knew all the tricks. Against the mountainous Eaton, one of the top shot-blockers of all time, Malone would always lean in, always create contact. "I needed about six inches of space as a shot-blocker to get the right angle," Eaton said. "Moses would soak that space right up and make it impossible for me to get at his shot."

And while Malone was one of the finest offensive rebounders ever, many of his contemporaries (Schayes included) believed he padded his stats by missing close-in attempts on purpose, then reclaiming the board and going back up with it. It is a claim Malone has long denied, but as Schayes said, "If he had opportunities and he was inside and had position, he'd punch the ball to the rim and get it back. He did that all the time.... It was amazing how that shot hit the low part of the front of the rim and came right back to him. He never missed over [the top]. He never rolled the ball off the other side of the rim. It always touched short and came right back to him."

Schayes also believes Malone set picks for teammates that were "just good enough to get you open, but not good enough to get you open for a shot." That way a guard or small forward would catch the ball on the wing and likely be compelled to throw it into the post, to Moses. And there the slam dance with his defender would begin anew.

A good night against Moses, Schayes said, was making him as inefficient as possible—holding him to a low shooting percentage, keeping him off the boards and the foul line. A good night, really, was weathering the assault and living to fight another day.

20 Bond between Doc and A.I.

"When people tell me it's Doctor and A.I. when they talk Philly basketball, and that's like one of the biggest compliments that someone can give you. Doctor and A.I. You put my name in the same sentence as Doc. That's why this day is so special, because of days like that."
—Allen Iverson talking at his retirement about being grouped with Julius Erving

Doc did it with class. He was the elite of the league. A.I. was the renegade. He created a new movement. Yet the fans seem bonded to both, even though both did it so differently.

"I think the fact that once you get on the hardwood, once you step on the court, then it doesn't matter who you are competing against," Erving said during Iverson's retirement announcement. "You were competing for your team, your fans, and your house, and you were the guy who was the leader of the team. You were the ultimate warrior."

Both players had a warrior mentality, though both went about it in different ways. Erving and his Afro and Iverson and his cornrows. Both were odd sights. Both were cool in their own way. Dr. J was the high-flyer who made playing above the rim acceptable. A.I. was the little guy with a big heart who brought the hip-hop culture to the NBA.

The two had similar childhoods. Both were raised primarily by their mother. Both grew up having to take care of the family, and both lived in or near housing projects. But the two approached their backgrounds differently. Erving looked back on his old neighborhood as a way to collect a memory; Iverson never wanted to leave the past behind, fearing it would make him a sellout.

In 1994, Erving was named by *Sports Illustrated* as one of the 40 most important athletes of all time. Iverson's mark on history has not been set, but his influence on today's players is immediately evident. Just look at the amount of players with tattoos.

Scoring and coming up in the clutch for their team, none were much better than these two.

While playing for the ABA's Virginia Squires, New York Nets, and the NBA's 76ers, Dr. J won three scoring titles, four Most Valuable Player awards, and three championships. A.I. won four scoring titles, one MVP, and played in the NBA Finals.

Both also entered the NBA with a lot of fanfare.

"My journey with Philly very much parallels Allen's—first-round pick, a lot of expectations," Erving said. "They gave me the ball and said, 'All right, you are going to be our franchise player and we are going to live with you and what you bring is going to determine how far we go.'

"So we were on parallel paths in that regard. When I look back in years after I got out and the torch was passed along to Charles Barkley and Barkley did very well with the torch and then moved on to Phoenix and Houston and then Allen came in. It was an exciting time for Philadelphia. I was almost a generation removed from following basketball and being emotionally tied to the franchise, but I got a chance to see him and cheer for him and pull for him."

Erving, who was inducted into the Naismith Memorial Basketball Hall of Fame in 1993, said the Sixers are the third team in the trinity of teams that have had the most success in the NBA—third-most wins in the regular season, third-most wins in the playoffs, three titles for the franchise, which is not quite third,

Two generations of Philly greatness: Julius Erving and Allen Iverson embrace before the 76ers' 2005 season opener.

but from a winning standpoint, is still impressive. Those are longevity stats, he said.

"And that means the franchise has been around for a long time and that has opened the door for it to have, for certain decades, certain people who are identifiable with the franchise," said Erving, who played from 1976 to 1987 with the Sixers. "Wilt certainly was in the '60s and I was so in the '70s, early '80s; Allen in the '90s, entering the 2000s. You had the Billy Cunningham era [1965–72], of course, and the Barkley era [1984–92], which overlapped and connected me with Allen. So it is what it is."

What it is, in many ways, is a bond between two players Philadelphia fans embraced like few others. Wilt and maybe Sir Charles are in the conversation, but A.I. and Doc have a special place in the hearts of Philly fans.

"The fans are me," Iverson said. "I am Philadelphia. When you think of Philadelphia basketball you think of Allen Iverson and I fought for that and I earned that."

On some special occasions Erving said he had the opportunity to be with Iverson, who was humbled that Dr. J showed up to see him at an All-Star party and also at his 30th birthday party.

"Allen has cried in my presence, and that just shows his sensitive side," Erving said. "We may have been a generation removed, but when I came and made my cameos here [in Philly for games] and peeked at him, at what he was doing, I was impressed by him on the court.

"Off the court, it was a bit of a turnoff, because of my background and my conditioning. I moved from a housing project and a broken home to a situation with mentors, teachers, and guidance and learned the value of stepping on the other side of the tracks and providing an example for others and kind of paved the way."

Bobby Jones, who was a teammate of Doc's, sees the one big difference Between Erving and Iverson.

"Julius changed the game. He was athletic, but also so smart with the ball," said Jones, who played for the Sixers from 1978 to 1986. "It was hard to guard a guy like him. He controlled the ball and he was unselfish. He was way ahead of his time, because he could score whenever he wanted to, but he knew he had to get other guys involved and he did.

"Allen didn't have that luxury. Allen had to play by himself a lot. That's a difference. Julius recognized what he had and took advantage of it."

Henry Bibby, who played with Erving from 1976 to 1980 and was an assistant coach on the Iverson-led Sixers, believes A.I. isn't given enough credit.

"They're the best. Both those guys are the best," he said. "Allen was very good to coach. He knew what he needed to do to play. As he moved through his golden age he knew more about the game of basketball and how it should be played. He is an icon of a basketball player. I just hate to see him go out where he didn't get all the accolades he needed to have gotten, like Julius and people like that. To me, he's a Hall of Famer. Allen Iverson should be in the Hall of Fame, and hopefully one day he will be."

What was it like playing with Erving?

"The most important thing was being friends with him," he said. "I was friends with him. We went out to eat a lot. My family, his family spent a lot of time together. Just a superstar, but I didn't see him as a superstar. I saw him as a great, great man. Personable, loved people, would do anything for people. That's the Julius Erving I knew. I didn't know Dr. J. I knew him as Julius."

Maurice Cheeks, a former NBA head coach with Portland, Philadelphia, and Detroit, also played with Doc, starting in 1978. He was an assistant coach with the 76ers (1994–2001) and head coach (2005–08) during much of the time Iverson was with the Sixers.

"Playing with Doc, he was a great player. Coaching Allen, he was a great player," Cheeks said. "You got two guys that just captivated when they played. Allen, his size was a major factor, because he was small in stature but his game was just so huge. And Doc was huge all over, so I think they go hand in hand."

21 Where's the Ball?

Harvey Pollack has worked with the NBA and its Philadelphia bas-ketball franchises since 1946. He was in Hershey, Pennsylvania, when Wilt Chamberlain scored 100 points on March 2, 1962. He did stats and public relations for the Philadelphia Warriors.

"See that sign he's holding?" Pollack said, pointing to a photo in his Wells Fargo Center office in October 2013. "I'm the one that wrote that 100 sign."

The rest of this chapter is written in Pollack's words, about what happened to the basketball Chamberlain used to score 100 points.

There is a picture in the Hall of Fame of him holding a basketball and that sign. That ball—it's a mystery where it is. Wilt may have known, but he's gone, so you can't ask him.

Some people said they had the ball. Wilt died in '99. The spring the following year some guy in Hershey said he had the ball and he went to an auction house to auction off the ball.

When I heard about this and the story came out that they were going to auction off the ball, I cast a lot of doubt about it. I traced the ball. The guy said he was 12 years old and grabbed the ball out of Wilt's hand. He took it from a 275-pound man. If you know Wilt, that didn't happen.

I was the PR director of the team and the game statistician when he got the 100 points. The game was late in the season and the [Philadelphia] *Inquirer* didn't send anyone to Hershey and they asked me to cover the game. The AP and UPI asked me to cover it. So I'm the one that let the whole world know about this feat.

I had the Zink [Dave Zinkoff] in the second half, when he got to about 65 points, announce every point. "Dipper Dunk, Chamberlain. That's 72." "Layup, Chamberlain, that's 74." "That's two free throws, 76."

By the time the game came down to the 90s, nobody was even thinking about 100, that he'd get that close.... When he got 100, there were 4,000 people there, but 50,000 say they were there. But there were 4,000. When [he got 100], the 4,000 people, everybody in the stands flew to the floor; there was nobody left in the stands. They were shaking his hand and talking with him.

Finally, they cleared the floor. They had 46 seconds to play. Meanwhile, the referee in charge, his name was Willie Smith, came over to me at the table. I was the highest ranking official he could reach. He said to me, "I think we should take this ball out of the game." I said, "Why, is something wrong with it?" He said, "No, I think it should be in the Hall of Fame."

"Good idea," I said.

There were no locks on the doors for the dressing rooms in Hershey. So when the game started, this was our home game, Philadelphia—the Knicks were the visitors, so we had to supply the balls for them to warm up. The Knicks didn't want their balls stolen, so they put them at my feet in the press area on the floor during the game. So [Smith] asked, "Where are we going to get another ball?"

I said, "You won't have to go too far. Here they are," and I pulled one of them warm-up balls from my feet. I took a ball out and Willie Smith felt it and bounced it and said, "It feels all right to me."

So that's how they finished the game. But Wilt never participated in the [last] 46 seconds. He stood on the side of the court with his arms spread out to the side and watched the last 46 seconds. Never touched that ball. That's an important part.

The game ended and Wilt went right to the dressing room. Meanwhile, I had to finish the box score with the official scorer, to make sure we both jived and we had 100 each. We gave it to one of the runners to run it off on the ditto machine—they didn't have a mimeograph machine—so we brought the ditto machine up from Philadelphia.

Then I went back to the dressing room, after putting out a one paragraph lead to the *Inquirer* story saying, "Wilt Chamberlain

Wilt holds the sign, but where's the ball?

broke all NBA scoring records tonight by scoring 100 points in a 169–147 victory over the New York Knicks."

I was sending copy during the game. I had a portable typewriter sitting beside me, and at every timeout I typed. My son, who was at the game, was the runner and he took the copy to Western Union, which was on the second level in the arena.

Other than the *Inquirer* and people at the game, no one else knew about the 100-point game. When the game started, there was not one photographer there. No television. This was '62. Bill Campbell was there broadcasting the game on radio. A photographer for AP was there. He brought his son to see Wilt. He was just at the game with his son. He came in the locker room. He was the only guy to have pictures at that game.

I said, "Did you get all the pictures you want of Wilt?"

He said, "No, I don't have anything that really tells the story."

I said, "Why don't you get something to illustrate it?"

"What can I get?" he asked.

I said, "I'll tell you what you can get."

A ripped off a sheet of notebook paper and wrote the 100 on it. I said, "How about Wilt holds the paper?"

Let me go back.

After I gave the referee a new ball, I called the equipment manager over and said, "Take this ball into the dressing room and put it into Wilt's duffle bag, and that's what he did. So when Wilt came in the room and took the ball out, he had the equipment manager, the ball boy, sign the ball. So all the players signed the ball, the owner, the official scorekeeper, the timer…everybody. So the ball was being passed around the room at the time.

I said, "How about I get the ball being passed around and the sheet?"

The photographer said, "Will Wilt do that?" I said, "Wilt will do anything for me."

I walked over to Wilt and said, "Wilt, there was only one photographer here at this game tonight and he's got exclusive photos. He wants to get a shot of you holding the ball and holding up this sign, 100."

Wilt said, "You want me to do this, Harv?"

"Of course. Why else do you think I asked you for?" I said. "Okay, I'll do it," he says.

I went over and got the ball and gave Wilt the sign. The guy took the photo; he took more than one. The guy said, "Boy, that's a great picture." It's so great that they already call it the greatest piece of memorabilia. Then I took the ball back and they resumed signing it.

Then I left and started calling newspapers, AP, and UPI and my son read them the box score. I went back to the scorer's table and wrote a completely new story for the *Inquirer*, which appeared on page one of the paper. Not page one [of the] sports page, but page one of the paper. But they didn't give me a byline. It said "Special to the *Inquirer*. Don't think I didn't let everyone know that I wrote that story.

But I have said that was the biggest mistake of my life, because if I had taken that sheet of paper [with 100 on it] and held on to it…collector's items were not as big as they are today. A collector told me that if I still had that sheet I could sell it and be a rich man. [That sheet] was probably swept up and trashed.

After we left, Wilt, who lived in New York—and we were playing the Knicks the next night in New York—traveled back to New York with the Knicks.

The next day I got back to the Sixers office and asked Zink if the ball was there. He said, "Yeah, it is here." The office had pictures in the windows. Zink got the ball from the picture window. One panel on the ball was blank, while all the others had signatures on them. Zink wrote [on the blank panel] THIS IS THE BALL WITH

WHICH WILT CHAMBERLAIN SCORED 100 POINTS IN HERSHEY, PA., AT THE HERSHEY ARENA ON MARCH 2, 1962, and put it in the window.

Shortly after that we lost to Boston in a seven-game playoff series and the owner decided to sell the team, saying he couldn't afford to pay Wilt what he's worth. So he sold it to San Francisco. Now this I can't prove, but he sent everything about the Warriors to San Francisco. In my case, all my pictures of players, all my bio sketches of players, all business records. There was nothing left in that office that had anything to do with the Warriors.

What I think happened is [Warriors owner, general manager, and coach] Eddie Gottlieb called Wilt and asked if he wanted the ball or should we send it to San Francisco as a piece of memorabilia? I think he said he'd come in and get it. Anyone who could confirm this is dead.

Remember, this was the year 2000. Wilt died in '99. Zink was dead. Eddie Gottlieb was dead. I can never prove it. But the fact is that Wilt said he had the ball.

Then comes that auction and I don't believe the story. I called the *Inquirer* and told them the story, how I traced the ball from the referee to me, to the ball boy to Wilt to the people signing the ball, the trainer who took the ball to our office and it was in our window.

I told them I believe Wilt came in and got the ball. And I don't believe the story about a 12-year-old stealing the ball away from Wilt. I know he didn't do it, because I had the ball and Wilt never touched that ball.

It became a national story. Is that the ball? Meanwhile, they are bidding on it. One week of bidding. The story became so big, Tom Brokaw, NBC; Dan Rather, CBS; Peter Jennings, ABC; all came to Philadelphia, at different times, to interview me. The story went all across the country.

The guy who bid on the ball paid $550,000. He reads this in newspapers and television. You have one week from the time you make your bid to put up the money. They canceled the auction for further investigation.

When they first posted the auction, they said, "This is the ball with which Wilt Chamberlain scored 100 in 1962." Three months later, they say, "This is the ball that was used in the game in which Wilt scored his 100 points." Remember, Wilt stood on the sideline and never touched the ball for the last 46 seconds.

I didn't care about this ball. But it is still a mystery where the ball [with which] he scored 100 points is at. People came out of the woodwork saying they had the ball.

The former owner of the Warriors told me Wilt gave him the ball. I asked if there were names on the ball. He said, "No." I said, "Who is listed as the commissioner on the basketball?" He said the name, but that wasn't the commissioner when Wilt scored 100. So I said, "How can you have the ball?"

I think Wilt, having fun the rest of his life, was giving balls away and telling people this is the ball that I scored 100 points with.

22 Game Night: Tom McGinnis

Chicago Stadium had always been a special place to Tom McGinnis. It is where he saw his first NBA game as a kid, having made the two-hour drive from his home in Spring Valley, Illinois, with his bank-president dad, Philip. It is where, on subsequent visits, he developed an abiding affection for the game and the league.

He returned there to call a game in 1995, as the rookie play-by-play man on the Sixers' radio network. Again his father joined him. In Tom's younger years Philip had waited patiently in the stands while his son, the third-oldest of five children he had with his wife, Joan, wandered down to the court during warm-ups, so that he might get as close to the players as possible. Usually the visiting players, Tom said.

Security being what it was in those days, Tom could eavesdrop on their conversations, learn what the guys were all about. And in time he would be shooed back to his seat.

So now there he was, all these years later, free to go wherever he wanted. As he walked into the building alongside his dad, he reached out and grabbed him by the hand.

"Thank you for the dream, Dad," he said.

"Thanks for being a good son," the older man said.

Tom buried his dad in January 2013, and was still holding on to him. As he sat courtside at the Wells Fargo Center a few weeks later, with tipoff of a Sixers-Pacers game less than an hour away, he recalled his final conversation with his dad, just a few days before he died at age 89—one in which Philip wondered how Coach Doug Collins was holding up, since the team was coming off a loss to Toronto and would surely never beat Houston in its next game (which turned out to be incorrect).

And Tom thought back to the time his dad sat alongside him as he broadcast a playoff game years earlier, also against the Pacers. Tom had lectured his dad about the fact that cheering was strictly forbidden on press row, and Philip adhered to that rule—until Indiana star Reggie Miller was slapped with a technical foul. Then he allowed himself a small celebration. (Tom shared that story with Miller when he was done playing, and he could only laugh. "C'mon, Pops," he said, in mock indignation.)

After his father died, Tom couldn't help but turn the clock back even further, to his freshman year of high school. Diagnosed with scoliosis (curvature of the spine), doctors fitted him with something known as a Milwaukee device, a metal neck-to-ankle brace he was required to wear 20 hours a day for 10 months.

Tom and his dad were driving home from Milwaukee after Tom donned the thing for the first time, and they stopped at a nice restaurant. As they were being seated Tom couldn't help but notice the stares from the other diners. It was more than he could take. He broke down. They were moved by the staff to a lunchroom, where they could eat in peace, and where his dad could console him.

Alas, Philip could only shield Tom from so much. He drove him to school the next day, intentionally arriving late to spare him the indignity of the morning rush. It turned out that the first kid Tom saw was the class clown. "Hey, Tin Man, what's up?" the kid teased.

But there were also times when patrons at the local restaurant where Tom washed dishes would see him and take pity, stuffing dollar bills in the waitresses' hands to pass over to him.

Looking back at that time, he said, "It taught me a lot about people. I was looked at differently."

On the trip back from another appointment in Milwaukee, Philip tuned the radio to a station carrying Game 5 of the 1976 NBA Finals between Boston and Phoenix. And, Tom said, "It keeps going and going and going."

It would, in fact, extend to three overtimes—so long that the two McGinnises stopped by a tavern not far from home to take in the final minutes of the Celtics' victory. There are those who have written that that was a watershed moment for young Tom, the moment when he grew certain he would follow the NBA's siren song. In truth, he had already been bitten by the pro basketball bug during those trips to Chicago Stadium; hearing that landmark game was just another step in the process.

By his sophomore year of high school he shed the brace; years later Sixers doctors would inform that him the thing did him no good whatsoever—news, Tom said, that "crushed" his parents. As it was, he played three years of basketball and two of football in high school, before devoting himself exclusively to hoops for two years at Illinois Benedictine.

He then transferred to Northern Illinois, earned his degree in broadcast journalism, and began an extensive apprenticeship. Weekend sports anchor in Charleston, South Carolina. Sports director in Panama City, Florida. Minor league basketball play-by-play man in Cedar Rapids and LaCrosse, Wisconsin. Minor league hockey voice back in Charleston, as well as in Cleveland.

Finally he landed in Philadelphia. He has become known for his enthusiastic calls, for bellowing out "Are you kidding me?" Sometimes that's said with wonder, as when the Sixers make a spectacular play, sometimes with derision, as when the referees make a decision incomprehensible to him.

But in truth he likes the quieter times, those times courtside before the game, when the arena is just coming to life. As in his younger years, he is curious to hear what the players have to say as they warm up. He likes to visit with team officials, writers, other broadcasters. He likens it to the time spent around the batting cage before a Major League Baseball game. "It's my way to be around the game still—the human drama," he said.

By tipoff he is off on his own, for while he has had on-air partners through the years, more often than not his has been a solo act. Turns out that's not completely true, though. Turns out he has always had someone to hold onto, whether he's there in the flesh or not. And that's still the case.

23 Andre Iguodala

His first game back in Philadelphia as an opponent, Andre Iguodala was booed *and* accorded a standing ovation. It had to be a first, and it neatly summed up the fans' view of the ex-Sixer: *We're really, really glad you're gone, but on the other hand, you weren't all bad.*

The issue was money, as it almost always is. The Sixers gave him a superstar contract—six years, $80 million—in the summer of 2008, and he simply wasn't a superstar; there were even those within the organization who acknowledged as much over time. He was a brilliant defender, one of the best in the league at checking high-scoring wings, but he was inconsistent at the other end of the court.

He would have been fine as a complementary piece on a great club. But it never sat well with many fans that he was instead cast as the team's centerpiece. They always expected more than he seemed capable of giving. And when he didn't deliver, they wanted to see him on the next flight out of town. He always exuded indifference toward the fans' disdain, never lashing out but never making much of an attempt to build bridges during his eight years in town either. As a result there was detachment. There was uneasiness.

All of which was on display when he returned to the Wachovia Center as a Denver Nugget for the 2012–13 season opener, having been sent to Denver a few months earlier in a four-team trade in which the Sixers acquired Andrew Bynum. (It would be the only season in Denver for Iguodala, who was traded to the Golden State Warriors the following year.)

Iguodala was the second Nugget introduced, and the ovation was mixed but intense, loud boos and loud cheers entwining for just a moment before the public-address announcer quickly moved on. Iguodala nailed a wing jumper on Denver's first possession—he later admitted he wanted to "destroy" the Sixers in the game—but missed his next two shots and then turned it over twice before turning a steal into a dunk.

Every one of his touches was greeted by boos, not only because of the past but because Iguodala had been quoted a month earlier as saying that his last two years in Philadelphia had been "draining" due to the constant criticism. He complained that he was asked to be a facilitator but was ripped when he didn't score enough. That Doug Collins, the last of five coaches for whom he played in Philadelphia, asked him to attack the rim as opposed to settling for three-pointers, something Iguodala did in Collins' first year but spurned his second. (Iguodala shot a career-best 39.4 percent from the arc that season.)

So all that was percolating when Iguodala took the court that night in 2012. He would say afterward that he was unsurprised at the fans' booing. After all, he said with a smile, "They'll get on their team sometimes, if they're not playing too well. It's been worse."

But during a timeout with 5:40 left in the first quarter a video was shown on the huge screens on the scoreboard of the final seconds of Game 6 of the Sixers' playoff series against Chicago the previous spring. The Sixers were poised to close out a Bulls team crippled by injuries to star guard Derrick Rose and center Joakim Noah, but trailed Chicago 78–77.

Then Iguodala rebounded a missed free throw by Bulls center Omer Asik, sped the length of the court, and drew a foul from Asik on a layup attempt. Immediately there was consternation in the arena, for Iguodala had struggled all season at the free-throw line. But he swished both attempts cleanly; he would later say that he pretended he was teaching his son, Andre II, to shoot foul shots. And when Bulls guard C.J. Watson narrowly missed from beyond midcourt at the buzzer, Iguodala climbed atop the scorer's table and stared out into the celebrating crowd, an unmistakable how-you-like-me-now gesture.

The video shown at his homecoming did not include that part, but at the end words of thanks appeared on the screen. And then the crowd rose to its feet and bathed Iguodala in warm applause. If there was an acknowledgement on his part, it was small and brief, but he later seemed genuinely grateful for that moment, calling the video "classy" and the crowd "great."

He had to admit, though, that it was odd to hear boos and get a standing O the very same night. "That's the first time," he said. "I don't know too many guys that have had that."

He finished the night—one that overall had been "taxing," he said—with 11 points on 5-for-13 shooting, as well as four rebounds, four assists, and four turnovers. And the Nuggets had lost, 84–75. It would be his only visit of the season to Philadelphia, and he figured that perhaps things could get back to normal.

But before he left, he was cornered by an Associated Press reporter and asked to explain why his final seasons in Philadelphia had been so draining. He reverted to the knee-jerk response about things being taken out of context, and said he had no problem with Collins—though he admitted earlier that they had not spoken that night.

"I was really saying I didn't get to enjoy success," he said. He noted that the previous season he had made the All-Star team and played for the gold-medal-winning U.S. team at the Olympics in London. And in 2010 he had been part of the national team that won gold at the World Championships.

Nonetheless, he said, "It seemed like every time I stepped back on the court, it wasn't enough."

"Money," he added, "always plays a role in how someone is perceived or looked at as far as production.... I feel like I made a huge impact on my team night in and night out, whether it showed up on the stat sheet or not, and it was always brought up. Every night, you're thinking, *This last game I played good, but it's still not enough, not enough, not enough.*"

The frustration cut both ways. The fans wanted more. Iguodala, feeling he had given all he had to give, sought more appreciation. But in the end, that would be doled out sparingly.

Lou Williams

There is a moment early in Lou Williams' online documentary, *Peace of Mind*, when the former Sixer appears on camera and says, sure, he makes his living as a basketball player. "But day in and day out," he adds, "I turn into whatever I want to be." In an attempt to prove it he is shown prowling clubs and playing with his infant daughter, cutting rap videos and passing out winter coats in a downtrodden Philadelphia neighborhood.

He was forced to adopt another guise in January 2013—that of hospital patient—after tearing the ACL in his right knee while playing for his hometown team, the Atlanta Hawks. He had landed there as a free agent after spending his first seven NBA seasons with the Sixers, only to see his year end after 39 games.

It was the first major injury of his career, and its effects were felt back in Philadelphia. "It made me sick," Sixers coach Doug Collins said. "Lou is one of my favorite people."

It was not mere lip service. Collins had identified Williams as the team's "heartbeat" in the two years he played for him, when Williams routinely trundled off the bench (usually in tandem with Thaddeus Young) and scored in droves. But more than that, Collins said, was "that personality and energy he brought every night to the arena, and what he meant in our locker room."

Williams, listed at 6'2", has never been much of a ball handler or defender. Nor, really, has he been much of a shooter—not in the strictest sense, seeing as he made just 42.1 percent of his attempts as a Sixer, and barely more than 40 percent during his last two seasons in town. But he was a scorer, an ignitor.

He will always be remembered for the three-pointer he made to beat Miami in a 2011 playoff game. For becoming, in 2011–12, the first nonstarter to lead his team in scoring since the Charlotte Hornets' Dell Curry did so in 1993–94. He finished second in Sixth Man of the Year voting that season.

And Williams will be remembered for a herky-jerky game that often allowed him to create scoring opportunities and get to the foul line. His body control was such that he often slithered through the tiniest of crevices in the defense. He also made great use of the head fake he stole from former Sixers teammate Andre Miller. And few players benefitted so much from NBA rules changes prohibiting hand-checking as the 175-pound Williams. "He's so quick and he's such a good three-point shooter, you have to pick your poison," Turner Sports analyst Steve Kerr said during the 2011–12 season. "He's got enough skill and speed that he can kind of dictate the way the play is going to evolve."

Especially since Williams, like many veteran players, had earned his share of favorable whistles by then. "Referees are like players—they have scouting reports," he said. "They understand how different guys want to play, and the things that a lot of guys try to do on the basketball court.... I think with me they recognize that I try to draw contact and get fouls."

Williams was born in Memphis but moved to the Atlanta area at a young age, after his dad died and his mom remarried. He came to the Sixers out of South Gwinnett High School in the second round of the 2005 draft, the last selection process that included prep players. Armed with a guaranteed contract—unusual for a second-round pick—he languished for a year, appearing in just 30 games but never once being sent to the NBA Developmental League, which he appeared to need.

He finally requested to be sent down early the following year, staying a week in Fort Worth, Texas, before returning on December 8, 2006, 11 days before the Sixers dealt Allen Iverson to Denver. "No looking back since then," Williams told the *Philadelphia Daily News*' Zach Berman in April 2012.

He became a double-figure scorer the following year, and remained so throughout his tenure in town, while almost always appearing in a reserve role. He made just 38 starts among the 455 games he played for the Sixers, all of them in 2009–10, when Eddie Jordan was the coach. Other than that, he excelled as a supersub.

"When you go to Thad Young and Lou Williams," Collins said, "and say, 'I really think you can help us better coming off the bench—you're [two] of our best players, but you can help us better coming off the bench'—you've got to justify to them why you think this is going to work."

For the most part it did. But in the playoffs, when defenses become more intricate and games more physical, Williams was not nearly as effective. His accuracy from the floor plummeted well below 40 percent in each of his last two postseasons with the Sixers.

That, combined with a desire on the part of management to shake up the roster, led him back to his hometown. The guy who claimed he could be whatever he wanted to be was forced to reinvent himself all over again.

25 Game Night: Marc Zumoff

Still lurking within Marc Zumoff is the heavyset kid from northeast Philadelphia who used to narrate the games of basketball he played by himself in his basement, using a rubber ball and two chairs as hoops. This is the same kid who would pretend to broadcast neighborhood games, since the other kids never picked him when they chose up sides. And the one who used to cozy up to his television set, turn the dial to a static-laden station, and pretend that was the roaring crowd as he called another imaginary game into a tape recorder: "Greer throws inside to Chamberlain.... *Yes!*"

Somehow he imagined something much bigger, too. Somehow he saw himself doing exactly what he's done since 1994—serve as television play-by-play man for the Sixers, the team for which he has rooted since he began going to games with his dad when the franchise moved to town from Syracuse in 1963. If his on-air enthusiasm appears at times to be over the top, it is without question genuine, as deep-seated as the belief he harbored as a kid.

"It's funny, because as a kid I always felt like I was destined to do something like this," he said one day in January 2013, as he sat in the stands before a game. "There are a lot of things I can't do. I'd be a terrible attorney or doctor. But I was born with this, and I would show up at Sixers games and do them into a tape recorder. That's how long I've been doing it. I felt confident that I could announce a game."

When he was promoted the Sixers were amid the "Dark Ages," as he called it, the fifth year in a six-year stretch when they managed to win fewer games than the season before. They finally bottomed out at 18–64 in 1995–96. Then Harold Katz sold the club to Comcast Corporation, and Pat Croce was put in charge. Croce drafted Allen Iverson, hired Larry Brown, and within five years had them in the Finals. But before long, all three were gone, and the team settled back into the middle of the pack.

Zumoff remains. He's gone through another ownership change—in 2011, Josh Harris headed a group that bought the club from Comcast-Spectacor—meaning there was, he said, some "breath-holding" on his part, since there was no telling if the new regime would want him to continue. He's also cycled through five color men during his tenure—Steve Mix, Bob Salmi, Eric Snow, Ed Pinckney, and now Malik Rose—which always involves an adjustment. But to him, every day is a good day.

"The greatest satisfaction is that I'm living a life that a lot of people would like to live," he said, "that for some reason a kid who wasn't a very good athlete, who wasn't real popular, who was kind of chunky and was sort of afraid of his own shadow growing up, for some reason that kid is the TV voice of the Sixers. It's been an amazing metamorphosis in that regard."

By his own description he was a "nerd" growing up, and during his time at George Washington High School, unathletic and uncomfortable talking to women. He went to Temple because it was close and inexpensive and because it was known for its communications department. And it was there that he began to find himself. Veteran newsman Bob Bradley was a professor there, and he became a mentor to Zumoff, teaching him the ins and outs of the profession and giving him some confidence in himself. (Young Marc also slimmed down by taking a summer job at a scrap-iron yard. "It made a man out of me," he said.)

He cut his teeth at some small radio stations in New Jersey. The first, in Trenton, was hanging on by a thread. The owner wanted to sell the place, and it seemed to Zumoff they were off the air more than on it. They were also six weeks behind in paying him for reading wire-service news dispatches, but when he finally received his first check—it was for something like $85 after taxes, he recalled—he was elated: *They're gonna pay me to do this? Yes!*

He spent some time at PRISM, the old cable outlet, doing the Flyers, Big 5 basketball, and the Fever. Then he did some Sixers sideline work for Comcast, where in his first year he scored an interview with Kareem Abdul-Jabbar, the notoriously reticent Lakers Hall of Famer. "He just chewed me up and spit me out," Zumoff said.

The consensus is that things have gone considerably better for Zumoff since then, that he long ago left his inner nerd behind.

26 Danny Biasone

Danny Biasone invented the NBA's 24-second shot clock. Any self-respecting pro basketball fan knows that. Biasone—late owner of the 76ers forerunner, Syracuse Nationals—says so himself in Terry Pluto's book *Tall Tales*, which was published in 1992, the same year Biasone died of cancer at age 83.

Except it's not that simple. A plaque on a shot-clock monument in Syracuse's Armory Square mentions that three men named Howard Hobson, Emil Barboni, and Leo Ferris were instrumental in its creation, along with Biasone. They are, respectively, a long-ago college coach, a Nationals scout, and the team's general manager, all deceased.

This is not to minimize Biasone's role in the birth of the shot clock, which came at the beginning of the 1954–55 season, put an end to the rampant stalling that plagued the NBA, and probably saved the league itself. A member of the NBA's rules committee, he had been pushing for it for three years, ever since the Fort Wayne Pistons stalled their way to a 19–18 victory over perennial power Minneapolis on November 22, 1950—the lowest-scoring game in NBA history. And his contributions to the game were such that he was elected to the Basketball Hall of Fame eight years after his death. (The first shot clock had been put on display there years before.)

But the other three played pivotal roles, roles that have been forgotten with the passage of time. Start with Hobson, who

Danny Biasone poses in 1992 in front of his most famous invention.

coached at Oregon and Yale from 1935 to 1956 (save one season), winning the inaugural NCAA Tournament with the Ducks in 1938–39 and later making the Hall of Fame on the strength of his work on the bench. He was a longtime advocate of a shot clock in the college game, to no avail, and while serving in World War II made Barboni's acquaintance. The *Syracuse Post-Standard*'s Sean Kirst wrote in 2006 that the two of them coached in Italy during the conflict and talked incessantly about ways to improve the game.

So it's not hard to draw a straight line from there to the Nationals' brain trust—to Ferris and Biasone. When the shot-clock monument was unveiled in March 2005, the Associated Press' John Kekis wrote that the two of them settled on the 24-second clock by dividing the number of seconds in a 48-minute game (2,880) by the average number of shots taken by both teams combined (120)—a calculation made on the back of a score sheet in the Syracuse bowling alley owned by Biasone.

A 2004 *New York Times* story by Richard Goldstein also credits both men. But the *Times'* Harvey Araton wrote in Biasone's obituary 12 years earlier that Ferris actually settled on this formula on his own. Biasone insisted otherwise in Pluto's book, telling the author, "I looked at the box scores from the games I enjoyed, games where they didn't screw around and stall. I noticed each team took about 60 shots. That meant 120 shots per game.

"So I took 48 minutes—2,880 seconds—and divided that by 120 shots. The result was 24 seconds per shot. "That was it—24 seconds."

No mention of Ferris, or any of the others.

But again, it was Biasone who gave the idea legs. He invited his fellow owners to witness an exhibition showing the worth of a 24-second clock on August 10, 1954, at Blodgett Vocational School in Syracuse, his alma mater. Nats star Dolph Schayes told Pluto it featured some of the Nats, as well as college and high school players from the area. There was no clock, but it was decided that league publicist Haskell Cohen would track the time on his wristwatch and call out whenever the limit was reached.

At first the players were rushing themselves, putting shots up after eight to 10 seconds. Biasone told them to slow down. "He had complete confidence in his formula," Schayes told Pluto. And after a while everyone realized there was plenty of time to work the ball around and get a decent shot opportunity.

The owners quickly saw its worth as well; a dry run in the pre-season confirmed it once and for all. It was implemented for the regular season, and in the very first game in which it was used, the Rochester Royals beat the Boston Celtics 98–95. The mark would have been the seventh-highest-scoring game of the previous season.

According to NBA.com, each team averaged 93.1 points per game in 1954–55, an increase of 13.6 from the previous year. The Celtics became the first club to average more than 100 points per game, and four years later, every team in the league did.

The Nationals saw a direct benefit from the change that season, rallying from a 17-point second-quarter deficit in Game 7 of the Finals—something that would have been nearly impossible during the "stall-ball" era—to beat Fort Wayne and win the first title in franchise history.

All because of Danny Biasone. Though not without help.

Irv Kosloff

By 1963 Syracuse Nationals owner Danny Biasone, the driving force behind the NBA's implementation of the shot clock nine years earlier, had come to the realization that time was winding down on his franchise, a relic of the league's inaugural season. With two teams now playing on the West Coast, costs (especially those related to travel) were on the rise—no longer were the Nats a mere train trip from every road venue—while attendance, the club's sole source of revenue, had flatlined.

In the meantime Ike Richman, a Philadelphia attorney, reached the conclusion that his city needed a pro basketball team—something it did not have during the 1962–63 season, after Eddie Gottlieb moved the Warriors to San Francisco. Richman, made aware of Biasone's straits by Gottlieb (one of his clients), was interested in making an offer to the Syracuse owner, but needed a backer with deep pockets. He turned to Irv Kosloff, an old friend from their days at South Philadelphia High School.

Kosloff, owner of the Roosevelt Paper Company, agreed to pony up the lion's share of the $500,000 it would take to wrest the franchise from Biasone, but did so under the condition that Richman oversee the club's day-to-day operations; he was busy enough with his business and would serve as the club's silent partner. Richman agreed, a deal was made, and the team was moved to Philadelphia. Their new name, chosen by fans in a contest, would be the 76ers.

Richman enjoyed being the face of the franchise. Author John Branch wrote in his 2005 book *The Rivalry* that Richman aired out the team after a game one time, then emerged from the locker room and asked reporters, "You guys got all that?" He also liked to sit courtside and berate the referees, as he did on the night of December 3, 1965, when the Sixers were battling the Celtics in Boston Garden. Suddenly he slumped over, the victim of a massive coronary. Efforts to revive him proved fruitless. Ike Richman was dead at the age of 52.

Kosloff, who had been among those watching on television when Richman collapsed, was left as the sole proprietor of a franchise just beginning to gain traction in its new environment. The Sixers had gone just 34–46 their first season in town, as fans were slow to warm to a team that had been one of the Warriors' primary rivals. But on January 15, 1965, Richman engineered a trade with San Francisco for native Philadelphian Wilt Chamberlain, ensuring success on the court and at the box office.

With Chamberlain joining holdovers Hal Greer, Chet Walker, and Luke Jackson, the Sixers improved to 40–40 in 1964–65 and 55–25 in 1965–66, both times losing to Boston in the Eastern Division Finals. It was left to Kosloff to do some fine-tuning, replacing Dolph Schayes as coach with Alex Hannum after the latter season.

That led to the magical 1966–67 season, during which the Sixers won 68 games and the first of two NBA titles they have claimed since moving from Syracuse. But success was short-lived. The team flamed out against Boston in the '68 playoffs, and afterward Kosloff was forced to trade Chamberlain.

At issue was a secret verbal agreement between Wilt and Richman, ensuring Chamberlain a piece of the team upon his retirement. Branch writes that such a deal was against league rules, but Richman would have surely been able to finagle it in such a way to avoid any legal issues.

The problem was, Kosloff had no knowledge of the agreement, and refused to honor it when Chamberlain raised questions about it after the championship season. Instead Kosloff gave him a lump sum for his supposed share of the team, ripped up his three-year contract, and signed him to a one-year, $250,000 deal. When that was up in the summer of '68, Kosloff had little interest in re-signing Chamberlain, and instead shipped him to the Lakers for center Darrall Imhoff, forward Jerry Chambers, and guard Archie Clark, a pennies-on-the-dollar exchange that signaled the franchise's demise.

In 1972–73 the team bottomed out to a degree not seen before or since, going 9–73. Again Kosloff presided over a build-up, this time keyed by the signing of free-agent forward George McGinnis in 1975. It would be the last major move of the Kosloff era, as he sold the team to Fitz Dixon in May 1976.

After the team won a title seven years later on Harold Katz's watch, Pat Williams, whose stay as general manager spanned the stewardships of all three men, wrote in the book *We Owed You One* that Kosloff once told him the only things that should matter to the owner of an NBA team are winning and selling tickets.

"Don't get sidetracked by anything else," Kosloff told him. "Otherwise you're just spinning your wheels and you're not helping the team."

There were clearly times when Kosloff, who died in 1995 at age 82, was spinning his wheels. But often enough he had the Sixers heading in the right direction.

28 Fitz Dixon

Noted in the 2006 obituary of F. Eugene "Fitz" Dixon in the *Philadelphia Inquirer*—after the fact that he was born into great wealth, lent to great acts of philanthropy, and was instrumental in bringing Julius Erving to Philadelphia—was that he once owned a basketball team that played the seventh game of a playoff series in its home arena before just 6,704 fans.

That game, the last in the 1981 Eastern Conference Semifinals against the Milwaukee Bucks, might also have been the last straw of Dixon's five-year tenure as 76ers owner. His team had lost twice in the Finals during his stewardship. Attendance in the 18,000-seat Spectrum had slipped from 17,000 a game when Dr. J came to town in 1976 to 12,000 in 1980–81—a season in which the team won 62 games, a total equaled by only one other NBA club that year.

That Dixon failed to galvanize the fan base is no surprise, for only occasionally has Philadelphia cottoned to the Sixers in the half-century they have spent in town. They have always been no better than fourth in the city's sports pecking order, behind (in order) the Eagles, Phillies, and Flyers. There are many years, like 2012–13, when they lag behind Big 5 basketball as well.

Surely Dixon, who was born in Maine but spent nearly all of his 82 years living on a 500-acre estate just outside Philadelphia, understood the lay of the land in his adopted hometown. At various times he owned pieces of the Eagles, Flyers, and Phillies, and was majority owner of the Philadelphia Wings, a professional lacrosse team, before its league tanked.

He took his shot with the Sixers anyway, purchasing them from Irv Kosloff for $8 million in 1976. He trusted in general manager

Pat Williams, who told him soon after that purchase that it would be prudent to part with some $6.6 million in order to acquire Erving. But the Sixers, while very good on Dixon's watch, were never the last ones standing. Nor did they ever manage to raise pro basketball's profile in the city.

April 19, 1981, the day of that playoff game against the Bucks, happened to be Easter Sunday. Across the street from the Spectrum, in Veterans Stadium, the Phillies drew more than 30,000 fans for their early season game against the Cubs. But there was, as usual, little buzz about the Sixers, despite the importance of the game and the fact that it had been a hotly contested series.

They won, 99–98, and moved on to face the Celtics in the Eastern Conference Finals. There they assembled a 3–1 lead in games, only to lose the final three—the last a one-point heart-breaker in Boston Garden—to drop the series. "The financial impact of this is so great that, with the current attendance and the current costs, it's just impractical for me to continue much farther," he told reporters at the time. Within months he sold the team.

Heir to the combined fortunes of the Widener and Elkins families, Dixon did great deeds—his obituary identifies him as a "civic jack-of-all-trades"—but preferred to look at himself as an ordinary man. He taught English and French for 17 years at his alma mater, Episcopal Academy, and once told a reporter that while he surely didn't need the paycheck, he would be "a martini drunkard at the end of six months" if he sat home and did nothing.

He was known for ponying up $35,000 to return the LOVE statue to Philadelphia when the city was unable to cobble together the necessary funds to prevent its creator from reclaiming the beloved statue, originally lent for the bicentennial. And Dixon was known for making larger donations, like those he made to save from bankruptcy the Pennsylvania Military College (later renamed Widener University in his family's honor)…or the $5 million he gave the Dixon School of Nursing at Abington Memorial Hospital for scholarships and low-interest loans…or the $4 million he gave the Philadelphia Museum of Art to acquire a certain portrait.

The one thing he wanted for himself was a sports franchise. While he knew little about basketball when he purchased the Sixers, he got up to speed quickly enough. He sat not in an owner's box but courtside, and with his bodyguards preventing spectators and vendors from walking in front of him, he would spend game nights hectoring the referees.

He was also known for his disdain for Gene Shue, coach of the team when he first bought it. "What's your excuse tonight?" he reportedly asked Shue after a loss in 1976–77. Dixon insisted in a 1978 profile in *Sports Illustrated* that he was joking, while also admitting that he was "a spontaneous, outspoken and occasionally obstreperous fan." Whatever the case, he fired Shue six games into the 1977–78 season and replaced him with Billy Cunningham.

The Sixers improved, and could even be called great. But they could never get over the top, and in July 1981 Dixon sold them to Harold Katz for $12 million. The day of the sale, he was reportedly sailing his yacht on the Atlantic. He issued no statement but was later quoted as saying, "I, as an individual, was unable or did not desire to continue funding our losses at the gate. My only regret is, we couldn't bring a championship to Philadelphia. We tried hard. It was…elusive, shall we say. We came close…but we didn't win the title."

Fitz Dixon, a rich and powerful man, could only correct so many things in his corner of the world. The 76ers defied even his best efforts.

29 Dr. J As Trendsetter

Julius Erving had grace, artistry, and coolness. And that was off the court.

On the hardwood, Dr. J was all those things and more. The Doctor was the epitome of cool. He was the man.

Style was essential to the substance. Dr. J was the ultimate entertainer. He was instrumental in launching a modern style of play that emphasized leaping and play above the rim.

But he wasn't just a dunker. In the same way that players like Dominique Wilkins, nicknamed "the Human Highlight Film" for his spectacular dunks, could also score (he led the league in scoring in 1986), Erving was a dominant player in all aspects of the game.

Wilkins, who said young kids wanted to be Dr. J, patterned more than just his dunks after the NBA's 1981 Most Valuable Player. The Doctor was Michael Jordan before there was a Jordan in the NBA.

Before Erving joined the 76ers on October 20, 1976, he was already great. The legend of the player and man was already huge. Erving, who began his career in 1971 with the Virginia Squires in the American Basketball Association, played in a league with no major television exposure. Rarely were his games seen on TV. Just highlights, newspaper clippings, and word of mouth. It added to his legend, as tales of his high-flying and scoring prowess were passed along among basketball fans.

"I developed a style of play which is a playground style, which is real loose and real freelance in style," said Erving, who brought street ball to the NBA long before Allen Iverson.

Dr. J wanted to be the man to determine the outcome of the game, whether it was with a rebound, a key steal, fadeaway jump shot, or dribbling the length of the court for a dunk or finger roll.

In five seasons in the ABA he won three scoring championships, three MVPs, and two ABA championships. In 1976, his last season in the ABA, Erving averaged 34.7 points and was named MVP of the playoffs. His team, the New York Nets, beat the Denver Nuggets for the ABA championship. In the Finals against the Nuggets, he averaged almost 45 points and 15 rebounds a game.

Bobby Jones, a teammate of Erving's on the 1983 Sixers championship team, was then on the Nuggets and had the assignment of guarding Dr. J in the '76 finals. Jones, credited by many former pro basketball players as being one of the best defenders in the sport, couldn't find a way to stop Erving from scoring.

"He was not only above the rim, but he had a fadeaway that you couldn't stop," Jones said. "As a defender you wanted to take out one of three things. Either cut out the drive, the shot, or the pass—and you really couldn't with him. He was too good and his hands too big. He could do all three of those things. It made it difficult for me to do something with him."

After retiring following the 1987 season, Dr. J was in the leagues all-time top five in steals (first), field goals attempted (fifth), and field goals made (third).

He gets credit for his almost balletic flair on dunks, his Afro flowing during another fierce throwdown at the rim, after launching several feet from the basket. But there was more to his game.

"That's the part of the game that everybody forgets," Darryl Dawkins, his former teammate with the 76ers said about Erving. "A scorer can score with the clock not moving. He's moving around. He finds a way to get a shot, oftentimes on guys bigger than him.

"He'd go between guys' arms and reach around guys. He was amazing and he was the best player I ever played with. People always say, 'Why don't more people say how great he was?' and I say that people are afraid that someone else is going to get mad at them. They can get mad at me and stay mad at me."

Erving said he kind of considered himself to take a side entrance into basketball, joining the ABA before moving on to the 76ers. Besides the pressure of joining a new league and living up to high expectations, he was supposed to lead a very unique group of talented players on the Sixers.

"There was a lot of responsibility with coming in and being made captain of a ship that had a lot of very unpredictable characters, sailing along with George McGinnis, Darryl Dawkins, World B. Free, 'Jelly Bean' [Joe] Bryant," said Erving, who during his career scored 30,026 points, third-most on the NBA/ABA all-time list when he retired.

On a team with this many options, the Doctor sacrificed his scoring opportunities. Think about that. He combined on the NBA/ABA scoring list, for more than 30,000 points, and he took less shots once he arrived in Philly. He still hit big shots and was the leader of the team.

"There will never be a guy who will come from one league and dominate and come to another league and dominate," Bibby said about Erving. "That's the iconic part of being the pro that he was."

Added Jones, "Julius changed the game. He was athletic, but also so smart with the ball. It was hard to guard a guy like him. He controlled the ball and he was unselfish. He was way ahead of his time, because he could score whenever he wanted to, but he knew he had to get other guys involved and he did.

"We knew our roles, but we also got rewarded. Julius, during a timeout, would say, 'Bobby hasn't gotten a touch' or 'Maurice hasn't gotten a shot, let's get him a shot.' He thought about others. That made a difference."

Moses Malone appeared to be the missing piece for the 76ers. The three-time NBA MVP was coming off a big year when he joined the 76ers. A dominant inside force, he added a dimension

Erving had not played with in his career. They seemed to complement each other's games.

Malone, who played in both the ABA and NBA, said Erving brought fans out to games when made the switch to the NBA. "Back in the days when Dr. J played, Dr. J was the man," Malone said. "Dr. J is the one who brought the ABA to the NBA. When Doc came to the NBA all the fans started coming out, because he was the best player that people had ever seen. All the credit goes to Doc. He's the one that brought everyone to the NBA. We had a lot a of great ABA players, but Doc was the greatest, and all the praise has to go to Doc."

Malone, the 1983 MVP, led the Sixers in scoring and rebounding. The Doctor appeared to take an even further backseat on the '83 championship team. At times Andrew Toney, a deadly shooter, became the second option, behind Malone. But Malone knew whose team it was. He knew Erving was still a dominant player who could still get his shot when he wanted it.

"Doc could score, Doc could play defense. Doc could do a lot of things," Malone said. "Doc was not only a shooter, Doc was a scorer. Some guys [have] to shoot 40 times to get 40 points. Doc could shoot the ball 25 times and get 30, 40 points, because he could do other things. Doc was great....

"I used to watch Doc when I was in high school, when he played for the Virginia Squires, and he was the best. They had a stacked team. Charlie Scott, George Gervin, and Dr. J—and he was the man back then. When he came to the NBA, man, he uplifted the NBA and took it to another level."

Advertisers noticed, too. Major corporations saw the buzz Dr. J was creating and they wanted their name associated with his. In the 1970s and early '80s having a black man endorse a national product was a big deal. Converse and Coke were just two of many companies jumping on his bandwagon.

Besides his flair on the court, his presentation and the way he articulated his words when he spoke made him stand out. When asked about sacrificing his offensive game, he said, "Winning is paramount." Not "Winning is big with me, or I only care about the 'W.'" No, he chose a more impactful phrasing. He just sounded smarter than most athletes.

Dawkins said Erving was the complete package on and off the court. The Doctor was the role model for a new way to play the game as well as how to market oneself. Other players dunked before the Doctor, but no one made playing above the rim such a big part of their game, Dawkins said.

"Michael Jordan did all this one-hand stuff, but it wasn't done before Dr. J did it," Dawkins said. "Doc played in the air. He was the original above-the-rim guy. He had air breaks. He went side to side. And he was always double-teamed.

"He was a great trendsetter because he always dressed fancy, he always wore hats, he was always speaking clearly, and he was a leader—and that's what we needed. We need more leaders today. We have to get some more of them."

30 Iverson As Trendsetter

On October 30, 1996, Allen Iverson's hair was short—no corn-rows—and he had few tattoos.

Barely six feet tall, A.I., then better known as "the Answer," invited a young reporter onto the court after the media session ended at training Camp at the University of Delaware in Newark.

Iverson shot a short jumper from the left of the key.

Swish.

He took a few dribbles, pulled up for a three-pointer, an area where his teacher rarely shot, and stopped. He spun the ball in his hand, allowing for backward rotation, and said, "I watched him as a kid—yeah, Mo Cheeks. We call him Maurice now."

Respect can start with a name. It's a beginning, anyway. But true respect between basketball players comes from the court.

Prove you can play, and I will listen.

Prove you belong, and I will teach.

Sometimes the way you listen depends on who is speaking the words.

Iverson, the new point guard for the 76ers, learned to appreciate his teacher, Cheeks, then entering his second year as an assistant with the team, while watching the Sixers on television. Those early lessons helped develop Iverson, who respected the voice enough to listen to the advice—something the young guard didn't do with everyone.

He proved he could play and earned the respect of peers and retired NBA greats.

Media Day was ending when someone standing under the basket where Iverson was shooting asked him, "What excites you the most about your first NBA season?"

"Winning," Iverson said without hesitating. "That's the only thing that matters." It is a hard answer not to respect.

The electrifying guard was always about winning, but sometime after that rookie season, image became important, too. Being true to himself and his roots often became the story, as much as his winning ways on the court.

He was a forerunner in making street ball acceptable in professional basketball, in displaying tats, wearing cornrows, and introducing hip-hop style to the league. He became known as much for bandanas and backward baseball caps as his slashes to the basket.

"I had a Fro back then," said Iverson, who still has cornrows and wears his Yankees hat sideways or backward, joking about his rookie year.

Allen Iverson ushered in a new era of style among NBA players.

He may have started out with a Fro, but he was to cornrows what Erving was to the Afro. The 76ers had two cultural icons. Iverson was a trendsetter in the 1990s and 2000s, just like Julius Erving was in the '70s and '80s.

"It's all about being who you are," Iverson said. "I had no problem with people who misunderstand who I was. I wanted to be the same person that I was. I didn't leave my house and then turn into somebody else. I wanted to be me.

"I never wanted to go home to Virginia and look at my mom and she look at me and be like, *Who is this guy?* I always felt like it was cool being me. I felt like that was the style. I think that was the style. Being me, being who I am, it rubbed people the wrong way because they didn't accept the way that I wanted them to, but I didn't care. I wasn't doing anything wrong with being who I am.

"I didn't like wearing suits. I still don't. I dress the way and look the way I want; you only live once and it's over. And whether you are going to heaven or hell you'll find out then, but you live to go to heaven. So that's how I lived my life and I had no problem with it."

Cheeks was a reserved person, very much trying not to draw attention to himself or his game. He was a complementary player. For 11 seasons, he dished the ball to his Sixers teammates during a 14-year career. He finished fifth (now 11th) all-time in assists with 7,392, and was one of the top defensive guards, finishing second (now fifth) all-time in steals in NBA history, with 2,310.

Many of his assists came from Erving baskets. He played with a great player (Erving) and coached a great player (Iverson). He saw the brilliance of Iverson's game, a style completely different from his own.

"Oh definitively [they are] trendsetters, for sure, the way they played, the way they changed the game," Cheeks said.

The term "hip-hop" was coined and became fashionable, and A.I. was somewhat the poster child of that subculture. Fans, especially younger ones, had someone they could look up to and emulate in style.

"When you stepped off the court, there [were] the Walt 'Clyde' Fraziers of the world and there were the Bill Waltons of the world," Erving said. "Everybody has their style off the court, but on the court I think that's what the fans appreciate. I think that's what the fans relate to. They can clearly relate to Allen because he was there for the rise of the hip-hop era."

Evan Turner, a member of the 76ers from 2010 to 2014, said he always respected that Iverson played his heart out. The tats, the cornrows, he made that hip.

"That's who he was," Turner said about Iverson. "Obviously, a lot of kids in the world could relate to it in the inner cities and places like that. I think the most important thing, in general, was what he represented. He gave his all every time out on the court. He may have looked cool, but he wasn't too cool to play hard. I think that showed a lot."

Dwyane Wade was an inner-city kid who grew up watching Iverson. Wade, who broke into the league in 2003, is a three-time NBA champion and a 10-time NBA All-Star. He said he will always appreciate what Iverson did for guys like him.

"He made it cool to be a hip kid," said Wade before the 2013 season opener. "He made it acceptable to want to play basketball but also love hip-hop and all those things. He was a trendsetter in his own way."

Spending four months at Newport News City Farm—a correctional facility—when he was 15, making rap music and even missing practice, helped cement Iverson's image as a renegade, someone who played by his own rules.

Going under his moniker "Jewelz," Iverson recorded a rap single in 2000, but the song, which featured controversial lyrics, and ensuing album were never released. But no one would have paid attention to his look, his dress, his music, or his practice habits if he hadn't played well on the court.

"With Allen Iverson, there will never be a small player like that who will dominate the game of NBA basketball," said Henry Bibby, who was an assistant coach for the 76ers in 2006.

"A.I. is a great ballplayer," Sixers great and basketball Hall of Fame member Moses Malone said. "He is quick and he brought a lot to the NBA. He is from Virginia and I love A.I. He's a great guy."

Iverson came across like a tough guy, but the younger players admired him and the NBA greats appreciated his heart and ability. For Iverson, his look, the way he dressed, was just about him being himself. His appearance on the court is still evident in today's game.

"Now you look around and see all the guys in the NBA—now all of them have tattoos, guys with cornrows," Iverson said. "You used to think the suspect was the guy with the cornrows, now you see the police officers with the cornrows.

"I took a beating for those types of things. I'm proud to be able to say I changed a lot in this culture and in this game. It is not about how you look on the outside; it's who you are in the inside."

Harold Katz

During his 15-year tenure as the 76ers' owner, Harold Katz traded Moses Malone and Charles Barkley, and seriously considered trading Julius Erving—twice. He also drafted Shawn Bradley and gave thought to moving the team to Camden, New Jersey.

By the time he sold the Sixers to Comcast-Spectacor in 1996, the team was a laughingstock. It had slogged through five straight losing seasons, each worse than the one before, and the last an 18–64 nightmare in 1995–96.

There are those, like former general manager John Nash, who have argued that Katz's legacy should be more positive, an argument based on the fact that he delivered a long-sought championship in 1982–83, his second year as owner. "Without his desire to succeed," Nash once told this author, "we might not have been able to climb that mountain."

That might be true, but most of the pieces were in place before Katz arrived—Malone being the very notable exception. And in the intervening years Katz systematically and impatiently dismantled that team. (He did the same after the Sixers won an Atlantic Division championship in 1989–90.)

So the question for any Sixers fan is whether they were (and are) willing to accept the tradeoff of one exceptional year for several lousy ones—because that is Katz's legacy in its entirety.

Bryan Abrams, a former longtime season-ticket holder, once told this author that Katz was "good and bad." Good, Abrams said, in that "he would have done anything to win." Bad, in that Katz "thought he was a great talent evaluator." While accurate, that only begins to tell it, considering how pitiful the franchise became by the end of his stewardship.

Don Benevento, who covered most of the Katz era for the *Camden Courier-Post*, said that while the owner was not the cheapskate he was sometimes perceived to be, he didn't always spend wisely. "He was willing to invest money in the team," Benevento said. "I just don't think he was a basketball expert. He absolutely wanted to win. He just didn't know how to go about doing it."

After selling the team, Katz told the *New York Times* that his only goal had been to win. "If I made mistakes, if I didn't do some things right, it was never done for the wrong purpose," he said. "It was done because I was too impatient to win."

But the victories became fewer and further between as the years went on. And that gnawed at him. "Winning was everything to me, not making money," he told the *Times*. "Pro basketball is not a regular business, and losing is not fun. I was very fortunate. I got in at the right time and sold at the right time."

Phil Jasner, late beat writer for the *Philadelphia Daily News*, once said that he appreciated the fact that Katz always put himself out there, that he never hid from the media. "You didn't always agree with everything he said, but that was okay; he was the owner," Jasner said. "He always did what he thought was right, sometimes to a fault."

And *Delaware County Daily Times* columnist Jack McCaffery appreciated the fact that a journalist could "go to the bank with

Harold's word." As McCaffery said, "There was no spin. He was the no-spin zone before there was a no-spin zone."

But Katz's straightforward nature was not without cost. Nash said the former owner was "a public-relations nightmare" who might have been regarded much differently had he held his tongue more often. Katz did not disagree, saying he was often "too open" with reporters. "And as I look back, there are many things I wish I hadn't said," he acknowledged.

One other specific regret is trading Charles Barkley to Phoenix in the summer of 1992. Barkley wanted out and was disruptive during his final season with the team. Still, Katz said, "I shouldn't have allowed Charles to force me to trade him. That's not me." And while the deal with the Suns was the best they could have made, it did not turn out to be a good deal.

The deal he made with Comcast was infinitely sweeter. He sold for some $130 million, more than 10 times as much as he had spent to buy the team from Fitz Dixon in July 1981. It was on the latter occasion that Katz, who had made his fortune in the weight-loss business, promised to be a hands-on owner.

"The main problem with the 76ers was the lack of someone at the helm, a lack of direction," Katz told *Philadelphia* magazine in November 1981. "Dixon ran it as a hobby, and he had very little involvement with the team. I don't think sports should be treated as a hobby. It's a business, and I intend to run it as I run my other businesses."

A native Philadelphian, he opened up his first weight-loss center in the suburb of Willow Grove in 1971. Five years later, at the age of 38, he was a millionaire. And five years after that, when his chain had expanded to some 500 centers nationwide, he was worth $300 million.

Upon buying the Sixers, he vowed to provide whatever it was that had prevented the team, infamous for its postseason failures, from getting over the hump. "Maybe," he told *Philadelphia* magazine, "it's motivation. Maybe it's luck. Whatever it is, I'm going to supply it."

In his first season, 1981–82, he announced to reporters after a frustrating loss to Boston that the team was "too nice." That led to his decision to sign Malone to a six-year, $13.2 million offer sheet the following summer, and a subsequent trade for the Houston center. And that proved to be the final piece to the puzzle.

But it is only one piece of Katz's legacy, too. The complete picture has more than its share of blotches.

Pat Croce

Pat Croce still has David Stern's clock. Small and basketball-shaped, it was still sitting on the desk in the office of Croce's suburban Philadelphia mansion in 2012, the year before he put the place up for sale. Croce removed it from the former NBA commissioner's desk when he was being approved as a minority owner of the Sixers in 1996, telling Stern he would one day exchange it for a championship trophy.

The Sixers came close, reaching the Finals in Croce's last year as team president (2000–01), only to lose to the Lakers. Then Croce moved on, but kept the clock anyway.

That is in keeping with his customary no-holds-barred, go-for-it mentality. You never have to ask how he feels, because you always know he feels GREAT!!!—capital letters, with multiple exclamation points—and that he will tell you so. You never have to wonder if he's keeping busy, because he's always reaching for something more.

This is the guy who went from rough-around-the-edges North Philly kid to slick entrepreneur. A guy who opened a single sports medicine center in 1979, and over time transformed that into a 40-shop empire—while also serving as strength-and-conditioning coach for first the Flyers and, later, the Sixers. Then he sold all that for $40 million. Then he badgered Harold Katz into selling the Sixers to Comcast-Spectacor. Then he drafted Allen Iverson, hired Larry Brown, and watched the whole operation take off.

It should come as no surprise that Croce holds a special place in his heart for pirates, that he admires (and, of course, emulates) their swashbuckling approach. He has an encyclopedic knowledge of pirate history and over the years has collected so much memorabilia that the Pirate and Treasure Museum he opened in Florida can't hold it all; some of it remains on display in his home.

So of course he took David Stern's clock. But does that also mean Croce will have to get back into basketball at some point?

"Never say never," he said one day in the fall of 2012.

In truth, Croce does not seem so inclined, having already conquered that world. He talked that day about the six bars he owns in Key West. About how he plans to develop the two acres surrounding his St. Augustine–based pirate museum into a historical theme park. "Think of it as Williamsburg[, Virginia,] meets Epcot," he said.

He does some motivational speaking. He has written books. He rides motorcycles and holds a third-degree black belt in karate. He was part of a diving expedition that explored the sunken wreckage of Sir Francis Drake's fleet off Panama, in hopes of finding Drake's remains, which are said to lie in a lead-lined coffin.

"If we found it, I was going to bring it back with a royal frigate, across the Atlantic, up the Thames, and give it to Queen Elizabeth II," Croce said with his customary gusto. "You'd be calling me *Sir* Pat Croce."

He can overwhelm people with his energy, and leave others shaking their heads, wondering whether he could possibly be genuine. "I hear that all the time," he said in a 1999 interview. "If it's fake, it's a long-term fake. I'm not smart enough to lie twice."

But it's also true he's crazy like a fox—that he's shrewd and determined and a quick study. When he approached Katz about selling, the Sixers owner said he wasn't ready to do so...yet.

"He never said no," Croce said.

It was all Croce needed to hear. In time a deal was done, for $147 million. Croce put up $5 million of his own money and served as the team's president. And as expected he tirelessly promoted the team, climbing the Walt Whitman Bridge to hang a banner, rappelling out of the rafters before a game one night, presiding over various giveaways.

He quickly understood that while he owned the team, this business venture was unlike any other he would ever undertake—that while he put up the money, he would have to share the team with the city. "People think that spotlight is precious, but it also can burn," he said. "So you're always in the spotlight—whatever you do, any decisions you make."

He had never fired anyone in the 16 years he ran his sports medicine centers, but after his first year with the Sixers he parted company with general manager Brad Greenberg and coach Johnny Davis, well aware that the team's modest fan base might forgive such mistakes once, but never twice.

So he brought in Brown, a respected (if quirky) coach, as well as Billy King to serve as GM. It was not always smooth sailing—Croce had to mediate the nearly constant disputes between Brown and Allen Iverson—but the team improved year by year, until making a spirited run to the Finals.

Iverson was named MVP that year. Brown was Coach of the Year. But the Lakers beat them in five games.

Croce departed soon afterward, after failing in a bid to gain greater power and influence within Comcast-Spectacor. He does not believe he overreached; rather, he said, he and Comcast chairman Ed Snider talked about Croce moving up in the hierarchy.

"It's not like I pulled something out of a hat," Croce said. "We discussed succession, and I thought, as I said in that [farewell] press conference, he had dangled the keys to the empire, then pulled them back. So no, I wasn't going to stay, because listen, I had the Sixers humming, and I had talked about it with him, running everything."

So Croce moved on and by that fall day in 2012 was fast approaching his 58th birthday. There were, of course, no plans for retirement.

"Never," he said. "I'm retired now."

Then he laughed, a pirate looking at 60—albeit with clear eyes and clearer ambitions.

33 Game Night: Matt Cord

Sixers public-address announcer Matt Cord has rules and he has rituals. Rules like never speaking into a live microphone without knowing what he is going to say beforehand. And rituals like always warming up his voice before leaving his home to drive to the Wells Fargo Center.

Even so, things go wrong. One of the mistakes that still makes him cringe came in 2002. It was just a routine substitution—Alvin Jones replacing Dikembe Mutombo at center for the Sixers. Only Cord said Alvin *Williams* was going into the game, likely because the team was facing Toronto that night, and Williams then played for the Raptors.

Mutombo walked by Cord as he returned to the bench. And in that deep rumbling voice of his—the one that calls to mind the

Cookie Monster from *Sesame Street*—he said, "There is no Alvin Williams on our team. Ha. Ha. Ha."

Cord was crestfallen. Does it get any worse than having Dikembe Mutombo critique your use of the English language?

Most nights are better. Most nights Cord enjoys his job immensely. "The best part, I always say to people, is the intros—especially the way we do them," he said.

The lights are turned down. A highlight video is shown on the scoreboard video screen. The music swells. And then Cord calls out the starters' names, one by one, as they emerge from a tunnel at one end of the arena. "That's what sets the tone for the entire night," he said.

The other thing he really likes is interacting with the players. He recalled in particular Michael Jordan passing by his position and asking, "Can you believe I missed that dunk?"

"I'm like, *Oh my god, he's talking to me*," Cord said. "That kind of stuff is what really blows you away. You're so close to these athletes. You take any other PA announcer—in football, baseball, or hockey—and that doesn't happen. They don't get that interaction."

A Delaware County native, he started out in radio upon graduation from Plattsburgh (New York) State, working at one station on Long Island, then another. But in time he took a job at WMMR in Philadelphia (a job he still holds), while also doing PA work for the Phantoms and Wings.

In 1997 he started working for the Sixers and managed to stay on board, even when he put his voice under extreme duress during All-Star Weekend in 2002. He consulted a voice coach, who taught him his 20-minute pregame warm-up routine, and he has not had any problems since—at least not with his voice. He did ram his car into a pole in the arena's parking lot one day in 2008, leaving him with a neck injury so severe that he wore a brace for three months.

He said the accident occurred when he spilled coffee on himself and looked down. It didn't help that he had already unbuckled his

The Mailman

Matt Cord once had a memorable encounter with "the Mailman," Utah Jazz forward Karl Malone.

Cord accidently omitted announcing Malone's name during pregame introductions. Here is Cord's take on things:

It was a preseason game. In a preseason game you introduce the entire team, all 15, 20 guys. You have the guys on cards. You do the reserves first and then you go into the starters.

[Malone] was starting, obviously, for Utah. His card got stuck. So I flipped it, I skipped him. I knew I skipped him. You can't go back. Finally, I introduced them all and he comes up to the table. He comes walking up and says, "Who's the announcer here?"

I say, "Me."

He said, "Let me introduce myself to you. Thirteen year All-Star, 6'8" power forward, Karl Malone.

I said, "Your card got stuck."

Malone said, "What?"

I'm showing him the card.

Malone said, "My card got stuck?"

I said, "Yeah, yeah. You see?"

He comes in later in the year and I don't mess up at all and he comes up to me and says, "I knew you had it in you."

He totally remembered. It was pretty embarrassing.

seatbelt, either—something he always used to do upon arrival at his destination but never does anymore. But armed with a swivel chair and a wireless microphone, he did not miss a game that year, and was on the job all the way through the 2010–11 season.

Then the Sixers' new ownership group decided to try a new voice—that of veteran broadcaster Tom Lamaine—while Cord did video features for the team's official website. That arrangement lasted a year, and before the 2012–13 season Cord found himself among 107 candidates trying out for his old job. That was whittled down to five finalists, and Cord beat out two PA guys, Kevin Casey of the Union and Kevin Linton of the Wilmington Blue Rocks, as well as two radio guys, Brian Startare and Mark Sheppard.

"Stepping away from it," Cord said, "made me realize, *Wow, that was a really cool job. I want that back.*"

He is well aware of the tradition of great PA men in Philadelphia—of the late Dave Zinkoff with the Sixers and the late John McAdams at the Palestra. Cord's dad, in fact, wondered aloud when his son was hired if he would someday have a street named after him, as the Zink once did. The younger Cord had no such goal in mind.

Rather, he would settle for not having Dikembe Mutombo remind him of the errors of his words.

Alex Hannum

Delivering a championship to Philadelphia in 1966–67, Alex Hannum knew, meant demanding something different from Wilt Chamberlain. It meant that the Sixers' new coach would have to ask his star center to score a little less (for there were plenty of scorers on the roster), defend a little more, and rebound as much as ever.

All of that happened. After leading the NBA in scoring each of his first seven seasons, Wilt slipped to third, at an ordinary (for him) 24.1 points a game. But he again paced the league in boards (24.2) and finished a surprising third in assists (7.8). And after years of being continually frustrated by Boston in the playoffs, he was finally a champion. Not only that, but those Sixers set a record by going 68–13, and would later be tabbed the greatest team of the league's first 35 years.

Chamberlain, who died in 1999, would in time say that Hannum was one of his favorite coaches. Hannum, who passed away three years after Wilt, was just as complimentary of his fellow Hall of Famer. At his news conference when he departed Philadelphia in 1968, Hannum said coaching the Big Dipper was "one of the most pleasant experiences" he had had in sports. And years later he would say in an interview with NBA Entertainment that Wilt was "one of the world's best athletes…in the history of time."

Despite that, it would be a mistake to say it was always smooth sailing between the two. Hannum had served in the U.S. Army during World War II—one of his nicknames was "Sarge"—and at 6'7" and 225 pounds was a rugged former player (though not a terribly effective one; he averaged just six points a game in eight seasons). He wanted things his way, and was not averse to challenging his players—physically, if need be. Shortly after becoming coach of the San Francisco Warriors in 1963 (the third stop in his 16-year coaching career, after the St. Louis Hawks and Syracuse Nationals), he and Chamberlain had to be separated during a locker-room confrontation in Vancouver on the eve of the regular season.

Then just three years later, Hannum asked Wilt to scale back his scoring that season, and Chamberlain did so. The result was that the Warriors unexpectedly won the Western Conference, losing (naturally) to the Celtics in the Finals.

According to Robert Cherry's 2004 book *Wilt: Larger Than Life*, Hannum and Chamberlain had some heated exchanges during the 1966 preseason, too. And in an interview for this book Matt Guokas Jr., a rookie guard on the 1966–67 team, said this about Chamberlain: "He and Alex did not speak. Alex would speak about him in front of the team, but not to him. And Wilt would speak to Alex without looking at him, in not-very-nice terms."

Guokas did not know the root of the problem, only that it dated back to their time with the Warriors. "I think Alex, being a relatively new coach, thought he was going to coach Wilt—in other words, correct him and tell him what he wanted him to do," he said. "By then Wilt was like, 'No, I tell you what I'm going to do.'"

Only occasionally did it seem to distract any of the other players, according to Guokas. "Alex used to get upset because Wilt wouldn't be hustling on the boards or something like that," he said. "And he'd say [during halftime], 'Come on, we've got to get on the boards. We're never going to win a game if we don't.' All that ranting and raving, and good coachspeak. And Luke [Jackson] would say, F-bombs interspersed, 'Who are you talking about? Who's not rebounding? I'm rebounding. Who are you talking about?'"

When asked about this in April 2013, Jackson said, "I don't remember those conversations." Nor did he remember any rift between Hannum and Chamberlain.

"It was a different type of communication from the way [Hannum] communicated with the rest of the team," he said, "but it was a good communication, I think, that they had."

Hannum told author Terry Pluto for the 1992 book *Tall Tales* that he and Chamberlain "always had an understanding and mutual respect" and added that he consulted Wilt about various matters, such as re-signing veteran guard Larry Costello, cutting back on Wilt's minutes, and playing him at the high post to take advantage of his passing ability, not to mention the explosiveness of teammates like Chet Walker, Hal Greer, and Billy Cunningham.

And where Chamberlain was concerned, Guokas said, "Every practice was optional." That was the thing about Hannum: tough as he was, he gave his players latitude. It has often been said that the 1966–67 team might have posted an even greater record if the players had not made a side trip to Las Vegas before heading to the West Coast, where they lost the first three in a seven-game road swing.

But generally speaking, all parties knew where to draw the line. "Alex was a man's man," Jackson said, "and he let us do things with the understanding that *if you do this, you're going to pay the price for it in practice and in games.* With that in mind, athletes have to drink sometimes, so we'd be in a bar and he'd pass by and he'd say, 'Okay, guys—remember, tomorrow we have to play.' And that's all he had to say, and we were on our way to the room to go to sleep and get ready for the game the next day."

The championship season was followed by a 62–20 season in 1967–68, but also another playoff disappointment, the Sixers frittering away a 3–1 lead to Boston in the Eastern Finals and losing in seven games. Then Hannum departed, saying he never intended to remain all that long in Philadelphia anyway. He would win an ABA title in 1968–69 in Oakland, becoming the first coach to win championships in both leagues, and remained in the profession through 1974.

After that Sarge marched away, forever in lockstep with his most famous player.

35 Billy Cunningham

There have never been any comparisons. For the purposes of discussion, there have never been any. Not when it comes to Billy Cunningham, sixth man on the Sixers team that won the 1966–67 championship and coach of the one that won the 1982–83 title.

Oh, he has dropped hints through the years about which of the two teams he might favor. He was always a big Wilt Chamberlain guy, always in awe of the Big Dipper's abilities. (He was also among those who spearheaded efforts to have a statue honoring Chamberlain erected outside the Wells Fargo Center.) And Cunningham thought the world of his other 1966–67 teammates—fellow Hall of Famers Hal Greer and Chet Walker, as well as Luke Jackson, Wali (then Wally) Jones, and the rest. But he would never make any definitive statements about how they might fare against the 1982–83 club.

"It would be a great game, wouldn't it?" he said in the fall of 2012. "I'm not going one way or the other."

Not at the expense of the guys he coached. They had fought an uphill battle for years before finally breaking through behind the newly acquired Moses Malone. Cunningham was again reminded of how much they meant to him when they gathered at his home in the Gladwyne section of Philadelphia after appearing at a nearby memorabilia show in October 2011.

He and his wife, Sondra, had rebuilt the place after it was largely destroyed by fire six years earlier, a blaze ignited by a welder's torch while some work was being done. No one was hurt, but the fire destroyed, by Cunningham's estimate, a third of the home where he and his family had lived for more than 40 years. The rest was so badly damaged by smoke and water that the Cunninghams decided to level the structure and start over.

Certainly a great many things of sentimental value were lost, and that was difficult to swallow at first. But as Billy said, "You get past that and you move on." And really, what had been lost? Material things, yes. But not his memories. Nothing could destroy those. He was happy to rekindle them with "a wonderful group of men." Besides all the ex-players, just about everybody was there, from former owner Harold Katz to the ball boys.

It was as if the championship season "just happened the day before," Cunningham said. Guys fell into familiar roles, told familiar tales. They snapped photos. They autographed mini-basketballs for one another; Cunningham had arranged a bunch of them, all in a row, so that everyone could sign. It was, perhaps, the first time they had had a chance as a group to contemplate what they had accomplished all those years before.

Back then they had enjoyed the victories, sure. But there was always another game, and never a chance to savor the one that came before. That night at Cunningham's house, they were finally afforded that opportunity. "I thought guys just sort of sat there and smiled and looked at one another," said former assistant general manager John Nash, who was also present. "It was really a night to just enjoy what had been accomplished a couple decades earlier."

Cunningham himself had been incredibly consumed by the task, but then again, that had always been his default setting. A product of the New York City playgrounds, he had starred at North Carolina before the Sixers plucked him in the first round of the 1965 draft, with the idea of converting him from forward to guard. One torturous outing against Celtics defensive hound K.C. Jones led to a change in plans, and Cunningham settled in as a reserve behind Jackson and Walker, the starting forwards on that 1966–67 club.

The Sixers breezed to the title that year and might have won another the following year if Cunningham had not broken his wrist in the first round of the playoffs against the New York Knicks. Cunningham missed the Eastern Conference Finals as the Celtics erased a 3–1 deficit in the best-of-seven set by sweeping the last three games. And for the ninth time in 10 years, they went on to win the championship.

The Sixers quickly slipped into irrelevance. Wilt was traded after the 1967–68 season, Walker went one year later. Jackson shredded an Achilles in 1968 and was never quite the same. Cunningham established himself as an All-Star, but he too slipped away, to the ABA's Carolina Cougars, in 1972. And while the Sixers slipped to 9–73 in 1972–73, Cunningham was named MVP in the new league.

But he also underwent two kidney surgeries while playing for the Cougars, and he told Jason Wolf of the *Wilmington News-Journal* in 2013 that he was "never able to have the same energy" he had previously. He did enjoy another big year when he returned to the Sixers in 1974–75, but 20 games into the following season he blew out a knee in a game against the Knicks in the Spectrum, a horrid noncontact injury that left him lying on the floor, shrieking in agony.

"I was disappointed with the way my career ended," Cunningham told Wolf. "I wish I could have played a longer career. It was a great game to be a part of."

Pictured here as a newly minted draft choice in 1965, Billy Cunningham enjoyed a number of years with the Sixers as a player and a coach.

126

Cunningham became a successful businessman but was approached about coaching the Sixers when Gene Shue was fired after going 2–4 to start the 1977–78 season. Cunningham had never coached a game on any level, but the idea, presented to him by general manager Pat Williams, appealed to him. And in his first game, on the road against the New Jersey Nets, he sweated right through his sport coat as the Sixers came from behind to win.

More sweat would be required. He sought to remake a defense he thought had gone soft under Shue. That was curious, since Cunningham had never been much of a defender himself. As he once told this author, "I'd have had issues with me as a player, if I'd been coaching [myself]."

And more than anything, he knew the roster needed an overhaul. Such players as World B. Free, Joe Bryant, and George McGinnis were jettisoned—the latter a particularly difficult decision, since Cunningham and McGinnis were close. Players including Maurice Cheeks, Andrew Toney, and Bobby Jones were added, the result being that the Sixers became more Julius Erving–centered, more defensive-minded.

Cunningham, in the meantime, became a more polished coach. He sought the counsel of friends in the profession—Villanova's Rollie Massimino, Cal's Lou Campanelli, and Billy's old coach at North Carolina, Dean Smith. He leaned on veteran assistants Chuck Daly and Jack McMahon. "I felt like he improved every year as a coach," Jones once said. "I enjoyed Billy because he didn't play favorites. He played the guys that were getting it done."

But year after year, the Sixers couldn't quite get it done, losing in the Finals in 1980 and '82 and coughing up a 3–1 lead to Boston—another one—in dropping the Eastern Conference Finals in 1981. And each loss gnawed at Cunningham. "If he had any fun during those years, he kept it to himself," former *Daily News* columnist Mark Whicker said.

Malone appeared to be the last piece to the puzzle, but Cunningham knew as well as anyone there were no guarantees. He said he and his staff "just pushed and pushed and pushed" the players that season. And finally, they made it to the mountaintop. But in Cunningham's mind, the view was one that was meant to be shared.

Brett Brown

Brett Brown is a runner. The man hired to coach the 76ers in 2013–14 runs six days a week, for an hour at a pop (and always outside). He doesn't run fast, but as he said in midseason, "My legs don't stop."

He appears to apply the same one-foot-in-front-of-the-other approach to his job, believing that he will get somewhere while at the same time knowing some pain will have to be endured along the way. Okay, a lot of pain.

The plan all along was for the Sixers to be terrible in 2013–14, in an attempt to enhance their position in a talent-rich draft. Sam Hinkie, the new general manager, said that would be the case from the start. So too did Brown, a former San Antonio assistant.

He continued to say it as his team meandered down the road to nowhere, in a voice betraying both his Maine roots and an extended stay in Australia during his salad days. (San Antonio star Tim Duncan once described Brown's accent as "Bostralian.")

Everybody seemed to be on board with the Sixers' approach, but like sausage-making, it was not easy to watch. The Sixers lost 26 games in a row in one stretch, matching the longest skid in pro sports history, en route to a 19–63 record.

Yet Brown for the most part remained upbeat, and mindful of the big picture. "I think in an inverted way, it's exciting times," he said before a February loss to Dallas.

Atlanta Hawks coach Mike Budenholzer, who worked alongside the 53-year-old Brown in San Antonio, called him "one of the most competitive guys I've ever been around." It is something that revealed itself at different times during Brown's first season with the Sixers, notably when he was asked about the Spurs' wrenching loss to Miami in Game 6 of the 2013 Finals. It was a game San Antonio appeared to have won, only to give it away in the closing seconds—and with it, eventually, the title.

"A defeat like that," he said, "is so frustrating you just want to flip a desk." But as far as anyone knows, there was no desk-flipping in 2013–14. Not even as Trevor Ariza, the Wizards' journeyman forward, was putting up 40 points against the Sixers—the first time Ariza had scored 40 at any level of competition. And not even as marginal guys (Miles Plumlee, Tyler Zeller) or guys apparently on their last legs (Steve Nash, Elton Brand) were enjoying big nights against them.

Brown was critical of his players at times, as when he said their effort was "extraordinarily poor" in a 20-point defeat by Milwaukee, the team that wound up with the league's worst record. But mostly he conveyed the idea that there was only so much they could do, and only so much he could do. "I actually deal with [the losing] fine, because I see the endgame," he said.

There were times when he was out running during the season when fans would stop and ask him, "When are you going to win?"

"Said," he added with a smile, "in a really aggressive tone."

But he didn't mind the question, calling it "a reflection of this city's personality and the mentality."

"And I know," he added, "that if we can ever pull this off, then the city's going to come right along with us and be proud to grow with us."

He played point guard for his dad in high school, then for Rick Pitino at Boston University. And after college Brown went to New Zealand on a backpacking trip and wound up staying in that part of the world, having met the woman who would become his wife.

He got into coaching in Australia, and even after his hire in San Antonio years later remained head of the Aussies' national team, leading it to a 3–3 finish at the 2012 Olympics in London. (The highlight was a victory over the host team. Down by 15 points in the third quarter, Australia turned the tide incredibly and decisively, winning by 31.)

Brown was part of the Spurs organization for the first four of its five championship runs. And in 2013 he found himself part of something else. "We're trying to flush people out," he said at one point. "The whole purpose of this year has been about identifying people to move forward with."

He promised that the organization would be "ruthless" in that pursuit, and he showed his player-development chops most notably by working individually with rookie center Nerlens Noel, who tore up a knee in his lone season at Kentucky and did not play at all in 2013–14. Before every game Brown could be found on the court at the Wells Fargo Center, attempting to reconstruct Noel's jumper.

In his mind's eye Brown could see Noel, a live-bodied 6'11" athlete, developing a passable offensive game to supplement his dynamic shot-blocking. In time Brown could see him becoming a complement to point guard Michael Carter-Williams, the NBA Rookie of the Year in 2013–14, and part of a cast augmented by two high draft picks in June 2014.

So Brown keeps plodding along, his eyes fixed down the road. Because there is no question in his mind that he is getting somewhere, the pain be damned.

37 Jack Ramsay

Forever clear-eyed, Jack Ramsay had as firm an understanding of cancer as he did any opponent he had ever faced. Never mind that he was declared tumor-free in June 2010, after battling melanoma for six years. And never mind that he had survived prostate cancer in 1999.

"My commitment to living in the now means I'll never ever say that I've beaten cancer," he wrote in the introduction to his 2011 book, *Dr. Jack on Winning Basketball*. "To do so would be living in the 'tomorrow,' if you will, and melanoma is far too erratic an opponent to go around making predictions. But I can tell you for sure that I'll never give in to it. Life is too precious to give it up without giving everything you've got—*now*."

That's what he tried to do until the very end. He died of cancer on April 27, 2014, at the age of 89.

A coaching success in and around his native Philadelphia—notably at St. Joseph's University—Ramsay had first worked in the NBA for the Sixers, spending two years as their general manager and four as coach before fleeing to the Buffalo Braves in 1972, just as his former team was plummeting to 9–73 in 1972–73. He would make the Braves a winner, then head off to Portland and capture a title at the expense of the Sixers in 1976–77. That championship has always been hailed as a triumph of team ball over one-on-one selfishness, and it cemented Ramsay's reputation as a legend. (And never mind that he won exactly one playoff series the rest of his career.)

The other blots on his record are easily overlooked or explained away. While the Sixers' GM he traded Wilt Chamberlain, though there is ample evidence to suggest that Wilt wanted out. And as part of the Portland brain trust in 1984, Ramsay elected to use the second overall pick in the draft not on Michael Jordan but rather oft-injured center Sam Bowie. That too was an arguable decision, as the Trail Blazers already had an outstanding shooting guard in Clyde Drexler and needed a center.

Ramsay transitioned out of coaching and into broadcasting in 1989, working first for the Miami Heat and then ESPN Radio, and was always clear-headed and direct in his analysis, but never pedantic. Indeed, his on-air partners always marveled at his ceaseless curiosity. "He doesn't think he knows everything—and he frankly does know everything," one of them, Mike Breen, told *Sports Illustrated*'s Richard Deitsch in May 2013. Breen then wondered at the idea of Ramsay asking him for an opinion about a player or team. This was, after all, Dr. Jack, the guy not only with a doctorate in education from the University of Pennsylvania, but as much knowledge of the NBA as any man alive.

His prostate cancer was treated with radiation therapy and by injecting radioactive iodine pellets into the gland. He came out of that okay, not even bothering to tell his family about the extent of the problem, but his six-year battle with melanoma was another matter.

He wrote in the introduction to *Dr. Jack on Winning Basketball* that the problem began as three spots on the bottom of his left foot, which he first dismissed as some sort of injury incurred while running on the beach near his home in Ocean City, New Jersey, as he was always an exercise fanatic. Tests revealed that it was much more serious, and he recalled asking one of his doctors if it was a death sentence. No, he was told; some people live with it for three years.

Three years. Scant consolation, that.

When it was discovered that the disease had spread to his left calf, he underwent surgery to remove part of that calf and most of the sole of his left foot. Further tests showed the cancer was also in his groin, and he underwent chemotherapy to deal with that issue.

As he was about to be wheeled into the operating room for one procedure, a doctor told Ramsay there was a 2 percent chance he would lose his left leg. "If you have to take off my leg," Ramsay told him, "don't wake me up."

It was 18 months before Ramsay was able to resume normal physical activity, which in his case meant running, swimming, stretching, and a daily allotment of push-ups. But in March 2006 he was told the melanoma was in his lungs, necessitating more chemo. And in November of that same year tests revealed he had tumors in his brain.

That led to a treatment at Massachusetts General Hospital, in which high-dose radiation beams were trained directly at the tumors. He was also given a drug called Temodar, designed to prevent recurrence of the tumors. And not only did that affect those in his brain, it wiped out the ones on his lungs as well. There was, he was told, a 1 in 20,000 chance of that happening.

By June 2010 he was declared tumor-free, though any temptation he might have had to rejoice was tempered by the death five months earlier of his wife of 60 years, Jean, due to the aftereffects of Alzheimer's disease. "Jean's death was much tougher on him than the cancer," Bill Walton, center on Ramsay's great Portland team, told the *New York Times* in 2010. "Guys like Jack are so tough they would do anything to take away someone else's pain. I don't think I've ever made a rougher call than when I called Jack after Jean died. What do you tell an 85-year-old man whose college sweetheart is no more? She was always there, the gentle one, the quiet one."

Ramsay was hit by another broadside in November 2012 when his longtime broadcast partner, Jim Durham, died of a heart attack. While Ramsay continued to do games with a variety of play-by-play men (and was careful to give them their due), he acknowledged that it "wasn't quite the same." As Breen put it in his interview with *SI*,

"Jack lost a piece of a heart with Jimmy. Those two men truly really loved each other."

Ramsay began to hint at retirement, and in May 2013 he was forced to step down because of health concerns. At the time Beth Faber, the lead remote producer for ESPN Radio, told *Sports Illustrated* that she had always thought of Ramsay as "indestructible." But Ramsay, forever clear-eyed, knew better.

John Lucas

John Lucas saved himself, and in his lifetime has saved countless others. That he couldn't save the Sixers hardly seems to matter anymore.

He went 42–122 in two years as coach (1994–96), bottoming out at 18–64 the second of those seasons. He said upon being fired that the foundation had been lain for improvement, but it was two coaches and several players later before the Sixers began the climb to respectability.

Which, again, seems beside the point. Lucas, after failing one more head coaching trial with Cleveland from 2001 to 2003, returned to what he does best: rescuing those sidetracked by substance abuse. A recovering addict himself, he founded a treatment program in Houston when his 14-year playing career ended in 1990, and has been immersed in it ever since.

Through the years hundreds of athletes have passed through his program—which, he told ESPN.com's Jason King in 2012, represented "the last house on the block...the last stop on the escalator." Among those Lucas has worked with are former NFL players Dexter Manley and Johnny Jolly, former NBA player Rod

Strickland, and college coaches Kevin Mackey, Larry Eustachy, and Billy Gillispie—all of whom had some substance-abuse problem or other.

It wasn't all Lucas did—he also counseled emerging high school and college basketball stars, and offered tough love to athletes whose careers were sidetracked for other reasons—but it remained a sizable part of his mission.

"I cut through the bullshit," Lucas told King. "If you don't do what I'm telling you to do, you don't have the gift of desperation." Which means everything, he said. It is what drove him to seek help years earlier, to find his way along the road to recovery.

It was desperation of another kind that compelled Harold Katz to hire Lucas in the summer of 1994. After winning 53 games and an Atlantic Division title in 1989–90, the Sixers had managed fewer victories than the preceding season each of the next four years. The coaching baton had passed from Jim Lynam to Doug Moe to Fred Carter.

What better man to inherit such a sorry situation than Lucas? Not only was he hired as coach, but he also assumed the role of general manager and vice president of basketball operations. He wanted all the power, all the responsibility. And he jumped in with both feet.

On the eve of his first season, he was beating the drum for the organization at a golf tournament in suburban Philadelphia. He was talking, not playing, for golf was not his preferred sport. Tennis had always been his game growing up in Durham, North Carolina—tennis and basketball. He was good enough on one court to be named to the Junior Davis Cup team, good enough on the other to gain a scholarship to the University of Maryland.

He even played both sports professionally for a while, before the bottom dropped out. He had used drugs before beginning his NBA career with Houston in 1976 as the first overall pick, the first point guard so designated. He did LSD the night before his first game at Maryland, for instance, and then went out and drilled his first nine shots.

But early in his pro career, he became a heavy user. Cocaine was his drug of choice, and he drank, too. He was not an addict, he thought, because he was sure he could stop at any time. And besides, addicts sleep on steam vents; they do not play in glittering arenas and stay in ritzy hotels.

Then he began missing flights. And practices. And games. People covered for him, tried to help him any way they could. When he was with Washington, the Bullets hired two bodyguards to follow him around. When he returned to Houston in 1984—having bounced to three other teams between then and his first stay with the team— coach Bill Fitch made Lucas stay with him in his hotel room until 2:00 AM every night on the road, just to keep him from going out.

When he was home, Lucas' wife, Debbie, locked him in the house and hid his car keys. But nothing helped.

Only John Lucas could save John Lucas. Which is what he finally set out to do after awakening from a cocaine blackout in downtown Houston one morning in March 1986. He was wearing three pairs of socks but no shoes, having sneaked out of the house the night before when Debbie left the front door unlocked. His clothes were soiled. He had no idea where he was.

Asked that day in 1994 about his substance-abuse problem, he said that was not the problem at all. "What I had," he said, "was a living problem."

The biggest reason he became an addict, he writes in his book, *Winning a Day at a Time*, was that he had achieved everything he could athletically. There was nothing else to reach for, no other mountain to climb.

"Drugs made me feel that wonderful wholeness I wanted so badly to feel," he writes. "Drugs made me feel connected and happy.... I still didn't know that all along I was using drugs to fill a big hole inside me."

He finally sought treatment, and something clicked. He has been clean and sober since March 15, 1986.

But that wasn't enough. He began an exercise program for recovering addicts at Houston International Hospital late in his playing career, then founded three treatment centers of his own. He also became the owner/coach of the USBL's Miami Tropics, and stacked the team's roster with addicts such as Roy Tarpley, Richard Dumas, and Pearl Washington.

Hired to coach the San Antonio Spurs in 1992, he became known for his unorthodox methods. He would turn timeout huddles over to players like David Robinson. He would have the team decide the punishment for someone who was late to a meeting or practice. Empowerment, he called it.

But that still wasn't enough.

He reached out to other recovering addicts. He bristled in '94 when then-Dodgers manager Tommy Lasorda reacted to Darryl Strawberry's entrance into a rehab center by saying his addiction was "a weakness, not an illness."

"He doesn't have any idea," Lucas said that day on the golf course. "It's not a lack of willpower.... You have all the best intentions, but your mind tells you something different.

"The other thing that makes it so difficult is that it's an emotional and spiritual bankruptcy. A person has lost his soul, and it attacks a person's ego. And when you attack a person's ego, it makes you violate all your values. It attacks your pride.

"It's almost like the 'poor me' syndrome: 'Poor me, I don't want to go to work today.' 'Poor me, it's raining.' 'Poor me, the owner is on me.' And the next thing is, 'Pour me another drink.'

"Those are living problems. And we handle our living problems by drinking."

As he followed his foursome to a green in a golf cart Monday, somebody wondered whether a reassuring voice ever told him, "Go ahead, John, have a drink. Take a snort. It's okay. You've got this thing licked."

"I don't hear that anymore," he said quietly.

So John Lucas turned out a lousy basketball coach. Like that even matters.

39 Game Night: The Dream Team

Being part of the Sixers' Dream Team is not without glamour— having actor Mark Wahlberg pay a visit to one's workplace isn't a bad perk, for starters—or mystique. The 22 women comprising the dance team are listed on the club's official website only by their first names, which besides giving them a certain aura also offers some protection from online stalkers and the like. (Although that works only to a point, as a quick scan of Twitter reveals.)

As for interviews, forget it. "I can't," the Dreamers' coach, Dayna Hafetz, informed this author when the subject was raised in February 2013. The higher-ups apparently wouldn't allow it. Then she brightened, saying that speaking with her was akin to speaking with a dancer anyway. Which is true. Hafetz was a member of the team from 1999, her junior year at Temple, to 2006, and a captain four of those years. She succeeded Debbie Apalucci as coach in 2009.

Hafetz, whose mother was a Sixers and Eagles cheerleader, had been dancing since age three. She called her time on the Dream Team "probably one of the most memorable experiences of my life."

"It's really neat to be on the other side and see the dancers experiencing [it]," she said. "I know how it feels to be on the floor, and how awesome it is."

The dancers do only three routines each game night, though they are on the court at other times, as when T-shirts are launched into the crowd from a Gatling gun–like contraption. A platoon of dancers is also stationed along each baseline during the game, meaning some of them were within Wahlberg's orbit when he was seated in the front row for a game in 2012–13.

"Mark Wahlberg is just as beautiful in person," one of the dancers tweeted, "as he is on TV."

"That moment where Mark Wahlberg makes eye contact with you and then says, 'You ladies are fantastic,'" another tweeted, adding the hashtag #inlove.

Two other dancers posed for a photo with him after he was presented with a souvenir jersey.

On other nights, there are opportunities for photos with people like Will Smith, a part-owner of the team; Hafetz herself joined in on that one. But there are also other responsibilities, such as visits to club boxes and appearances at various team-sponsored events, including Read to Achieve or Get the All-Star Vote Out (as well as more intimate gatherings like bar mitzvahs, Hafetz said). Squad members also have to attend twice-weekly rehearsals and submit to monthly weigh-ins.

Hafetz wouldn't say how much the Dream Teamers make for all their trouble, but as a guide, consider that the Cincinnati Bengals' cheerleaders make $75 a game, according to a 2008 story in *GQ* magazine.

Hafetz estimated that somewhere between 120 and 150 women try out for the squad each summer. She said it is not hard to make initial cuts, as some would-be Dreamers lack technical training. But the process grows increasingly difficult after that, as do the challenges faced by the dancers.

"It is stressful," a candidate identified only as India said in a video report that appeared on the team's website in June 2012, "because you never know what the combination [of moves] is going to be."

She added that she had majored in dance at Philadelphia High School for Creative and Performing Arts. That she had been a cheerleader there, and for the Philadelphia Soul of the Arena Football League. It was her third time trying out for the Dream Team.

She learned roughly a month later, in mid-July, that she had made it. She was one of eight rookies on the 2012–13 squad, a team that featured six second-year members, and two each who had been around for four, five, or six years. There were college students and recent graduates—they accounted for nine of the Dreamers—as well as dance instructors (five) and elementary school teachers (two). There was also an accountant, an administrative assistant, a foster-care case manager, and a pediatric echosonographer.

It's safe to say they attract their share of attention—sometimes the unwanted kind. There are stories of guys contacting them via Facebook. Guys who go with eye-rolling opening gambits like, "Can I ask you an honest question?" Or, "I like the way you cheerlead." Or something equally mundane.

There was also a guy early in the 2012–13 season who noted on Twitter that the dancers had "guts and rolls."

A dancer had a ready answer, though. Not to mention a sense of humor.

"It was fajita night," she tweeted.

No, it's not all glamour. But it appears there's at least some.

40 Warm Memories of 9–73

Fred Carter, who has evolved into the spokesman for the team that compiled the worst full-season record in NBA history, said the 1972–73 76ers would slink through airports with the logos on their travel bags turned inward, toward their legs, making it difficult for other travelers to identify them.

Occasionally someone would see all the tall guys together and ask. And when they did, the players would mumble their response.

Oh. Those guys. The soon-to-be 9–73 Sixers.

But in time Carter came to embrace that ignominious mark. Took him a while, though. Took him a long while. Maybe two decades. But as he told this author in 2008, "When you go through life, you'd like to be remembered some kind of way. For me, it's 9–73. If someone goes 8–74, you're no longer remembered."

He put it even more eloquently in May 2013, in an interview for this book: "The first graffiti was written on the railroad trestles during World War II, and it said, 'Kilroy was here.'" That was indelible, unforgettable. So too was 9–73.

Carter, the team's MVP (yes, they had one), was there. So was Roy Rubin, the overmatched head coach. So were Freddie Boyd and Manny Leaks and John Q. Trapp and all the rest. It was, in a sense, an incomparable team.

But when there is a comparison to be made, reporters have not hesitated to reach out to Carter. They did so when Chicago started out 6–42 in 2000–01, when Orlando started 1–19 in 2003–04, when New Orleans opened at 2–29 in 2004–05, and when New Jersey was 7–63 in 2009–10. Yet none of those teams managed to finish with a worse record than the 1972–73 Sixers. The closest any club has come is 11–71, the records put up by the 1992–93 Dallas Mavericks and the 1997–98 Denver Nuggets.

And while the Charlotte Bobcats did manage to finish 7–59 in the lockout-shortened 2011–12 season—and thus fashion the lowest winning percentage (.106) of all time—Philadelphia's 9–73 looms as a record that might not ever be broken.

Certainly Carter believes (and hopes) it will be difficult to eclipse. A native Philadelphian who spent his first two-plus NBA seasons with the Baltimore Bullets before being traded to the Sixers in October 1971, he pointed out that there are 30 teams now, 13 more than in 1972–73. The talent pool has, as a result, been watered down. "You're going to get wins," he said.

And, again, that's how he is rooting. "It's better to be remembered than not to be remembered at all," he said. "I played in the NBA Finals [in 1971]. No one remembers that.... But they all remember 9–73."

By 1972, most of those who comprised the Sixers' 1966–67 championship team—including Wilt Chamberlain, Chet Walker, Luke Jackson, and Wali Jones—were gone. Replacements had not been found; the Sixers' first-round draft picks between '67 and '71 (made by Jack Ramsay, the general manager the first two of those years, and his successor, Don DeJardin) were Craig Raymond, Shaler Halimon, Bud Ogden, Al Henry, and Dana Lewis. None of them played more than 74 games for the Sixers, nor averaged more than four points a game.

Ramsay, destined for the Hall of Fame, coached the team for four years but fled in 1972 for the Buffalo Braves. His replacement, former Long Island University coach Roy Rubin, was hired the same day a judge ruled that the Sixers' star forward, Billy Cunningham, had to honor the contract he had signed with the ABA's Carolina Cougars three years earlier.

There were hints right away that Rubin had no idea what he was doing. In the team's very first meeting, the new coach laid down

The 9–73 Sixers, By the Numbers

Coaches: 2
Players: 19
Home Record: 5–26
Road Record: 2–36
Neutral-site Record: 2–11
Average Points For: 104.1
Average Points Against: 116.2

the law: No smoking in the locker room. Carter protested, saying he needed to light up; it relaxed him. Immediately Rubin caved, pulling Carter aside and saying he was free to do so. "He didn't say it to everybody, but he let me know that I could," Carter said.

In another private conversation Rubin told him to shoot every chance he got—"because we had guys that couldn't score," Carter said. Carter averaged more than 19 points a game that season, most in his career to that point, though it was not without cost, as some of his teammates complained about his selfishness.

The Sixers beat the Celtics (or, at least, the Celtics' backups) in a preseason game, and Carter said Rubin "just danced around the locker room afterward and said, 'Hell with the Celtics. We can beat them. I told you we were going to be good.'" The players were left shaking their heads, knowing full well the team's shortcomings.

Carter, who served as the Sixers' head coach years later, would tell *Sports Illustrated* that having Rubin in charge "was a joke, like letting a teenager run a large corporation." It is a stance he still maintains.

"He was definitely a fish out of water, coming in from…LIU," he told this author. "Had no idea or concept of NBA basketball. He knew basketball, but on a professional level, NBA level, it's a totally different game. You're not dealing with boys. You're dealing with men, and men who have boys."

Rubin died in August 2013. He argued over the years, notably in interviews with *SI* and the *New York Times*, that he was not the only one at fault. "Why can't someone else take some of the blame?" he moaned to *SI* during that season. "I'm not the one who misses the shots, who throws the ball away, who won't box out. They're killing me. They're trying to take my livelihood away from me."

He lost 45 pounds during his 105 days on the job, or roughly one for every game he lost (47, in 51 games). Relieved of his duties at the All-Star break, he never coached in the NBA again. One of his players, Kevin Loughery, succeeded him and went 5–26—but he would enjoy a long career on the sideline.

The season, which began with 15 consecutive defeats and included a 20-game losing streak, ended with 13 straight losses, the last to Detroit in Pittsburgh. And afterward, Carter said, the players scattered to the winds, as if to distance themselves from the disaster.

Carter did that for a long time, too. But not anymore.

Box Score Double Take

The weirdest box score in NBA history—one that lists three players as having played for both teams—came about because of a question about Maurice Cheeks. It was a ridiculous question as it turned out, one that needn't have been asked. But it was posed by someone in the 76ers' front office during the 1978–79 season, and before anyone knew it the dominoes had tumbled and a situation unfolded that might never be duplicated.

The question was this: how is this rookie point guard going to hold up in the playoffs? Again, it sounds silly all these years later, knowing now what no one could have known then—that he was unshakable, as steady as anyone who has ever played for the franchise.

But at that point he was just a second-round draft pick from someplace called West Texas State, muddling through a season in which he would average slightly better than eight points and a little more than five assists. No one could be completely certain as to how he would perform in the playoff crucible, and it led the Sixers to make a trade with New Jersey on February 7, 1979, in which they swapped backup center Harvey Catchings and reserve guard Ralph Simpson for guards Eric Money and Al Skinner.

The key to the deal from the Sixers' standpoint was Money, a tough little guard who was scoring nearly 17 points a game for New Jersey. He loomed as Philadelphia's insurance policy, the guy to whom the team could turn, should Cheeks collapse in the postseason.

Forgotten, at least for the moment, was the fact that the two teams had squared off in the Spectrum on November 8, 1978, with the Sixers winning 137–133 in double overtime despite Money's 37 points. The Nets protested the game, claiming forward Bernard King and coach Kevin Loughery should not have been assessed third technical fouls by referee Richie Powers with 5:50 left in the third quarter, at which point the Sixers led 84–81.

Commissioner Larry O'Brien upheld the protest, and ordered the teams to resume the game from that point on March 23, before they met in a regularly scheduled game in the Spectrum. O'Brien also suspended Powers for five games without pay "for failure to comply with league procedure." And after the trade, it was ruled that the players involved would be free to compete with their new teams.

As a result Money likely became the only player to score for both sides in a major U.S. sporting event. He was credited with 23 points as a New Jersey starter and four as a Sixers reserve, as Philadelphia won the do-over 123–117. And while he lost the 14 he generated for the Nets in the original game, he seemed unfazed when the topic was raised by the *Los Angeles Times'* Jerry Crowe in 2008.

"It wasn't like I didn't score them," Money told Crowe. "I scored them. They just didn't allow them."

Catchings and Simpson also played for both teams, but Catchings scored eight for the Nets, none for the Sixers, while Simpson scored eight for the Sixers, none for the Nets. Skinner did not get into the game for either team.

Julius Erving scored 32 points to lead the Sixers to victory. John Williamson had 34 for New Jersey. And there were a couple other oddities: There are six referees listed in the official box, as Powers, Ed Middleton, and Roger McCann gave way to Jack Madden, Earl Strom, and Bill Saar. Also, Phil Jackson, whose days as a legendary coach for the Bulls and Lakers were far in the future, ran a team for the first time after Loughery's ejection from the original game. Jackson was activated as a player before the resumption, and collected four points and three rebounds in 14 minutes.

The Sixers also won the regularly scheduled game that night, 110–98.

As for Cheeks, any questions about his ability to withstand playoff pressure proved to be unfounded. He averaged 18.8 points in nine postseason games that year, including a playoff career-high 33 in Game 4 of the Eastern Conference Semifinals against San Antonio, a series the Spurs won in seven. Money, who played often and well in 23 regular-season games for the Sixers, saw little action in the playoffs and was traded to Detroit early in the 1979–80 season. Though just 24, he retired at the end of that year.

He told Crowe he looks back on that Sixers-Nets fiasco fondly.

"It's probably kept my name out there," he said. "It was years later before people started asking me about it and I had to be reminded about it more than I remembered it, but it's the one game that has kind of made my career."

42 Doc Defies Gravity

On one of the signature moves of Julius Erving's career—his hanging, twisting, hard-to-believe-your-eyes reverse layup in Game 4 of the 1980 NBA Finals—his hang time was measured at 0.7 seconds. Yet it has hovered forever in memory.

His reputation for acrobatic moves was well established by then, having been forged in the old ABA. It was said if you didn't see him then—soaring through the air; cradling that red, white, and blue ball in one ridiculously large hand; his Afro flopping in the breeze—you never saw him at all.

Meaning few did.

Hall of Fame coaches Lou Carnesecca and Hubie Brown did. Carnesecca, who had the ill fortune to coach the New York Nets before Erving played for them (but later achieved great success at St. John's), was asked by Tony Kornheiser about Erving's ability to hang in midair, seemingly forever, for a story that appeared in the October 29, 1984, issue of *Sports Illustrated*.

"I always had the feeling," Carnesecca said, "that one time he would lift off and rise through the glass, out of the arena, and disappear into space."

Brown, who coached the ABA's Kentucky Colonels, once told this author that Dr. J would routinely swoop downcourt, catch a pass, tap the top of the box on the backboard—11 feet above the floor—and dunk. And when he did things like that, Brown said, "He would turn your building against you. If you let him come down on the three-lane break and take off at the foul line and dunk, people in your own building would give him a standing ovation."

The cheers only grew louder over time. In the 1976 ABA All-Star Game in Denver, Erving ran the length of the court, took off

Dr. J shows off his high-flying ability against Los Angeles' Kareem Abdul-Jabbar in a 1980 game.

at the foul line, and dunked en route to winning the slam-dunk contest. And when he joined the NBA the following fall, he continued his air show.

He peaked—pun intended—on Sunday, May 11, 1980, when the Sixers faced the Lakers in the aforementioned Game 4, in the Spectrum. The situation was this: The Sixers were up 89–84 in the fourth quarter, and would win 105–102 (their last victory in a series they would lose in six games). Erving took a pass from Bobby Jones on the right wing, and finding himself defended by lumbering forward Mark Landsberger, accelerated toward the basket.

At the right side of the lane Erving elevated, only to be confronted by Kareem Abdul-Jabbar, who had come over to help. Erving, waving the ball in his right hand, floated across the lane and seemingly made a left turn in midair before ducking under the backboard and successfully laying up the ball from the opposite side of the rim.

The building exploded. And the play became a longtime staple of highlight videos, to be joined three years later by Erving's dunk over Michael Cooper in a regular-season game in the Spectrum. "He hung up there so long," Landsberger told the *Los Angeles Times* in 2011, "I was already down by the time he got to the other side."

Magic Johnson, then a Lakers rookie (and a man who would forge his own indelible memory two games later, when he subbed for an injured Abdul-Jabbar at center and piled up 42 points, 15 rebounds, and seven assists in the series clincher), was similarly awed. "Here I was, trying to win a championship, and my mouth just dropped open: *He actually did that*," he later told ESPN.com. "I thought, *What should we do? Should we take the ball out, or should we ask him to do it again?* It's still the greatest move I've ever seen in a basketball game, the all-time greatest."

Erving summarized his memory of the moment in an ad that aired to promote the 2011 NBA Finals: "I actually elevated and held the ball out of bounds, and watched to see what was going to happen."

That would suggest he had the ability to dawdle in midair before firing off some invisible booster rockets. And, well, maybe he could. "Sometimes on a straight rise," Erving told Kornheiser, "you sort of put your air brake on and wait for the defense to go down—that's pure hang time."

He also said in that same story that he did not take his maximum leap every time, believing that when he did so, he sacrificed body control.

"If you put all your energy into your leap, go up in a tube as it were, you're usually committed to a particular direction," he told Kornheiser, "and when you get there, if there's no light, there's nothing more you can do. You've expended all the energy your bottom half has to give you. A good defender can make you eat your shot. Whereas if you've just used three-quarters of your jump, now you can kick your legs up or what have you. I think you have to leave something in reserve. And believe me, it's nice to have something left."

There was also something of an optical illusion to his hang time, Erving said. When he picked up his dribble before liftoff, it might have left the impression that he was in the air longer than he actually was.

But that shot in the '80 Finals was no illusion. It happened, and it lives on in memory.

# "The Line for Apologies Forms Here"

In 1982, the Internet was but a pipe dream. Sports talk radio was still clearing its throat. ESPN was all of three years old. Newspapers remained a very big deal, and the words of a columnist carried considerable heft.

So when the Sixers lost Game 6 of the Eastern Conference Finals to the Celtics that year, they were subjected not to 140-character volleys delivered to their smart phones and tablets, but to a series of print broadsides delivered to their front doors the following morning.

It was not undeserved. For the second straight year they had led their hated rivals in the best-of-seven set, three games to one, only to see the Celtics rally to force a decisive seventh game in the fabled Boston Garden. The year before the Sixers had lost in the same venue, by a single point, and then watched as the Celts beat an eminently beatable Houston Rockets club (one featuring Moses Malone and little else) for the title. A similar heartbreak appeared inevitable.

No one was tougher on the Sixers than Bill Lyon, the *Philadelphia Inquirer*'s respected columnist. "Oh, the series isn't over yet…. But is there anyone who thinks Boston need do anything more than mail in the score?" he wrote

And also this: "There is a word for the Sixers' predicament. It is called hopeless." He compared them to the cliff divers of Acapulco. He wrote that they had folded like the bellows of an accordion. That the writers accompanying the team to Boston would be little more than pallbearers at a funeral, with interment underneath the parquet floor.

In the meantime the Sixers went about their business. The St. Joseph's University women's basketball coach, Jim Foster, watched them practice the day before Game 7 in the school's field house and sensed confidence, not dread. "I knew they'd win at Boston," he said years later. And on the bus ride from the team hotel in Cambridge to the Garden the morning of the game—a Sunday—Julius Erving kept talking to his teammates about the places they might visit in Los Angeles during the Finals. George

Shirk, the *Inquirer*'s beat writer, overheard and thought it to be a transparent ploy. *No way*, he thought, *do they win this game.*

And yet they did, decisively—120–106. Andrew Toney scored 34, one of many big games against the Celtics for the guard who inherited World B. Free's "Boston Strangler" nickname. Erving scored 29. And with the outcome no longer in doubt in the closing minutes, the Celtics fans memorably chanted "Beat L.A.," a chant that would echo throughout various arenas in the years to come.

The Sixers then proceeded to lose to the Lakers in the Finals, spoiling the perfect storybook ending. But the victory in Boston Garden still stands as one of the signature games in franchise history, the ultimate gut-check. "This feels too good to be bitter," point guard Maurice Cheeks told reporters afterward.

Team owner Harold Katz took a pragmatic viewpoint. "If we had lost, this franchise would have been very, very shaky," he told reporters. "We would have lost the confidence of an entire city. We probably would have sold only a handful of season tickets. Now this team should be all-time heroes. This is probably the greatest feeling I've had in my entire life."

Coach Billy Cunningham had been in a foul mood all day. During warm-ups he pulled his team off the court and told them in the locker room to go win it for themselves. And Lyon still swore, years after the fact, that the coach called a timeout late in the game just so he could glare at him.

Cunningham's mood had not improved by the time he met with reporters afterward. "I'm gonna be real quick," he said. "I only have two things to say. Number one, I want to thank the Celtics' fans for the way they responded at the end, because that showed real class.

"Number two, I'm ecstatic for the 12 guys and the coaches—and that's it. Everyone else buried us. Period. Good-bye. That's it for me, babe. I've had enough of you guys."

Then he repaired to the locker room and lit a victory cigar. A television crew approached him for an interview, but he waved them off.

Lyon, swallowing hard, tiptoed over. "The line for apologies forms here," he said, extending his hand to Cunningham.

For a moment he thought the coach might hit him, but he did not.

"That hurt a lot," he said of Lyon's pregame column.

"It was supposed to," Lyon said.

Then they shook hands and moved on. Lyon led his column with the line about apologies. Cunningham forgave and forgot.

"I'm not so sure I would have let me off the hook," Lyon, now semiretired at 76, recalled in 2012.

Again, it was a different time. Maybe better in many ways, too.

44 Erving, Bird Square Off

The last salvo in the Sixers-Celtics rivalry consisted of a series of ineffectual right hands from Julius Erving to the head of Larry Bird on November 9, 1984. Before that, the teams had been on opposite sides of a feud stretching back to 1953, their animosity fueled by geography and lofty ambitions. Afterward, things would never quite be the same.

Bird might have been the first one to realize an era was coming to an end, for it has long been rumored that as he was dismantling Dr. J that night in Boston Garden, he began taunting him. Did Bird really say "Take two and call me in the morning" after raining a jumper on Erving's head? Did he really remind the good Doctor that he was being outscored, 42–6, right before their most memorable brawl began? Bird, a notorious trash-talker during his career, has never admitted as much. Erving has only said that Bird started the fight, while never getting into the specifics.

What is known is that that meeting early in the 1984–85 season featured the NBA's two previous championship teams, the Sixers having won in 1982–83, the Celtics in 1983–84. They had not met in the playoffs in either of those seasons, but they had squared off four times in the previous six years, the Sixers winning three of those series, and 16 times dating back to 1953, when the Sixers were based in Syracuse and known as the Nationals.

Both teams were off to hot starts in 1984, with the Sixers winning their first five games, the Celtics their first four. So as usual there were claims to be staked, turf to be established. Bird did so, shooting a blistering 17-for-23 from the floor—and, perhaps, letting Erving know about it. This was not a role to which Dr. J was accustomed. He was the one who, through the years, had dominated opponents with his soaring dunks and acrobatic shot-making. He was also a regal presence, someone opponents treated with the utmost respect.

But Larry Bird had 42 points—42!—before the end of the third quarter. And the Celtics were spanking their longtime rivals by 21. Adding to the volatile mix was the fact that one of the game officials, Jack Madden, had been forced to depart with a leg injury, leaving Dick Bavetta to work the game by himself. It was, wrote *Boston Globe* columnist Dan Shaughnessy, "like leaving Barney Fife in charge of Hill Street District."

With 1:38 left in that third period, things boiled over. Elbows were exchanged, and suddenly two of the NBA's marquee players were squaring off. It was, of course, far from the first time the two teams had brawled. Back when the Warriors were in Philadelphia, in 1962, Boston's Sam Jones had grabbed a stool from a court-side photographer to fend off Wilt Chamberlain after the two exchanged words.

One of basketball's greatest rivalries: Erving versus Bird.

155

Four years later, Wilt and Bill Russell had had to be separated during a playoff game. And in the 1983 preseason—the preseason, mind you—Celtics patriarch Red Auerbach had come out of the stands during yet another fight and confronted Moses Malone, the Sixers' hulking center (a brawl also remembered for the fact that Sixers coach Billy Cunningham split his sport coat up the back while trying to break things up).

But for sheer star power, it was hard to beat Erving-Bird. And at the height of the melee, Malone and Charles Barkley grabbed Bird, apparently in an attempt to break things up, only to see Erving fire a few punches at the Celtics star. None appeared to do any damage. By this point, players from both sides had rushed the court. Celtics scrub M.L. Carr seemed bent on getting a piece of someone, anyone. That didn't happen, and before long order was restored.

Bird was ejected. So too was Erving, for the first and only time in his career. The Celtics went on to win the game 130–119, and in time the league handed down $30,500 in fines to the 18 participants in the brawl, including $7,500 each to Erving and Bird—large sums for that day and age.

The two teams met again the following month in Philadelphia, with Erving reportedly entering the Celtics' locker room beforehand to smooth the waters, then greeting Bird warmly when the two captains met the referees at midcourt. The Sixers won that one, and had an excellent season, going 58–24. It's just that the Celtics were even better at 63–19. They eased past the Sixers in the Eastern Finals, winning in five games.

Boston lost to the Lakers in the Finals that year, but with Bird at the absolute height of his powers—he was the MVP in 1984–85 and 1985–86, just as he had been in 1983–84—they won another league title in 1985–86 and another Eastern Conference championship in 1986–87.

Erving, while still a viable player, was in decline. He retired after the 1986–87 season, and his former team was left to languish. The Sixers did not return to the conference finals until 2000–01, when Allen Iverson led them past Milwaukee and into an ill-fated meeting with the Lakers in the Finals. The team is still looking to end its championship drought.

And as for the rivalry with the Celtics, that's as obsolete as the short shorts Erving and Bird wore that night in November 1984. The two teams have met in the playoffs just twice since 1985—in 2002 and 2012—with Boston winning both times.

45 Uniform Success

Whenever Maurice Cheeks comes up for Hall of Fame consideration—and in 2013 he was a finalist for the third straight year—few people are more interested than Scott Brooks. "I still have his uniform," Brooks said.

Brooks coaches the Oklahoma City Thunder. Cheeks was one of his assistants for four years, ending in 2013. But in 1988–89 Cheeks was in the last of his 11 seasons as the Sixers' starting point guard. (He would play four more years elsewhere.) Brooks, his backup, was in the first of his 10 NBA seasons.

Because he was a rookie, Brooks was required to perform all sorts of menial tasks for Cheeks, one of them being that he had to carry the veteran's uniform on all road trips. And after the last game of that season, Brooks kept it. Years later he asked Cheeks to sign it, and he held on to it.

"That's the main reason I really want him to be a Hall of Famer—so I can sell it for more on eBay," Brooks said.

He was kidding, probably. "It's a 25 percent premium if he becomes a Hall of Famer," Brooks said. "That's oceanfront property all of a sudden."

Not yet, though.

Cheeks retired in 1993 as the NBA's all-time leader in steals, and No. 5 in assists. While he remains fifth and 11th in those respective categories, he had to be seen to be appreciated. And the closer you were, the better he looked.

"To see him practice every day, you see why he was so good, because he was just so consistent," Brooks said. "His personality was ideal for a point guard. He was just levelheaded. He understands the game. He has a great passion for the game.... Playing against him every day in practice made me a better player. I saw the tricks that he would use on me."

Cheeks was traded to San Antonio for a younger point guard, Johnny Dawkins, the summer after he and Brooks spent that single season together. That was a messy piece of business in that Cheeks learned of the deal not from the team but from a TV reporter. He would later tell the *Philadelphia Daily News* he felt "betrayed."

He also made stops in New York, Atlanta, and New Jersey before his career came to an end.

In the meantime his former backup was becoming something of a vagabond himself. After a year as Dawkins' backup, Brooks went to Minnesota, then Houston (where in 1993–94 he was part of a championship team), then Dallas, New York, and Cleveland.

Their lives would once again intersect in Oklahoma City in 2009, the year after Cheeks was fired as the Sixers' head coach.

But really, they had always been tethered together, by a years-old uniform.

46 Iverson Gets the Better of Jordan (Briefly)

Michael Jordan owned an era, but Allen Iverson grabbed a moment.

Jordan's Chicago Bulls won six NBA championships between 1990 and 1998, failing to do so only when he skipped all of the 1993–94 season and most of 1994–95. And it was during the romp to the 1996–97 title—on March 12, 1997, to be specific—that the Bulls found themselves in Philadelphia to face the downtrodden Sixers and Iverson, the fearless rookie guard.

This was Iverson post-prison but pre-tattoo. Post–John Thompson but pre–Larry Brown. There was some sketchy idea of what he would become—he was well on his way to being named Rookie of the Year—but only some. Another hint came in the second half of the game, which the Bulls went on to win 108–104.

That's when Iverson found himself at the top of the key, isolated against Jordan.

"Michael, get up on him," Bulls coach Phil Jackson yelled from the bench. (An odd command, in retrospect, since it always seemed better to concede Iverson a jumper, as opposed to letting him invade the lane.)

But Jordan did as he was told, getting right in Iverson's face. The sellout crowd rose in anticipation, recognizing a potentially special moment involving an established star and a game newcomer. This was the game at its very essence, the way it is contested on every playground and in every gym. A challenge had been issued and accepted. Who would meet it?

Iverson tested Jordan with his signature crossover dribble, a move he had appropriated just a few years earlier from a teammate at Georgetown named Dean Berry. "I [saw] that he was biting on it," Iverson said in a 2011 video produced by the *New York Times.* "Then I hit him with the second one."

Jordan bit even harder that time, swiping at (and missing) the ball as Iverson maneuvered from left to right, enabling him to launch an 18-foot jumper from the right side of the circle. He swished it, and the crowd exploded. "The craziest thing about it," Iverson told the *Times,* "is I hit him with my best move, and he still almost blocked it…. That just lets you know how great of a defensive player he was."

Iverson finished the night with 37 points, Jordan with just 23, on 9-for-24 shooting. The Bulls, bound for a 69–13 season, won in large part because Scottie Pippen scored 31 points and Dennis Rodman seized 17 rebounds. And while the Sixers were headed for a 22–60 finish, Iverson had given one more indication about the direction in which he was headed; he would lead his team to the NBA Finals just four years later.

The moment also brought some degree of notoriety to Berry. He was mentioned in Larry Platt's 2002 Iverson biography, *Only the Strong Survive,* and would sit for an interview with the *Times* nine years later.

A Brooklyn native, he was a four-year walk-on at Georgetown, his career intersecting with Iverson's in 1995–96. They knew each other from the AAU circuit, and Iverson was obviously the superior player. But Berry had studied the great practitioners of the crossover—guys like John Stockton, Kenny Anderson, and Tim Hardaway—and had mastered the move himself. So when he and Iverson squared off in one-on-one games, as they frequently did after practice, Iverson found that he couldn't stop it, even when he knew it was coming.

Iverson finally swallowed his pride and asked Berry how to do it. And this lowly walk-on—a guy who averaged 2.3 points per game in his college career—passed it on to the future Hall of Famer.

Who famously used it on the night of March 12, 1997. "I used to always tell my friends when I get on that stage, I'm going to try my move on the best," Iverson told the *Times*.

In that same video, Miami Heat star Dwyane Wade says Iverson's move on Jordan "made it cool for everyone" to want to perfect his crossover.

Of course Berry laughingly claims in the video that his crossover remains superior to Iverson's, that "the student can never beat the teacher." Of course Iverson says his is the best "by far," because he "put it on that platform on the biggest stage ever."

The argument is far from settled, though. "I'm pretty sure there's going to be some guy that's [going to] come along, that's going to learn it and get it better than I got it," Iverson told the *Times*, "and his is going to be better than mine. Hopefully it's my son."

He laughed. It was the laugh of a man who had once met the biggest of challenges.

47 Mark Hendrickson's 15 Minutes

It was a nothing play, Mark Hendrickson has always insisted, just a simple layup by Michael Jordan in a nothing game at the end of a long season.

It became something more when a Time-Life photographer captured the moment on April 7, 1997. Jordan soared over the earthbound Hendrickson, then a 76ers rookie forward, and cradled the ball in his right hand. It appeared Jordan was about to throw down a particularly majestic dunk that night in the United Center, in a game that saw the championship-bound Bulls whip the lottery-bound Sixers 128–102.

The photo made Time-Life's Pictures of the Century collection. It appeared on the cover of the 1997–98 *NBA Register*. And it
was made into a poster, one that was prominently displayed in the
Florida Marlins' clubhouse in 2008, when Hendrickson, by then a
journeyman left-handed pitcher, played for the team.

"He straight up got posterized," pitcher Scott Olsen told the
Palm Beach Post.

While that is literally true, Hendrickson has said things are not
quite as they appear—that it was a two-on-one fast break and he
attempted to draw an offensive foul on Jordan, which explains why
Jordan's right leg is shown hitting him in the chest. "He hit me
pretty hard," he told the *Post*, "and it just makes me amazed that
someone could pose after hitting me that hard."

The 6'9" Hendrickson had starred in baseball and basketball growing up in Mount Vernon, Washington, and again at
Washington State University, but had spurned the Major League
Baseball teams that drafted him each year between 1992 and '96—
five times in all. The Toronto Blue Jays also drafted him in June
1997, nearly a year after the Sixers had taken him in the second
round of the same draft that netted Allen Iverson.

He spent just that single season with the Sixers, then signed
with the Blue Jays in May 1998 and juggled both sports for
three years, playing in the minors each summer and the NBA—
Sacramento, New Jersey, and Cleveland were his other stops—each
winter. He spent some time in the CBA as well.

With his basketball career at a standstill—his NBA norms were
just 3.3 points and 2.8 rebounds—he decided in 2000 to devote
himself fully to baseball. He would later tell the Associated Press
that he was proud of what he had done in hoops, proud of how far
he had gone in the sport and believed he could have had "a decent
career" if he had devoted himself full-time to it. "But just the lure
of what I could be in baseball," he said, "is something that is very
attractive to me."

And, he added, "Being 6'9" and left-handed [as a pitcher] is like being a seven-footer in basketball."

He made his major league debut two years later, becoming just the 12th player to appear in the NBA and the majors, and one of the tallest big-leaguers of all time. Never a hard thrower, he went 58–74 with a 5.03 ERA while pitching for five teams over the following decade.

Out of the game in 2012, he attempted a comeback with the Baltimore Orioles in the spring of 2013.

48 We're *Still* Talkin' 'Bout Practice

It is the ultimate irony: Allen Iverson, clearly no fan of practice, will forever be associated with it. That was assured when, in his 2001–02 season-wrap-up press conference with the Sixers, he uttered the word "practice" some 24 times—and nearly a 25th—when asked about his practice habits, long a bone of contention between him and coach Larry Brown.

Certainly it is one of the most memorable pressers ever, ranking with one in which then–Indianapolis Colts coach Jim Mora spewed the word "playoffs" with singular incredulity and another in which then–Arizona Cardinals coach Denny Green exploded after his team blew a game to the Chicago Bears: "We are who they thought they were! And we let 'em off the hook!" (Both sound bites were immortalized in popular ads for Coors Light.)

But Iverson's rant resonates as much as any of them. Actor Charlie Sheen referenced it in 2011, when asked how often he missed rehearsals for the TV show *Two and a Half Men*. Brown himself dredged it up in 2012, when he was introduced as the new coach at SMU: "I don't love games, but I love practice. I'm talking about practice…. I love practice."

Four years earlier, Iverson was introduced to reporters after a trade from Denver to Detroit. Seated at a table alongside general manager Joe Dumars, the former Pistons great, Iverson assured everyone he was going to do everything coach Michael Curry asked of him.

"Even practice?" Dumars deadpanned.

"Practice?" Iverson said, laughing along with everyone else. "We're talking about practice?"

Everyone laughed some more.

"I set myself up for that one," Iverson said.

The origins of his rant were far from amusing. Indeed, it had its basis in his deep-seated philosophical differences with Brown. Brown thought practice extremely valuable, the place where Iverson could bond with his teammates, where the team could become whole. Iverson believed the best way to do that was to play his heart out every game night.

There are differing reports as to how many practices Iverson missed during that 2001–02 season, which ended with the Sixers losing in the first round to the Boston Celtics. Some said it was just a handful; Iverson himself said it might have been one. But Brown, never one to hide his feelings, made his displeasure known. And so too did Iverson, when he sat down before reporters in the Sixers' home arena on May 7, 2002, four days after the season ended with a 33-point playoff rout in Boston.

He started out by saying he was disappointed by the way the season ended, and that he and Brown were, contrary to popular belief, on the same page. Then there was this:

Reporter: Could you be clear about your practicing habits since we can't see you practice?

Iverson: If Coach tells you that I missed practice, then that's that. I may have missed one practice this year but if somebody says he missed one practice of all the practices this year, then that's enough to get a whole lot started. I told Coach Brown that you don't have to give the people of Philadelphia a reason to think about trading me or anything like that. If you trade somebody, you trade them to make the team better...simple as that. I'm cool with

Iverson and Brown: still talkin' about practice?

that. I'm all about that. The people in Philadelphia deserve to have a winner. It's simple as that. It goes further than that.

Reporter: So you and Coach Brown got caught up on Saturday about practice?

Iverson: If I can't practice, I can't practice. It is as simple as that. It ain't about that at all. It's easy to sum it up if you're just talking about practice. We're sitting here, and I'm supposed to be the franchise player, and we're talking about practice. I mean listen, we're sitting here talking about practice, not a game, not a game, not a game, but we're talking about practice. Not the game that I go out there and die for and play every game like it's my last but we're talking about practice, man. How silly is that?

Now I know that I'm supposed to lead by example and all that, but I'm not shoving that aside like it don't mean anything. I know it's important, I honestly do, but we're talking about practice. We're talking about practice, man. [Laughter from the media crowd.] We're talking about practice. We're talking about practice. We're not talking about the game. We're talking about practice. When you come to the arena and you see me play, you've seen me play right, you've seen me give everything I've got, but we're talking about practice right now. [More laughter.]

Reporter: But it's an issue that your coach continues to raise?

Iverson: Hey, I hear you. It's funny to me, too. Hey, it's strange to me, too. But we're talking about practice, man. We're not even talking about the game, when it actually matters. We're talking about practice.

Reporter: Is it possible that if you practiced…you would make your teammates better?

Iverson: How in the hell can I make my teammates better by practicing?

Reporter: So they can be used to playing with you.

He responded by saying they should be used to him, since they play alongside him.

The question-and-answer period went on much longer, and some of it grew testy. But the part about "practice" is what everyone remembers.

It was left to Brown to have the last word.

"He said 'practice' more times than he's actually practiced," the coach told reporters the next day.

That would never be forgotten.

49 A Brief History of Iverson's Caddies

How do you build a team around Allen Iverson? That was the dilemma the Sixers faced, as long as he played in Philadelphia—finding the right combination of players to play alongside a point-guard-sized shooting guard, and a guy who was a high-volume (not to mention low-percentage) shooter.

It led to some disastrous draft decisions, like the selection of Larry Hughes in 1998, when Paul Pierce and Dirk Nowitzki were also on the board. It led to good ideas that turned out bad, as when Toni Kukoc was acquired from Chicago during the 1999–2000 season, only to make a modest impact during his abbreviated stay. It led to the Sixers reacquiring Derrick Coleman in '01, and in subsequent years trading for Keith Van Horn, Glenn Robinson, and Chris Webber.

Ultimately the best idea proved to be putting grinders around Iverson and letting him do his thing, as was the case when the Sixers advanced to the Finals in 2000–01. But that nucleus only remained intact for a year, and the Sixers slid back toward mediocrity during the latter stages of the decade-plus he played for them (not including his 25-game cameo in 2009–10).

Here is the list of the players who finished as the Sixers' second-leading scorers in each of the 10 full seasons Iverson spent with the team, along with his average and the team's record:

1996–97: Jerry Stackhouse, 20.7 (Iverson: 23.5) (Team: 22–60)

1997–98: Derrick Coleman, 17.6 (Iverson: 22.0) (Team: 31–51)

1998–99: Matt Geiger, 13.5 (Iverson: 26.8) (Team: 28–22)

1999–00: Toni Kukoc, 12.4 (Iverson 28.4) (Team: 49–33)

2000–01: Theo Ratliff, 12.4 (Iverson: 31.1) (Team: 56–26)

2001–02: Derrick Coleman, 15.1 (Iverson: 31.4) (Team: 43–39)

2002–03: Keith Van Horn, 15.9 (Iverson: 27.6) (Team: 48–34)

2003–04: Glenn Robinson, 16.6 (Iverson: 26.4) (Team: 33–49)

2004–05: Chris Webber, 15.6 (Iverson: 30.7) (Team: 43–39)

2005–06: Webber, 20.2 (Iverson, 33.0) (Team: 38–44)

Coincidence or not, the four years in which the Sixers' second-leading scorer was most productive came during the four losing seasons of the Iverson era. And Iverson's two lowest-scoring sidekicks performed alongside him during the team's two best seasons with A.I.—1999–2000 and 2000-01.

Translation: It takes a special group to play with someone who dominates the ball as much as Iverson did. It takes guys who understand they will only get a limited number of shots, and that they will have to have glory in the dirty work.

They're hard to find, as the Sixers learned during a decade-long search.

50 Cheeks' Greatest Assist

Thirteen-year-old Natalie Gilbert, winner of a contest to sing the national anthem before the Portland Trail Blazers hosted the Dallas Mavericks in a playoff game in April 2003, started out well enough.

But no sooner did the eighth-grader sing, "what so proudly we hailed," than she faltered.

"At the starlight's...stars..."

She knew that wasn't right. But neither could she retrieve the line from memory.

So she stopped.

Maybe it was the flu, which she had contracted earlier in the day. More likely it was simply nerves. There were 19,980 fans in the Rose Garden, the Blazers' home arena, that day.

She laughed nervously, put her hand to her head, started looking around for her parents. She would later say that it was as if she couldn't move; it felt like her feet were stuck to the floor.

Then Maurice Cheeks arrived.

"C'mon," the Trail Blazers coach said, putting his arm around her. "C'mon."

And the former Sixers point guard started leading her through it. She stammered for a moment, then picked up steam. And Cheeks waved his free arm, encouraging the fans to join in.

They did, and before long it was one of the loudest renditions of the anthem. Also one of the most moving.

When it was over, Cheeks hugged Gilbert. She thanked him and he walked back toward the Blazers' bench, head bowed.

"That's just so Maurice," Laurie Telfair, one of Cheeks' friends, said years later. "It does not surprise me in the least. That's the essence of him."

When he was asked about his timely assist after becoming the Sixers' coach in 2005, Cheeks recalled thinking only that he could not let Gilbert stand there by herself. He knew he would want someone to come to the aid of either of his two kids if they were in the same predicament, so he reflexively did the same. "I didn't know if I knew the words or anything," he said. "I just started walking.... I didn't know what I was doing. I just reacted."

Even his assistants were stunned. They had no idea where he was going, or what he might do. And when he arrived at center court, he saw the surprise on Gilbert's face. "I was scared myself," he said. "The crowd got me through it."

The Blazers lost the game 115–103 to go down to 3–0 in the best-of-seven series—a series they would somehow extend to seven games before losing. But reporters were more interested in asking Cheeks afterward about his act of kindness. And Dallas assistant Del Harris ducked his head into Cheeks' office as well.

"Forget the game," Harris told him. "What you did was so amazing."

Cheeks' act moved many to write him, including the mother of his former coach with the Sixers, Billy Cunningham. Cunningham himself told Ira Berkow of the *New York Times* he was moved to tears.

"I was so proud of him," Cunningham told Berkow. "But that was typical Maurice, to spontaneously do the right thing at the right time and generally without any fanfare. And so smart."

Because Cheeks is not, in his words, "an e-mail person," he did not realize at first how much of an impact he had made. But before too long the Blazers' public-relations staff had forwarded him hundreds of messages.

And he began to read.

"It was unbelievable," Cheeks said years later. "There were things that almost put me in tears. I had no idea it would rise to the level it became. There have been people who recognized me for doing that, and not playing or coaching in the NBA. I didn't know it would have that much impact, and I didn't do it for that reason."

In 2009 Cheeks, by then an assistant for the Oklahoma City Thunder, told *Daily Oklahoman* columnist Darnell Mayberry that he was merely doing what his parents had taught him to do, years before. "We didn't have the best life," he said. "But they instilled in us to treat people the right way. That's all that is. It's no secret. It's no recipe to it. It's just treating people correctly, and if you do it correctly it'll come back to you."

As for Gilbert, she was initially devastated by the events of that day. But she would come to realize that it was "one of the greatest moments" of her life, as she would tell *Good Morning America*. It was also an event that would long be remembered, even after she went to Hollywood and took voice and piano lessons, as well as some acting classes.

"I waited a very long time for people to get over it," she told *Portland Oregonian* columnist John Canzano in 2009, "but ultimately, I figured, messing up so bad was a good thing that happened to me."

51 Game Night: Allen Lumpkin

Allen Lumpkin knows things. He knows things because he's been embedded within the Sixers organization since 1977, first (at age 16) as a ball boy and in subsequent years in the ticket office, as the equipment manager, the director of team travel services, and currently the director of basketball administration. He has seen the players as few others have seen them. He has seen them in public and in private, at their best and at their worst. He knows their likes and dislikes, as well as their strengths and weaknesses (and not just whether they can go left or not).

He knows it all, but he says very little about it publicly. Which is, of course, one of the reasons he has managed to stick around as long as he has, through one generation of players after another, one regime change after another, one coach after another.

So when he was asked in February 2013 what he understands about the players that others do not, he wasn't about to give anything more than name, rank, and serial number. "They're just regular guys," he said. "You look up to them. In a sense, I do.... They laugh and joke. Sometimes they cry about stuff. Things happen to their families. They're just regular guys."

He has remained close with many of them through the years. Julius Erving and Andre Iguodala. Darryl Dawkins and Dikembe Mutombo. Larry Brown and John Lucas. Rick Mahorn is godfather to the oldest of three children Lumpkin has by his wife, Lea: Allen Jr. That very day, the elder Lumpkin had texted Tony Battie to wish him a happy birthday.

"These are relationships you just continue to build," Lumpkin said. "I'm fortunate. I'm very fortunate."

He became a ball boy when the *Philadelphia Daily News* held a contest in which entrants were asked to write why, in 25 words or less, they would be ideal for the job. He doesn't recall what he wrote, but he does recall that he was by himself in his New Jersey home on a Saturday afternoon when someone called to tell him he had won. He also recalled being "scared to death" when he worked his first game.

He was only supposed to hold the job for the 1977–78 season, but he was kept around for a second year, then a third. Before he knew it, he had gone from fetching coffee for Doug Collins the player to arranging flights for Doug Collins the coach. From shagging shots for Al Skinner to watching over Allen Iverson's jewelry. (Iverson would entrust his bling to no one else during games.)

After a while, Lumpkin's business became the family business. Allen Jr. worked as a ball boy for several years. So too did the youngest Lumpkin, Ryan. He started in 2003, when he was seven, and worked through the 2012–13 season, at which point he planned to give it up, as he was poised to graduate high school and go off to college.

He had been accepted to nearby schools like Drexel and the College of New Jersey, and if he chose either he could have continued to work for the team. "But," he said one night in March 2013, "it's my chance to get away." So his real hope was to go to Maryland, though Connecticut and St. John's remained possibilities, too.

He too knows things—not as many as his dad, of course, but some things. He was around for the end of Iverson's stay in Philadelphia, and still counts it as a great thrill to have met a player he regards as "a legend." Ryan also saw the relationship between his dad and Iguodala blossom. "They were so close," he said.

You get that far inside, you not only see everything, you feel it as well. Ryan said he doesn't mind picking up after the players on those nights when they have won, but that same locker-room routine becomes "kind of dreadful" after a loss. The players shower and dress quickly, maybe mumble a few words to reporters, then head out the door.

The ride home to New Jersey with his dad is no better on such nights. "After a tough loss: silence," Ryan said. "He just doesn't want to talk."

Allen Lumpkin knows and sees everything. And in his own way, he shares it, too.

52 Manute Bol

In the summer of 1991, Manute Bol returned to his native Sudan, an African nation ravaged by civil war and famine. A *Philadelphia Inquirer* reporter named Timothy Dwyer described in excruciating detail the scene as Bol—who had just completed his sixth NBA season and his first with the Sixers—trudged through a refugee camp. How with throngs of people in his wake he passed a place described as the camp's marketplace, which consisted of three men peddling a half-dozen ears of corn. How he came upon one young boy whose head was so swollen he could not hold it up on his own, and no one could properly diagnose his affliction, much less cure him. And how Bol saw an elderly woman lying by herself, wasting away from hunger.

Later, Dwyer wrote, Bol addressed the large crowd for 15 minutes. He struggled to find the right words, finally ending with, "Just ask God to get you through today and tomorrow and then start again."

Bol would over the course of his 10-year pro career contribute millions to his homeland. He would raise millions more, and raise awareness of Sudan's plight in his adopted country. Even after his playing days were over, he remained a positive force, tirelessly campaigning in 2010 for candidates of the Sudanese People's Liberation Movement (SPLM), an effort that resulted in an Election Day victory for that party. That led in turn to the passage of a referendum allowing south Sudan to secede from the rest of the country in 2011.

He didn't live to see the birth of an independent nation, having died of kidney disease in June 2010 (probably at 47, though nobody knew for sure, since Sudanese records were imprecise). But

Manute Bol and the Best Western Eden Resort Inn

The late Manute Bol was a giant of a man. At 7'7", Manute Bol had trouble getting comfortable in bed. Not too many beds could accommodate a man of his height. Besides being tall, Bol had exceptionally long limbs. He had a 49-inch inseam and a wing span measuring 8'6" inches.

Prior to the 1990 season, a staff member at the Best Western Eden Resort Inn mentioned to hotel owner Drew Anthon during a meeting about the team's upcoming training camp visit that "Manute Bol is a tall guy. How about a special bed?"

Anthon thought it was a good idea and called his friend, Stuart Herr, who owned a local bed company in Lancaster. Herr built a bed specifically for the NBA's tallest player, so his feet would not hang off the bed. "It made the room a little tighter," Anthon said, "but we were able to fit it into the room."

The Sudanese center, who enjoyed a 10-year career in the NBA with four different teams, had never had a bed made for him and he was very appreciative. While attending a pre-draft party for Sixers season-ticket holders in 2006, Bol's face lit up when a reporter brought up the bed. "I remember it well; that's the best I ever slept," Bol said.

Known for his play at the defensive end of the court, Bol finished his career with more than 2,000 blocked shots and was second all-time in NBA history in blocks per game.

His three training camps staying at the hotel were eventful. Besides having a special bed made for him, Anthon gave the green light to destroy property for a prank on Bol. All in good fun, Charles Barkley and Rick Mahorn planned a stunt for a bloopers video called *Basketball's Funniest Pranks*.

A hole was cut in a portable table and in a table cloth. A covered tin was placed over the hole. Inside Garfield's, one of the hotel's restaurants, Barkley walked Bol through a buffet, pointing out the food on the table.

Barkley: Right there is a little rice. [Bol lifts the covered tin and sees rice.] Right there is a little peas. [Bol lifts the covered tin and sees peas.] Right there… [Bol lifts the covered tin and Mahorn's head is sticking through the open hole, and he yells, "Ahhhhh."]

Bol jumps and says, "It was Rick Mahorn." Then Bol, laughing, high-fives Barkley.

"It was hilarious," Anthon said. "You still see clips from the video, and it was filmed in our restaurant."

Manute Bol (11): basketball player, humanitarian, extremely tall man.

he survived long enough to know his campaigning had not been in vain. It was the last act of a life of great consequence, one that stood in contrast to the way he was viewed in the comparatively artificial world of the NBA.

There he was seen as a novelty, a curiosity. As a 7'7" Dinka tribesman with an incredible backstory—a staple of which was that he killed a lion with a spear, though nobody was sure if that was true or not—Bol saw only limited use on the court. His frame was so slight that Orlando Magic vice president Pat Williams joked that he was built like 6:00. That made Bol useful as a shot blocker; as a rookie with Washington in 1985–86 he swatted 397, second-most in league history to that point, and ended his career with 2,086, 15th all-time. But his offensive game was so rudimentary it was akin to playing four-on-five when he was on the floor.

Manute Bol, a real-life hero, had limited worth in the Land of Make-Believe.

He came to the United States in 1983 and was in the NBA two years later. At first he was apolitical regarding matters in his homeland, but a freelance writer named Jordan Conn wrote in a 2011 piece for the Atavist, a website, that Bol was made to understand the gravity of the situation during an early-morning phone call from the Sudan. People were dying, Bol was told—dying in the southern part of that country in a civil war begun the very year Bol departed for the States. It was, sadly, nothing new for that beleaguered nation, as government forces had also clashed with rebels from 1955 to 1972, and in the renewed fighting Bol would lose some 250 family members, including his father. The village in which he grew up, Turalei, would cease to exist.

He threw his support behind SPLM, financially and otherwise. Conn wrote that rebel leader John Garang held meetings at Bol's home in Washington, DC, and that in addition to visiting the war zone and the refugee camps, Bol spoke before Congress. While doing so, Conn wrote, Bol warned of the threat posed to the U.S.

by a man named Osama bin Laden, who was at that point holed up in Sudan.

The contrast between real life and NBA life was not lost on Bol. "If I didn't have basketball, I might be dead now," he told the *Sporting News'* Dave Kindred in November 1994. "Sometimes I don't feel I should make a good living while my people are dying."

Bol played just five NBA games in that 1994–95 season, then a season in the United States Basketball League before giving up the sport. Years later he attempted to raise money for his homeland by agreeing to box former NFL defensive lineman William "the Refrigerator" Perry in an exhibition bout. He also donned skates for a minor league hockey team (though he never played in a game) and put on a jockey's silks (though he never rode a thoroughbred).

He was far from perfect. He liked to drink—Heineken was his beer of choice—and he liked to gamble. And his life was not without further complications. In the summer of 2004 he broke his neck when the taxi in which he was riding crashed after a WNBA game in Connecticut; it was later determined that the driver, who died of cardiac arrest, was under the influence and using a suspended license. And Bol, who had lavished so much of his wealth on others, struggled to pay his medical bills, as he did not have health insurance.

Bol recovered in time to return to Sudan the following year, where a treaty had put an end to 22 years of violence. (The death squads had moved on to neighboring Darfur.) Turalei was rebuilt, and Bol spearheaded fund-raising efforts to have a school constructed there, a school that came to bear his name.

Throughout his career he would often fret in interviews about being unable to do more, that his millions only went so far. But he did all he could. He was, in a real-life sense, a hero.

53 Armen Gilliam

Where the late Armen Gilliam was concerned, there was always the "Charmin" thing. Charles Barkley, his teammate the three years Gilliam spent with the Sixers, affixed the nickname to his fellow forward. There was a cruel truth to it, as Gilliam was a finesse player, not the sort of low-post tough guy his frame (6'9", 230 pounds) might suggest. But to label a teammate as such seems the handiwork of a bully.

Asked by this author about the matter in February 2013, Barkley said, "I never called Armen 'Charmin.' Never. Me and Armen, we never had an issue.... We did not mesh together, obviously, but I've never had a problem with Armen. Me and Armen were cool the entire time."

He then insisted that Gilliam was given the nickname while playing for the Phoenix Suns earlier in his career, but again said that he never followed suit. Others who were around the Sixers in that era remember it differently. They recall Barkley, so affable and approachable to so many, called Armen "Charmin" among many other unflattering things.

They were destined to have their differences from the moment Gilliam was acquired in a January 1991 trade from Charlotte—a deal that saw Barkley's good friend, Mike Gminski, go to the Hornets. Barkley was the Sixers' resident superstar and alpha male, a free-spirited guy who would seemingly say and do anything.

Gilliam, son of a minister, was more measured, more reserved. After he died in July 2011 of a heart attack at age 47 while playing pickup basketball near his hometown of Pittsburgh, one of his former teammates at UNLV, Leon Symanski, remembered Gilliam as "a real sweet guy" in an interview with the *Pittsburgh*

Post-Gazette. The legendary Jerry Tarkanian, the Runnin' Rebels' retired coach, wrote in a first-person story for the *Las Vegas Sun* that Gilliam was "warm and kindhearted, but tough as nails." And Jim Lynam, who coached him for two years with the Sixers and served as general manager for the third, pronounced himself "a fan" of Gilliam's in an interview with the *Philadelphia Daily News*, adding that he was "a really, really good guy."

In his autobiography, *Outrageous!*, Barkley took Gilliam to task for his passive play, then immediately backtracked after the book was released (as he did about a great many other things). Gilliam finally responded on December 18, 1991, in an interview with Phil Jasner, the *Daily News'* late beat writer, calling Barkley "our most visible player, but, to me, not the type to provide leadership."

"Not like Magic [Johnson], not like Michael [Jordan] or Larry [Bird]," Gilliam added. "What they do is all conducive to winning, to making [teammates] better, to building chemistry."

As a result, Gilliam said, "young players can look to Charles as a great talent, but not as a leader." And even veterans would be well served to look elsewhere for leadership, he added.

Gilliam said he had held those opinions even before the book came out, and Jasner wrote that Gilliam was "clearly offended" when Barkley spit in the direction of a heckler during a game in the Meadowlands the year before, only to hit a little girl. Barkley later expressed regret for the incident and befriended the girl and her family. But at the time, Jasner wrote, Gilliam was so appalled that he sought out those sitting near where the incident occurred and apologized for Barkley's behavior.

Barkley was traded to Phoenix after the 1991–92 season and in his first game against the Sixers, in Phoenix in March 1993, was lying in wait for Gilliam. A *Philadelphia Inquirer* account of the game—a 125–115 Suns victory in which Barkley had 36 points, 17 rebounds, and nine assists—said that after Gilliam was inserted late in the first quarter, Barkley immediately dunked on him, then knocked down a jumper. That he threw Gilliam to the floor and glared at him. That he later nailed a three-pointer and taunted Gilliam, saying, "I've been waiting for you for six months."

Gilliam, whether dispirited or fatigued, soon signaled to Coach Doug Moe that he wanted out of the game. "Obviously, it was a special game," Barkley told reporters afterward. "But I'm a little disappointed in myself. I was playing angry; I don't want to play basketball angry. It's not a life-and-death situation. I want to have fun. But I was so emotionally involved, I didn't enjoy playing basketball."

Gilliam told the *Daily News* he was surprised by Barkley's approach. "Whatever our differences, Charles is a great talent and doesn't need to play angry," he said.

He was much more expansive on the subject of Barkley in an interview that appeared in the *New York Times* on December 3, 1993, the day the Suns faced the New Jersey Nets, with whom Gilliam had signed four months earlier after being waived by the Sixers. "No, I won't be in the Charles Barkley fan club," Gilliam told the *Times*. "He had a problem with me because he couldn't control me or dominate me or tell me what to do. For him, it was a personal thing. My position is I forgive him for his ignorance and I have nothing that I'm holding against him."

Gilliam went on to say that Barkley was frequently critical of teammates but "took offense" when Gilliam fired back in the media. "It was like, how dare I stand up to Charles Barkley," Gilliam said. "He's just kept a grudge ever since. But that was just after my first year there, a half season. After that he didn't say much because I was having a good year, but if I had a bad game, he would let something drop to the press, and then say he didn't say it."

Gilliam concluded by saying what he had said two years earlier to Jasner—that Barkley wasn't a leader on par with some of the league's great players.

For the record, Barkley had 34 points, 16 rebounds, and eight assists in that game, a 104–103 Phoenix victory, while Gilliam had 27 points and eight boards off the New Jersey bench.

Gilliam averaged 13.7 points and 6.9 rebounds while playing for six teams over his 13 seasons, ending in 2000—impressive, considering he did not take up basketball until his junior year at Bethel Park High School, having wrestled until then. He spent a year at a junior college, then scored 1,855 points at UNLV and became the No. 2 pick in the 1987 draft.

Gilliam, who changed the spelling of his first name from Armon to Armen to reflect the correct pronunciation, was just 47 when he died. "Everybody loved him," Tarkanian wrote in the *Sun.* "I don't know anyone who didn't care for him or think highly of him."

There was just one person, apparently.

54 Breaking Down the 76ers Greats

Sonny Hill, 78, and Harvey Pollack, 92, known as "Mr. Basketball" and "Super Stat," respectively, have seen every great basketball player who played for the Philadelphia franchises, the Warriors and 76ers.

Both men are in the Philadelphia Sports Hall of Fame. Pollack is also a member of the Naismith Memorial Basketball Hall of Fame.

Both still have roles with the Sixers. Hill servers as executive advisor and Pollack is director of statistical information.

Here they break down Philadelphia's pro basketball icons, all of whom are in the Basketball Hall of Fame.

Adolph "Dolph" Schayes

"Dolph was one of the early outstanding big men with mobility," Hill said. "He could shoot the ball from the outside. Could put the ball on the floor. One season he broke his right arm and he played left-handed."

"He was the first coach of the Sixers," said Pollack, who has worked in the NBA since 1946. "He still comes down [to games in Philadelphia]. He's still close with the team. It's a joke that his son [Danny] played more years in the league, 18 years, and [was] never a regular [starter]. When Dolph played, most of his shots are three-point field goals today. You imagine how many times he would be in the record books."

Wilt Chamberlain

"Wilt could do everything in basketball," said Hill, who grew up playing with and watching Chamberlain. "He is the only player in the history of basketball to do the following things: [he] led the league in scoring; led the league in rebounds; he has the most minutes average per game of any player in the history of the game, 46 minutes a game; he led the league in assists, which is almost impossible, because no center has done that; and if they had kept blocked shots in the day he was playing he would have led the league in blocked shots."

"Wilt's been retired for more than 40 years. Right now he still owns 96 records in the record book," said Pollack, who produces *Harvey Pollack's NBA Statistical Yearbook*.

Hal Greer

"Hal Greer was a center at Marshall College, which is now Marshall University, and he was able to be converted to a guard in the NBA," Hill said. "He was noted for being one of the few players, if not the only player that you can identify with shooting a jumper from the foul line as his foul shot."

"He was a shooter, a backcourt man," Pollack said. "In 1972 the 76ers had a coach named Roy Rubin. He was coach at Long Island [University] and had a great record there. During training camp, when he spoke to the team for the first time, he said, 'I don't care who you are, how long you've been in the league. There's no starters on this team. Everybody is on the same footing. Here you got a guy, Greer, a 15-year veteran of the league still starting, but from that time on Greer wouldn't play. He was getting paid, he dressed for every game, but didn't start any game. And when Rubin tried to put him in, he wouldn't go in.

"He felt disrespected. That was the season when the team went 9–73, the worst record in the history of the league. When he finally retired that year—and he played with Syracuse before Philadelphia—he thought they'd hire him as a coach. When they didn't, he's held that against them ever since. He's never come to any functions."

Billy Cunningham

Billy was a hard worker," Hill said. "One of the early jumping guys, that's why his nickname was 'Kangaroo Kid.' When [team officials] first brought Billy in, they tried him at guard, but that's not where he should have been playing and they switched him to the forward position and he went on to be one of the great players of all time."

"My biggest memory of Billy Cunningham is after he hurt his leg [during the 1975–76 season]. I took him to the hospital. I drove him to Temple Hospital. Whatever he did to his leg [a knee injury], his career ended. He always used to remind me of the fact that I was his driver. He was a great player, a great rebounder, an inspirational type of player," Pollack said.

Tom Gola

"[Tom] is one of the greatest all-around college basketball players to ever play," said Hill about Gola, who died on January 26, 2014.

"His first year he played for the Philadelphia Warriors they won the championship.

"Gola was one of those early multidimensional players, just a little under 6'6", a guard who could play a little forward. A very excellent passer. Outstanding defensive player. Just a great all-around basketball player."

"I worked the games [doing stats] when he was in college," Pollack said. "My biggest memory with Gola was after his first year, as a rookie, we won the title, 1955–56, but he went into the service.

"But before he went into the service, there was a rule that if you were 6'6" they [the military] wouldn't take you—too big. But he was always listed as 6'6" in college and pros in the program. But [team owner] Eddie Gottlieb found out that he was 6'5¾".

"Gottlieb had me pick Gola up at his house and take him to army headquarters in Philadelphia. He lay backward in my car, his feet never touching the ground [trying to make himself smaller]. He stayed curled. We drove to the headquarters and I went in and said, 'Are you ready for Gola yet? He's saying good-bye to his wife.' His wife was back home. They said they weren't ready yet. I went out and told him to stay where he was, same position.

"Twice I went in and they weren't ready. Then they made him sit on a wooden bench for more than an hour. Finally, they measure him, 6'5¾", so he was eligible. I was the last one to see him before he left. And the famous quote is when I came back to the Warriors' office and told Eddie Gottlieb what had happened. He said, "Damn you. I give you one little job to do and you screw it up.""

Moses Malone

"Moses was the James Brown of basketball," Hill said. "You know James Brown, the Godfather of Soul, hardest working man in the business. Moses just took a tenacity and just turned it into something that made him an exceptional basketball player. Hard work, determination, and a fact that he would not be denied. That was his game. Nothing fancy about what Moses did. He just came and brought his lunch pail and you knew you were in for a long night."

Pollack said he was with a group of players in 1982 at a big shoe store in Atlanta, where he bought a pair of orchid-colored shoes.

"Somewhere along the line I wore the shoes to a playoff game and we won the game," Pollack said. "I said, 'Wait a minute, maybe they are lucky shoes.' So from then on, whenever we had a crucial game, playoff game, I wore those shoes—11–0 was my record. Never lost. In 1984, playoffs. We were the defending champions. We were [second] in the division [third seed for play-offs] and we played New Jersey [the sixth seed]. It was a five-game series then. There was no way we could lose to them.

"Two games apiece. Fifth game was in Philadelphia. I wasn't sure if I should wear those shoes. I don't know how many wins are left in them. So I didn't wear them, but took them with me and left them in the back of my car. Before the games I always went into the locker room to talk to the guys.

"And Moses sees me and he says, 'Hey Harv, where are the shoes? [Pollock making his voice deeper trying to imitate Malone's speech.] I said, 'Moses, you don't need my shoes for this game. We are [the higher seed]. We are playing on our home court. We wiped them out in every game we played this season. I don't think I should wear them.'

"And Moses said to me, 'Hey, Harv, [again Pollack makes his voice deep] you don't wear those shoes and we lose this game and we are going to blame you.' Well, we lost to Jersey in the first round of the playoffs."

Charles Barkley

"I think when you look at Charles Barkley you would put him in the category of maybe three players of his size," Hill said. "The first one is Elgin Baylor at 6'5" and the other is Adrian Dantley at 6'4", and now you look at Charles Barkley at somewhere around 6'5". If you look at all of them, the thing they had was tremendous strength, great hands, and an ability to not be denied. Height was a disadvantage, but they made up for it with a big body, and they made their body make up for their lack of height.

"In the case of Barkley, he had some guard skills, similar to Adrian Dantley and Elgin Baylor. He also had the strength of a forward. [There are] only three players in the history of the game that have had that combination."

"One of the incidents I had with him was when I used to go with the players when they made appearances," Pollack said. "We were practicing at Saint Joe's College and we were going to Children's Hospital in northeast Philly.

"I drove and he didn't like the way I drove. He said, 'Did you ever take a test?'

"'Yeah, I took a test. How do you think I got my license?' I told him. When we left, he said, 'I'll drive back,' and he drove my car."

Julius Erving

"He took the baton and took it to another level," Hill said. "Elgin Baylor is the first player that you think of who played above the rim, [had] hang time, and had a flair. People don't know about that. Dr. J will talk about that. The second player to do that was Connie Hawkins. After Connie Hawkins was Dr. J. After Dr. J was Michael Jordan. After Michael Jordan [are] the guys you have now.

"[Dr. J] was at a time when the media was beginning to cover the games more. He brought a flair to the game. He enhanced playing above the rim, creativity in the air, tremendous dunks on the fast break and over the top of people. He had the 'it' factor, certain pizzazz that flowed on the court and off the floor.

"He had to make the adjustment from an open league in the ABA to a more structured league in the NBA. People in the NBA never saw Dr. J. They saw flashes of Dr. J, but they never saw Dr. J."

"He and I were real close," Pollack said about Erving. "I went to his house for Christmas dinners. When I traveled with the team, I ate dinner with him and he never let me pay.

"When he retired, before the start of the 1987 season, he called me over one day. He said, 'Hey Harv, I want to tell you something, but I don't want you to tell anybody. Nobody. Not even your wife. I am going to retire this year, but I don't know when. I'll let you know when.

"I didn't tell anyone, but I prepared myself. I wrote a story all about him announcing his retirement. Then I went over his whole career, ABA, NBA. Then I made 50 copies of it. I carried it in a bag. I did it in the summer. I didn't know if he was going to do it in training camp, in the regular season, playoffs, or what he was going to do.

"It gets to be opening night of the 1987 season and the game begins. He's playing. Timeout comes. Ball boy comes down to me and said, 'Doc says, "Tell Harvey, now is the time."' Those were the words.

"I had my briefcase sitting right there with me. At the next timeout I walked down the press table handing out my sheets. Guess what? Everyone in the organization was mad at me because I didn't tell them."

55 Jack McMahon

Jack McMahon was an assistant coach and superscout in the late 1970s and early '80s—and something more.

Like a father figure, said Billy Cunningham, the coach at the time.

Even a grandfather, suggested John Kilbourne, the strength and conditioning coach.

But surely "a presence," as Jack's widow, Kay, once said. A guy who not only found players but nurtured them. A guy who not only assisted the coach but propped him up. He was, in the words of former *Inquirer* beat writer George Shirk, "a good talent evaluator and a good human evaluator."

McMahon had been around the league forever, it seemed—first as a pass-first, shoot-seldom guard for the old Rochester Royals and St. Louis Hawks, then as a head coach for four teams—most notably the Cincinnati Royals, where the great Oscar Robertson was one of his players—and finally as a scout.

The Sixers hired him late in the 1972–73 season—the year they went 9–73—meaning he would have a hand in deciding which player the team would draft No. 1 overall. He liked Doug Collins, a skinny guard from Illinois State University.

So too did the Chicago Bulls. The Bulls' general manager was Pat Williams, who was between front-office stints with the Sixers, and he called to offer center Clifford Ray and backup guard Bob Weiss for the pick. Jack politely declined, and the Sixers took Collins.

In the years that followed, McMahon would visit more places than Rand McNally. He always wanted to scout players in person, because video could only tell you so much. To see a player in the flesh was to see how he interacted with his teammates, how he responded to coaching, how he dealt with adversity.

He would recommend that the Sixers draft Darryl Dawkins and Lloyd (later World B.) Free. That they take Maurice Cheeks and Andrew Toney. And when they held the fifth overall pick in 1984—the one they acquired from the Clippers for Free—he recommended they take a roly-poly forward from Auburn he described as "a ballhandling Wes Unseld." A guy by the name of Charles Barkley.

McMahon missed on occasion, but he was right far more often than he was wrong. And he always seemed to display the right touch with the players, as well as with his fellow coaches. He mentored Cunningham, who was hired to coach the team early in the 1977–78 season, and it was something Cunningham always appreciated.

McMahon was the one who could calm Cunningham down, the one who kept him out of trouble. After a loss in Atlanta one night, a guy came up to Billy and started making racially charged comments about some of the players. But before Billy could go after the guy—and he was fully prepared to do so—Jack jumped in.

"You can't get in a fight," he told Billy. "I can get in a fight."

So Billy ended up dragging Jack out of the place.

The players called him "Uncle Jack" or, when his cheeks flushed after an adult beverage or two, "Jack O'Lantern."

"Every guy on the team loved him because they were comfortable and confident with him," Billy said. "They'd tell Jack things they'd never share with me. But Jack wasn't a pushover with the players. He'd tell them the truth, even if it was painful, and would never sugarcoat his answers."

In fact, Billy said, "Jack had the ability to tell you to your face you were a real so-and-so, and you'd smile and say, 'Thank you.'"

It reached a point where Billy wouldn't have to talk to a player when a problem arose. Jack would take it upon himself to pull the guy aside and smooth the waters.

"They understood," Billy said, "and responded."

McMahon's body was found in a Chicago hotel room, early on the morning of June 11, 1989. He was lying in bed, a paperback novel opened across his chest. The phone was off the hook.

He died in his sleep, and in his element. Then working as the Golden State Warriors' player personnel director—a position he had assumed after leaving the Sixers in June 1986—he was in town for a predraft camp when a heart attack took him at the age of 60.

He left behind a wife and three children. And virtually no enemies.

"I don't know of anybody," Cunningham said, "that was loved by everybody the way Jack McMahon was loved by everybody."

Phil Jasner

The scene was the parking lot of a Sheetz convenience store near Kutztown, Pennsylvania, in August 2003. I had made a quick stop at the place on the drive home after accepting a new job. Just then my cell phone rang: Phil Jasner, offering congratulations.

Mind you, I had told no one of this turn of events at this point—not even my wife. And there was Jasner, revered Sixers beat writer for the *Philadelphia Daily News* (and a man I knew from my own coverage of the team), passing along his best wishes. Dumbfounded, I asked him how he could possibly know about this.

"What, you don't think I have sources?" he asked, sounding happier than I felt. It was an unforgettable gesture by an unforgettable man.

Of course Phil Jasner knew. Of course he knew, because he always knew. He knew everything there was to know about the team he covered, the people who covered it, and—more important than all that—how to be a good friend. He was also a devoted husband to his wife, Susan, even as she spent some 35 years in the throes of the dreaded disease lupus, which took her life in 2006. And he was a great father to his son, Andy, who followed him into sportswriting.

Phil died of cancer in December 2010, at the age of 68. Some 750 mourners turned out for his memorial service, at a funeral home in North Philadelphia. There were so many that the line snaked out the chapel door and down a hallway. So many that the director of the place fretted about fire-code violations.

In attendance were his coworkers from the *Daily News*, where he had spent 38 years, 29 as the Sixers' beat guy (1981–2010). Also on hand were several team officials, college coaches, and friends. And while no current Sixers were present, Sacramento Kings center Samuel Dalembert, who played for Philadelphia from 2001 to 2010, flew cross-country to be there.

Former Sixers star Allen Iverson, playing in Turkey at the time, also tweeted his sympathies ("The world has truly lost a great man who will be sorely missed"). Doug Collins, the coach of the team at the time and a former player, was among those who eulogized Jasner. And former Sixers coach Larry Brown remembered him warmly while passing through town with the Charlotte Bobcats, calling Jasner "a real reporter" who cut to the heart of the matter, as opposed to getting caught up in peripheral issues.

His work ethic was second to none. He always had to make one more phone call, always had to ask one more question. Pat Croce, the Sixers' president from 1996 to 2001, said Jasner was not unlike a police detective in an old TV show by the name of Columbo, in that he would hang around after a practice or press conference broke up and pull a subject aside to ask him something that the rest of the reporters had failed to ask.

To former Sixers coach Jim Lynam, Jasner's tireless search for the truth set him apart "in an ever-changing world...headed in the wrong direction." The way Lynam saw it, reporters were increasingly apt to "throw anything out there just to try to get somebody, and hopefully a whole lot of somebodies, to read. Whether it's accurate, inaccurate, 60 percent, that's beside the point. It was the polar opposite to what Jasner was about."

The constantly changing cast of Sixers officials respected not only how he went about his job, but how much he knew about theirs. As a result, he became something of a confidant to many. Croce, for one, "ran a lot of things by Phil Jasner," especially early in his front-office tenure, aware of how much he could learn from a man who had seen so many fill the same position through the years.

Jasner saw the Sixers at their best—they won a title in '83 and reached the Finals in 2001, Croce's last year with the team—and at their worst (they went 18–64 in 1995–96). He covered greats including Iverson, Charles Barkley, Moses Malone, and Julius Erving, as well as players who were somewhat less competent. But his approach never wavered.

He soldiered on, even as his wife was withering away from lupus, the name given an array of autoimmune diseases that sees the immune system attack healthy tissue. She was diagnosed in 1970, some nine months after Andy, the couple's only child, was born. Phil seldom breathed a word to anyone, but Andy said those years were not easy for anyone.

"She had 42 surgical procedures through the years," he said. "She was so physically ill, and mentally ill in some ways.... The last five years of her life, Mom was so sick. She was in and out of nursing homes. We thought we lost her a half dozen times."

So grim was Susan's condition that Andy wondered if she would survive to see his wedding day in 2004. As it was, she was confined to a wheelchair; Phil pushed her down the aisle. "That couldn't have been easy," Andy said.

He believes his dad came to view his job as "an emotional outlet," something that "helped him keep his sanity." He had included Andy from the time he was very young, bringing him along to practices and games. Andy grew accustomed to doing his homework while waiting for his dad to wrap up his night's work. "Wherever he went, I went," Andy said. "I didn't have a choice to be anything but a sportswriter."

Andy went to Syracuse, then took jobs in North Carolina and Florida. His path continued to cross with his dad's. They covered three NBA Finals and 10 All-Star Games together. But in 2003 the younger Jasner returned to Philadelphia and took up as a freelancer.

"Continuing the name and legacy," Andy said, "keeps me going."

It is a sizable one, and one that extends well beyond the press box. Even to convenience store parking lots.

57 The Spectrum

By the time they began knocking down the Spectrum late in 2010, the arena was a small and insignificant part of the South Philadelphia landscape, dwarfed by Citizens Bank Park and Lincoln Financial Field a block to the east and by the Wells Fargo Center across the parking lot.

That belied its significance in the city's sporting history. Wilt Chamberlain, Julius Erving, and Moses Malone had played there, as had both of the Flyers' Stanley Cup winners. Joe Frazier had fought there. Most of the town's high-profile college basketball coaches, including John Chaney, Rollie Massimino, and Speedy Morris, had plied their trade there, at least on occasion.

The arena had hosted six Stanley Cup Finals, four NBA Finals, and two NCAA Final Fours in all, as well as the greatest college hoops game ever, Duke's 104–103 overtime victory over Kentucky in the 1992 East Regional Final. It had been no less significant in the nonsporting realm; Elvis and Michael Jackson and the Rolling Stones had all performed there. So too had the Grateful Dead—53 times in all, more than any other band. And a young singer from New Jersey was booed off the stage when he opened for the group Chicago in the Spectrum, in 1973. That singer—a guy named Bruce Springsteen—tended to be greeted much more warmly in subsequent appearances.

The building, which came to be dubbed "America's Showplace," opened in 1967 and served as the home to the Sixers and Flyers through the 1995–96 season, at which point both teams moved to the Wells Fargo Center (then known as the CoreStates Center). When it was constructed, it was viewed as a state-of-the-art arena, a marked departure from the dank, dingy places used by its teams in the past.

Spectrum vice president Lou Scheinfeld was the one who came up with a name for the place after brainstorming with the building's designer, Bill Belker, during construction. As Scheinfeld told the *Inquirer*, "We didn't want it named for some dead general." Arena president Hal Freeman was in favor of "Keystone," but Scheinfeld stacked the deck when the alternatives were presented to developer Jerry Wolman and his cohorts: "Keystone," Scheinfeld pointed out, was a name used in the name of no fewer than 60 businesses in the Philadelphia area alone.

They voted on it, and "Spectrum" it was. The first event in the place was the Quaker City Jazz Festival. The first Sixers game was a 103–87 victory over the Lakers on October 18, 1967. And if through the years there were times when fans seemed about to blow the roof off the place, it can also be said that the roof was literally blown off the place—twice. It first happened on February 17, 1968, during an Ice Capades show, then again on March 1 of that year. At that point Mayor James H.J. Tate ordered the place closed for repairs. The Sixers played the remainder of their games that season at the Palestra and Convention Hall.

There were moments in the place that became frozen in time: a brawl between Darryl Dawkins and Portland enforcer Maurice Lucas in the '77 NBA Finals...Magic Johnson's 42-point tour de force while filling in for an injured Kareem Abdul-Jabbar at center in the decisive Game 6 of the 1980 Finals...Erving's acrobatics, whether the impossible baseline floater in that same series against the Lakers or his soaring dunk over Los Angeles' Michael Cooper in the '83 regular season.

And there were other, less glamorous moments, like the time only a smattering of fans showed up for Game 7 of an '81 playoff series against Milwaukee, or the time the fans cheered an injury to Boston's Tiny Archibald a year later. Erving, addressing the crowd that gathered outside the Spectrum just before the wrecking ball flew in November 2010, recalled a fracas involving fans dressed as Santa Claus during a game against the Celtics in the early '80s. "I looked up," he said, "and the Santa Clauses were throwing haymakers at the unruly fans, and the fans were returning the favor. We had to stop the game and check that out."

The building died a slow death. It hosted minor league hockey and a stray college basketball game or two in the years after the Sixers and Flyers fled, until plans were drawn up to build an entertainment complex on the site where the arena stood. The Sixers played there one last time, beating the Bulls 104–101 on March 13, 2009. There were farewell concerts, by Springsteen and finally Pearl Jam. And the building's impending destruction morphed into a marketing opportunity.

A book detailing the Spectrum's history was published. Various items—seats and hockey glass and even freezable drink coasters containing water from the hockey ice—were put up for sale, with some of the proceeds going to the Comcast-Spectacor Foundation.

(In time, that organization would even sell the building's bricks, for $39.95 apiece—plus shipping and handling.)

On November 6, 2010, fans were allowed, for $25 a head, to comb through the building and take whatever they could carry out in one trip, including seats and posters and signs. And shortly thereafter, on November 23, there was a ceremony to mark the place's demise. Besides Erving, Comcast chairman Ed Snider, Philadelphia mayor Michael Nutter, and retired Flyers star Bobby Clarke addressed the fans who had gathered.

Then the wrecking ball flew. And did nothing. Not at first. It took a half dozen swipes before the walls finally began to crumble, and several months before the Spectrum was destroyed entirely. But in time the arena was gone, leaving behind only its many memories.

58 Harvey Pollack

As had been the case every day for nearly a decade, Harvey Pollack wore a new T-shirt on March 11, 2013, when the Sixers' director of statistical information was saluted for turning 91 during a game against the Brooklyn Nets. The front of the shirt read: 33,237 Days Old, but who's counting?

Just Harvey. Then again, he counted everything. Always had, from the time the NBA set up shop in 1947. Nicknamed "Super Stat," Pollack (who actually celebrated his 91st birthday two days before that game against the Nets) revolutionized the way pro basketball was quantified. He kept track of things like minutes, blocked shots, steals, and dunks long before the league did. He introduced things like the triple-double and the plus-minus rating, not to mention the media guide.

"Super Stat" Harvey Pollack does his thing at Philly's February 20, 2008, game against the Knicks.

His first one came out in 1967. It was 24 pages long. The 2012 edition was 354 pages in length, and as usual was a treasure trove of information—some of it pertinent, some of it arcane. If he once listed the nicknames of Darryl Dawkins' dunks (e.g., "Sexophonic Turbo Delight"), he now noted that Allen Iverson had no fewer than 23 tattoos. Need to know the league leaders in technical fouls? That was in there. How 'bout a player's little-known first name? That was, too.

Other teams were soon required to put out media guides as well, but his—which came to be known, simply, as "the Book"—was always the most exhaustive, the most unique. He told Jon Marks of Sheridan Hoops that even people from far-flung places like Croatia would request a copy. He was always happy to oblige. (Same for other teams' stats crews, who sometimes called him in the wee hours to double-check their totals.)

Pollack was a Philly guy, who lived in the same house in the Northeast section of town for 56 years. He wasn't the Sixers' full-time publicist until 1980—he actually worked for the city before that—but he liked to say that for years he did a part-time job full-time. And he was nothing if not diligent about his work.

"I had bypass surgery in 2002," he told Marks. "I think I missed three games."

His work did not go unnoticed, as he was named to no fewer than 13 Halls of Fame, including the one in Springfield, Massachusetts. There were also times he found himself in the middle of the fray, as was the case when he charted the rebounds collected by Wilt Chamberlain and Bill Russell during a typically furious Sixers-Celtics game one night in Boston Garden. By game's end Pollack had Wilt with 35 boards, Russell with 23, and he approached the Celtics' stat crew to compare notes.

They had it the other way around, which led to an argument that was overheard by a *Sports Illustrated* reporter. The story of Boston's alleged stat-padding made the next issue of *SI*, and raised the hackles of Red Auerbach, the late Celtics coach and president. "Any time we played the Celtics after that," Pollack recalled in 2006, "he wouldn't even go near me."

That changed several years later, when Boston's Dave Cowens was battling Washington's Wes Unseld for the rebounding title. On the season's final day, the Celtics played earlier than the Bullets. Cowens had a decent day on the boards, but Unseld, playing at home, was credited with a season-high 30 rebounds, allowing him to edge out his Boston counterpart. Pollack questioned the Bullets' stat-keeping in interviews, and Auerbach took note.

"So the next time I saw him after that article, he walked up to me and shook my hand, and handed me a cigar," Pollack said. "And for the rest of the time that he was the coach, he always gave me cigars, every year. Win or lose, he would give me a cigar."

Years earlier he was in Hershey, Pennsylvania, when Wilt exploded for 100 points in a game against the New York Knicks. Pollack was required to file stories for several publications, since few had seen fit to send reporters out to the wilds of central Pennsylvania. And when a wire-service photographer came looking for a shot of Wilt in the locker room after the game, it was Harvey who scrawled 100 on a sheet of paper and handed it to Wilt. Wilt held it up for the guy, and the result was an iconic photo.

Nobody thought to save the sign afterward, though—not even Pollack. It was, he told Marks in 2013, his "biggest regret."

Pollack overlapped the Wilt Era and the Julius Erving Era (not to mention the Charles Barkley and Allen Iverson Eras). Along the way he also served as the publicity director for the Philadelphia Department of Recreation. He kept the stats at various college games and wrote columns about the Eagles, Phillies (under the pseudonym "Curly Diamond"), and boxing (as "K.O. Battle") for a weekly newspaper called *The Guide*. He also reviewed movies and shows for various suburban publications.

Lousy Trades

Wilt Is Sent Packing

By 1968, it had long been clear that Wilt Chamberlain could do almost anything he wanted. He had led the NBA in scoring his first seven seasons; in rebounding his first four, and eight of his first 10. He even led it in assists in 1967–68.

He had scored 100 points in a game, and he had averaged 50 in a season—both while with the Philadelphia Warriors, early in his career. He moved with the team to San Francisco in 1962, returning to Philadelphia when the Sixers acquired him in exchange for Paul Neumann, Lee Shaffer, and Connie Dierking at the '65 All-Star break.

In his second season back in town Chamberlain finally beat his longtime nemesis, Bill Russell, when the Sixers took out Boston in the playoffs, en route to the 1966–67 title. But the following year the Celtics erased a three-games-to-one deficit to beat the Sixers, and all the familiar frustrations reemerged: he was too selfish, too uncoachable, etc.

Alex Hannum, the coach who had led the team to the title, departed at that point to take the job with the Oakland Oaks of the ABA, and the idea of Wilt becoming a player-coach (as Russell was in Boston) was broached. Author Robert Cherry writes in his 2004 book *Wilt: Larger Than Life* that Hannum was the first to mention the idea, during his farewell news conference.

But Jack Ramsay, then the Sixers' GM, writes in the 2004 book *Dr. Jack's Leadership Lessons Learned from a Lifetime in Basketball* that it was Wilt himself who had first suggested becoming coach— so long as Ramsay agreed to serve as his assistant, to help him with strategy.

Ramsay wrote that while he and owner Irv Kosloff were surprised by the idea, Ramsay was in favor of it. The brain trust had already interviewed Frank McGuire, John Kundla, and Earl Lloyd, but none of them wanted the job. Who better to coach Wilt than Wilt?

As Ramsay writes, Chamberlain "would play with added intensity knowing his name was on the line." While nothing had been decided in that first meeting, Ramsay promised Chamberlain they would revisit the matter when Chamberlain returned from visiting his parents in Los Angeles.

But at that point he said he had changed his mind: If the Sixers did not trade him to a team on the West Coast, he would sign with the ABA's Los Angeles Stars. And he had leverage, too, since he was at the end of a contract. He had the same sort of advantage he usually had on the court: he could do whatever he wanted.

Ramsay wrote that he was stunned, that he had entered the meeting "brimming with enthusiasm," and now found himself not only without a coach, but faced with the prospect of losing "the most powerful player in the game." Cherry fills in the blanks, writing that Wilt wanted a three-year contract worth $250,000 a year, and a piece of the team. (Chamberlain had made the latter demand of Kosloff before, claiming that the late Ike Richman, the team's previous owner, had promised Wilt a 25 percent share of the franchise when he retired.)

But Cherry, like others, wonders if Chamberlain had any intention of remaining with the Sixers. The belief is that Chamberlain was well aware Kosloff would not allow him to become a part-owner, and that he had many reasons for wanting to be in Los Angeles. His parents were there, and his father, William, was very ill. The California weather was great, Cherry wrote, and it was one of two towns (New York being the other) where he could have some degree of privacy, as he would be a star among stars there. (Nor did it hurt, Cherry added, that a black man could date white women there without a second thought.)

Whatever the reasons, on July 9, Wilt was traded to the Los Angeles Lakers for guard Archie Clark, forward Jerry Chambers, and center Darrall Imhoff.

Chambers never played for the Sixers, who traded him to Phoenix in 1969. Clark averaged 18.2 points over three-plus seasons in Philadelphia. Imhoff, who years earlier had been the Knicks' starting center when Wilt had his 100-point game in

Hershey, Pennsylvania, averaged 11.3 points and 9.6 rebounds in two seasons with the Sixers.

With the Lakers Chamberlain continued to put up numbers, continued to be his dominating self—save the 1969–70 season, when he was limited to 12 games because of a torn Achilles tendon. And in the last two seasons of his career he reinvented himself as a defender and rebounder, at the urging of coach Bill Sharman. The result was that the 1971–72 Lakers won 69 games, including 33 in a row. The season total, a record, was one more than the 1966–67 Sixers had won, and would not be exceeded until the 1995–96 Chicago Bulls went 72–10.

After the Knicks won the first game of the Finals that year, Sharman unleashed the Wilt of old against an undersized New York team. Chamberlain averaged just fewer than 20 points a game in that series, after scoring at a 13.2-points-per-game clip during the regular season, and the Lakers captured the title in five games.

Moses Departs

As incomprehensible as it seems now—as indeed it seemed soon after the fact—there was ample reason for the Sixers to turn their franchise upside down on June 16, 1986.

Moses Malone was in fact in decline.

Brad Daugherty did not seem like a great fit.

So the team's brain trust, to its everlasting regret, pulled the trigger on two disastrous trades the day before the NBA Draft, sending Malone to Washington for Jeff Ruland and Cliff Robinson and the top overall pick to Cleveland for forward Roy Hinson.

Ruland, slowed by a knee injury, played five games for the Sixers in 1986–87, and 13 in a short-lived comeback with the team in 1991–92. Robinson and Hinson, beset by knee injuries of their own, each departed Philadelphia within three years.

Malone, while not the player he had been during the Sixers' run to the 1982–83 championship, played until 1994. He even returned to Philadelphia for a one-year curtain call toward the end of his career. Daugherty, meanwhile, was an effective player for the Cavaliers for eight years, before his career was cut short by back problems.

But as terrible a day as June 16, 1986, proved to be, the Sixers' moves were not indefensible.

Start with the fact that there was no clear-cut No. 1 pick. "There was no Shaq, no David Robinson, no Tim Duncan," former Sixers general manager Pat Williams said in a 2011 interview.

The consensus top pick was Daugherty, a center from North Carolina. The Sixers worked him out at the home of team owner Harold Katz. And while they liked him, they weren't excited about him. They wondered, for starters, how his game would mesh with those of Malone and Charles Barkley. (And Jack McMahon, the team's late superscout, had nagging concerns about Maryland forward Len Bias. It wasn't drugs—Bias, taken second overall by Boston, died of cocaine intoxication two nights after the draft—for the team's background check in the weeks leading up to the selection process raised no red flags. But McMahon's doubts were such that the Sixers never even worked Bias out.)

In the meantime, Moses was slipping. His scoring average in 1985–86 (23.8) was virtually the same as it had been during the championship season (24.5), but his shooting percentage had fallen from 50.1 to 45.8, and his rebounding norm from 15.3 to 11.8. He had failed to lead the league in rebounding for the first time in six years (and indeed would never do so again).

There were other complicating factors. Malone got into a shouting match with coach Matt Guokas when Guokas yanked him from a game against Golden State. That came months after Malone's agent inquired about a contract extension, something Katz was loath to do. Relations between Katz and Malone had been strained since March 1984, when Katz asked an *Inquirer* reporter, "Is Moses Malone worth $2 million this year? No. The answer is absolutely no."

Then, late in the 1985–86 season, Malone suffered an eye injury that knocked him out for the year. The Sixers, playing a fast-paced style and featuring Barkley, won six of their last seven regular-season games, beat Washington in the first round of the playoffs, and extended Milwaukee to seven games in the second round.

Malone was not around for any of that, choosing instead to repair to his adopted hometown of Houston. Spotted in the stands during a Rockets playoff game, he agreed to an interview with Brent Musburger of CBS Sports.

"If he thinks the team is playing better without me," Moses said of Katz, "hey, it's up to him. But I know one thing…when I come to play, I'm coming to play."

Later, he added, "I would like to know before the draft. If Harold wants to trade me, I want to know [by] then, so I can get everything situated…. [But] please don't trade me to the east. I'd like to come back to Texas—Dallas or San Antonio. Don't trade me to the East Coast, 'cause Moses is going to be ready."

There had been no discussion of trading Moses before that. But now the calls came. From Detroit, which offered Bill Laimbeer, Kelly Tripucka, Vinnie Johnson, and their first-round pick, 11th overall. And from Washington, with the offer that the Sixers ultimately accepted.

In the meantime the Cavaliers called, dangling Hinson for the No. 1.

The Sixers' contingent—Katz, Williams, Nash, Guokas, McMahon, and assistant coach Jim Lynam—gathered. And the decision was ultimately made to go with the Washington-Cleveland plan.

Harold, in a first-person story that appeared in the July 1996 edition of *The Fan*, a now-defunct magazine, wrote the following: "I can assure you that those [draft day] moves were not my idea. We had a meeting and at least six of our basketball people were in favor of it, including Jack McMahon, [whom] we had relied on for so long and who had been a brilliant personnel man."

Guokas holds a slightly different view. "It's going to be Harold's decision," he recalled in March 2007. "There could have been 15 guys in that room. A decision of that magnitude was going to be Harold Katz's."

Whatever the case, it all blew up in their faces. "Add up all those years [among the assembled executives], and you've probably got 100 years of basketball experience," Williams said in 2011. "There was a sense that night of, 'Let's make deals.' Twenty-five years later, we would have been better off with no deals, and drafting Daugherty. I don't know how that would have worked. At some point we would have had to trade Moses."

Instead, they pulled the trigger on June 16, 1986—with disastrous results. But given what they knew then, their decision was not indefensible.

Barkley to Phoenix

Charles Barkley learned he had been traded from the 76ers to the Phoenix Suns on June 17, 1992, shortly before he boarded a plane in Milwaukee. He had just been acquitted on a battery charge as a result of an altercation outside a bar in that city six months earlier.

It seemed to sum up his career rather nicely. He was unquestionably one of the greatest Sixers ever, and one of the greatest players of his generation; his selection to the United States team that would compete in the 1992 Olympics in Barcelona—the fabled Dream Team—was testimony to that. But there was a constant litany of off-court troubles, and while that did not forever tarnish his reputation (a fact owing to his considerable charm and good humor), it did smudge it some.

His final season was particularly cacophonous and led to his exit. If he wasn't getting in a fight in Milwaukee, he was claiming he had been misquoted in his autobiography. If he wasn't ripping teammates, he was lashing out at the media. If he wasn't questioning the racial makeup of the roster, he was telling reporters he was a "'90s nigger."

Whether he did all this in hopes of getting traded—as the Sixers were a poor team, headed toward a 35–47 finish—was open to question at the time. He claimed in a March 1992 interview with Rick Reilly, then of *Sports Illustrated*, that he wanted to remain with the team. ("I don't want to pick up my bat and ball and go home just 'cause we're not winning," he said. "I don't want to bail out on the rest of the guys.") But it seemed then, as it does now, that his actions were a pretty obvious attempt to get out of town.

Sixers officials hinted at that when the deal with Phoenix was made, bringing guard Jeff Hornacek, forward Tim Perry, and center Andrew Lang in return. "We had to come to some conclusions," new coach Doug Moe said, "and the conclusion we came to was that Charles was unhappy."

But they also said Barkley was not the player he had once been, that he would not fit in with the motion offense Moe was installing, and that dealing him was the best way to upgrade the roster. "We won 35 games with this superstar," owner Harold Katz told reporters when the trade was complete. "Nobody can tell me we won't win more than 35 games next year. There's no doubt in my mind we'll win more."

That turned out to be wildly optimistic; ditto for the prediction by Dick Weiss, veteran *Daily News* sportswriter, that the Sixers were destined for "42 or 43 wins and a short-lived appearance in the playoffs." In reality they slipped to 26–56 in 1992–93, beginning a string of four straight seasons in which they won fewer games than the year before. (They bottomed out at 18–64 in 1995–96, earning themselves the right to choose Allen Iverson first overall in the NBA Draft.)

Barkley, meanwhile, was named MVP while leading the Suns to the '93 Finals, where they lost to Michael Jordan's Bulls.

He would never be quite so great again in his last three years in Phoenix, or the four he spent with the Houston Rockets at the end of his career. But his sideshow continued unabated.

It was nothing new by then. Not for a guy who accidentally spit on an eight-year-old girl during a game in the New Jersey Meadowlands in March 1991, having missed the heckler he intended to hit. ("I didn't get enough foam," he later said, by way of explanation.) And not for a guy who said during a radio interview on the eve of the 1991–92 season that he was sure the Sixers wouldn't have an all-black roster, after being asked whether he thought that seldom-used center Dave Hoppen, who was white, would be cut.

Barkley turned out to be right, but his remarks caused a stir, with the fans and within the front office. While Katz told *Daily News* sportswriter Phil Jasner he wasn't that "offendable," he did say Barkley didn't speak for the team or owner. "I speak for myself," Katz told Jasner. "He runs off at the mouth."

"People say I make outrageous statements, but nobody ever says if [they're] true or not," Barkley countered. "I don't think I said anything outrageous. If you bring up any controversial subject, it's a problem. When is [the right] time to discuss them?"

Early in the season, Barkley again rubbed the paying customers the wrong way when he asked to wear No. 32 instead of his customary No. 34 in honor of his friend Magic Johnson, who had just announced he had been diagnosed with HIV, the virus that causes AIDS. There was only one problem: the Sixers had retired No. 32 to honor Billy Cunningham. Cunningham gave his blessing, but it nonetheless rubbed some fans the wrong way. "I can't believe something so good turned so bad," Barkley said.

Next came the flap over his autobiography *Outrageous*, which saw Barkley claim his coauthor, Roy S. Johnson of *Sports Illustrated*, had misquoted or misinterpreted several remarks on Barkley's part—notably the ones where he criticized Katz or teammates

Charles Shackleford and Manute Bol. Barkley, who admitted he hadn't read the book before it was published, at first vowed to block its release, only to learn that wasn't possible.

He admitted that "a couple of things" were going to be wrong but added that "the majority" was correct. By sticking with this version of the book, *Inquirer* columnist Bill Lyon wrote, Barkley avoided "litigation history—the first man to sue himself for libel."

Former Sixers general manager Pat Williams, by then part of the Orlando Magic front office, also had a field day with this one. Tongue firmly in cheek, he claimed Barkley told him he would write his autobiography "as soon as he could figure out who the main character should be." The publisher had put out two books—"his first and last." That the sequel would surely be entitled *I Never Met a Problem I Didn't Cause.* One more thing about the book, Williams said: "Once you put it down, you can't pick it up."

The incident in Milwaukee came at 2:30 AM on December 22, 1991. Barkley broke the nose of James McCarthy with a punch outside a nightspot and was charged with misdemeanor battery and disorderly conduct. This came after McCarthy, by his own admission, heckled Barkley, yelling, "Hey, Charles, I hear you're the baddest guy in the NBA!" Barkley, who spent four hours in jail, later told Reilly he also broke a bone in his left hand punching McCarthy.

By the All-Star break in February 1992 there were persistent rumors that Barkley would be traded. One report had him going to the Lakers for forward James Worthy, with the Sixers then sending Worthy to the Charlotte Hornets for guards Kendall Gill and Rex Chapman. Another had him going to the Los Angeles Clippers for forwards Ken Norman and Charles Smith.

It was just about that time that a Philadelphia television station asked Barkley to film a public-service announcement. For the first he placed a towel over his Sixers uniform and said, "This is Charles Barkley of the Los Angeles Clippers saying stay in school. It's your best move." Then he doffed the towel and said, "This is Charles Barkley of the Philadelphia 76ers saying stay in school. It's your best move."

"Okay," he said to the TV people, "now you're covered."

But nothing happened. Not until June.

"This, by far, was the best deal offered," Katz told reporters at the time.

It turned out to be a very bad deal, of course. But by then, Barkley had to go. He had made that clear with his actions.

Oh, and They Thought About Trading Doc, Too

In the years after he helped the 76ers win a long-awaited NBA championship, Julius Erving found himself in a he-loves-me, he-loves-me-not dance with team owner Harold Katz. When Erving explored the possibility of signing a free-agent contract with the Utah Jazz in the summer of 1986—the summer before his final season—Katz grew indignant (mostly with Jazz owner Larry Miller) and moved to re-sign Dr. J.

But two years earlier, Katz had been all too eager to part with Erving, notably in a trade with Chicago on the eve of the 1984 draft. It was not just any garden-variety trade, either. It would have sent Erving to the Bulls for the third overall pick. The pick that became Michael Jordan.

Consider that for a moment. Consider how different NBA history might be had the Bulls pulled the trigger and the Sixers selected Jordan. Chicago almost certainly would not have won six league titles, as the Bulls did with Jordan. And it stands to reason that the Sixers would not have slipped into the doldrums. (It's also possible that Jordan and Charles Barkley would have been on the same team. The Sixers used the fifth overall pick in '84 on Barkley.)

"I thought I had a deal with Jonathan Kovler [then the principal owner] of the Bulls for the third pick," Katz told Pat Williams, once the 76ers' general manager, in an interview for the 2007 book

210

Pat Williams' Tales of the Philadelphia 76ers, cowritten by this author.

Ultimately, Katz said, "Rod Thorn [then the Bulls' general manager] killed that one and took Michael Jordan. I would have made that deal."

Rod Thorn, now the NBA's president of basketball operations, confirmed to Williams that Kovler approached him about such a deal, and that he quickly quashed it.

Katz, who sold the 76ers to Comcast Corp. in March 1996, also said he had "serious talks" with the Los Angeles Clippers about trading Erving for forward Terry Cummings before the 1984 draft. Billy Cunningham, then the 76ers' coach, talked him out of it, Katz said, though the Associated Press reported at the time that Erving also opposed the deal.

Publicly, at least, Julius did not say he was disappointed about the prospects of a trade. He did not have a no-trade clause in his contract, and he told reporters he appreciated the fact that Katz consulted him each step of the way. What Doc found more disappointing was all the leaks on the Clippers' end.

The trade eventually fell through, and Cummings was dealt to Milwaukee three months after the draft.

The selection process itself saw the Houston Rockets use the top overall pick on Akeem (later Hakeem) Olajuwon, who was everybody's consensus No. 1. The Portland Trail Blazers, needing a center, then made the fateful decision to choose Kentucky's oft-injured big man Sam Bowie rather than Jordan—their rationale being that they were already set at shooting guard with Clyde Drexler.

Jordan went next, and merely became the greatest player of all time.

As for Erving, he inevitably declined his last three years, his scoring average dipping to 20.0, then 18.1, then 16.8. He remained a serviceable player but was no longer the dominant presence he had once been.

Still, he told reporters he felt like he was "being toyed with" by the Sixers in negotiations for his final contract, in the summer of 1986. And Miller, sensing an opening, offered him a two-year, $3.8 million contract to come to the Jazz.

The Sixers thought they had reached a verbal agreement with Erving on a one-year, $1.465 million deal at the end of June, a deal that would have been finalized when the salary cap was raised on August 1. Instead, a three-week ordeal began in mid-July. It was one that saw Julius cut short a vacation in Jackson Hole, Wyoming, to visit with the Jazz. One that saw Doc's agent, Irwin Weiner, tell the *Daily News* that Harold Katz had "jerked Julius around for five months." And one that was ultimately resolved when Dr. J agreed to a one-year, $1.75 million contract after playing tennis at Katz's house.

"You are so in awe of this man who came here and tried to take away a player who belongs here," Katz said at the news conference announcing the new deal. "I'm tired of hearing about Larry Miller. I'm not in love with Larry Miller. If I said he was my best friend, I would be the biggest liar in the world. I'm happy everybody thinks he was so sincere [about signing Erving]. I'm happy that I'm sincere and that Julius Erving is here. Larry Miller belongs in Utah and we belong here."

60 Al Domenico

Nothing lasts forever. Former Sixers trainer Al Domenico, who died in November 2012 at age 83, understood that implicitly.

Whenever a player was traded or waived during his 26-year run with the organization (1964–89), he would cut that player's head out of the team pictures that hung in the Spectrum's tiny training room. Then he would take the head and hang it on a wall underneath a piece of athletic tape, upon which he had scrawled, Our Fallen Comrades, Lest We Forget. That was his way of reminding guys just how expendable they were, and just how fleeting their time was.

He never seemed to forget how true that was in a larger sense, either. It is why he made the most of every day, living large and laughing heartily (often at someone else's expense). It is why he never suffered fools and always cut to the chase, telling players and team officials what they needed to hear, as opposed to what they wanted to hear.

"He was truly a Damon Runyon character," former Sixers player and coach Billy Cunningham said.

Domenico was an ex-marine, and a father of eight. He also served as a trainer for roller derby and pro wrestling before NBA teams were required to have their trainers serve full-time—"full-time" being a very loose definition when it came to Domenico.

He hated practice, Cunningham said, because on the whole, he would rather be at Philadelphia Park. He hated rookie tryouts, believing that the organization could find all the players it needed from within the league. And he hated long games, believing that clubs should just play to 100 and be done with it. (His friends took to calling this the "Domenico Rule.")

But he served a very important function in that he realized it was his job not so much to tape ankles—a task he went to great lengths to avoid at times—but to massage egos. That it was his job not so much to administer analgesic balm as to assure that the whole operation worked smoothly.

Former Sixers general manager John Nash said Domenico was a "tremendous buffer" between the players and management. The players confided in him—something more likely to happen in that era, when organizations were far more streamlined and athletes were far less apt to go running to their agents.

Domenico would in turn shoot the players straight—when he wasn't busting their chops. "You have to be a funny guy in this job," he once told *Sports Illustrated.* "If you don't keep everyone up, get their minds off the bad games and the travel, throw things at them when they're getting on the bus at seven in the morning so they can laugh, then you're not worth a damn."

Charles Barkley told the *Inquirer* upon Domenico's retirement that he had never met a funnier man. Cunningham found out about that as a Sixers rookie in 1965, when he accompanied Domenico as he took Wilt Chamberlain's travel bag to a shop in town to be repaired. Cunningham dozed as he waited in the car, only to be awakened with a start when Domenico sneaked up and threw a firecracker inside. "And there I was," Cunningham said with a laugh, "chasing him down the street."

Domenico was also known for setting newspapers on fire as people were reading them. For shoving toothpick shards into the locks of hotel-room doors—back when they still required keys—so that his victims couldn't enter.

One time a seldom-used rookie guard named Coniel Norman showed up for a game against Portland without his uniform. Domenico told him not to worry, that he should just put on his sweats, for there was little chance Norman would get into the game.

Then Domenico informed coach Gene Shue what had happened. "You be ready, Coniel," Shue told Norman right before the game. "You'll be the first man off the bench tonight."

Oh, and about ankle-taping: It wasn't unusual for a rookie or fringe player to hop up on the training table, only to discover that Domenico was writing their name on a list. When the neophyte asked why he was doing that, Domenico would inform him that the coach always kept track of such things, since he didn't like players to have their ankles taped, thought it indicated they were soft.

Just like that, the player in question went on his way. And Domenico could get back to his copy of the *Daily Racing Form.*

"Obviously I wasn't aware of that," Cunningham said, "during that period of time. Ended up that we never knew about it till well after the fact." If a trainer dared to do something like that today, Cunningham said, "the person would be fired on the spot."

Nobody was spared from Domenico's wiles. Knowing that team owner Harold Katz was obsessed about the weight of star center Moses Malone, Domenico would approach Malone and ask, "What do you wanna weigh today?"

At the same time, Nash said, Domenico was vital to management. "Al could really assist us in the way in which we dealt with the players," he said. "He knew the good guys, and he knew the bad guys. He knew the guys who had bad habits, and he was invaluable in that manner as well. He could identify the problem child, and he could also rubber-stamp with approval somebody who was a solid citizen."

He had other roles, not the least of which was bench jockey. He used to call Celtics star Larry Bird "Harelip." One night Bird decided he had heard enough, and came after Domenico as he sat on the bench. Al, Nash remembered with a chuckle, "shriveled up to the size of a raisin." Sixers forward Steve Mix intercepted Bird before things went too far.

But mostly, Domenico took it upon himself to make sure the whole operation ran smoothly.

"He surely wasn't qualified to be a trainer of today," Cunningham said, "but he had an ability to do things with players—to talk to them, to get them mentally prepared for games, to help a coach—that was priceless."

He was a man for his time, knowing that his time was short. So why not live a little? Why not laugh a little?

61 Darryl Dawkins

Darryl Dawkins—once the Sixer who launched a thousand quips, and later decreed the father of the power dunk by no less an authority than Shaquille O'Neal—memorably destroyed a backboard more than three decades ago with a slam he labeled the "Chocolate-Thunder-Flyin', Robinzine-Cryin', Teeth-Shakin', Glass Breakin', Rump-Roastin', Bun-Toastin', Wham-Bam, Glass-Breaker-I-Am Jam."

The footnotes are these: Chocolate Thunder was Dawkins' nickname, Bill Robinzine the luckless opposing forward caught in the shower of glass.

The upshot was this: Dawkins obliterated another backboard three weeks later, which resulted in a talking-to from then–NBA commissioner Larry O'Brien, the introduction of the collapsible rim, and the assurance that Dawkins would forever be a cult hero.

And the update is this: Dawkins, now 57, doesn't dunk much anymore. "I dunk once a year, to make sure I can still do it," he said one day in the fall of 2012. "Once a year."

That's right, Chocolate Thunder no longer does much flyin'. Now he's much more grounded, in every sense. He and his wife, Janice, live in Allentown, Pennsylvania, with Tabitha, Janice's 19-year-old daughter from previous relationship, and the couple's two children, Nicholas, 12, and Alexis, 11.

Darryl, who has improbably done some coaching since ending his 19-year playing career (14 in the NBA, five in Italy), does community-relations work for the Sixers and another of his former teams, the Nets. He said he works with Native American players in the Midwest.

He also said he has become a more spiritual person, and a doting father. "I've grown up *some*," he said. Then he laughed, and talked about what a soft touch he is for his kids—how Janice will tell them no and he always says yes. And he talked about how he has water guns scattered throughout the house. How he goofs on his kids the way he used to goof on his coaches, something that is a lot more amusing now than it was then.

And he talked about how Tabitha, who is afflicted with Down's syndrome, has him wrapped around her finger. "Tabitha sees the world just for what it is," he said. "Here's a seven-foot black guy with a 4'6" little white kid, and people are saying, 'What's he doing with her?' And she says, 'That's Daddy Darryl. Do you love me, Daddy?'… She only knows how you treat her. She doesn't care about black or white or whatever."

Darryl taught her to shoot foul shots. And she loves to dance. Few other things matter, least of all the opinions of outsiders.

One time a guy came up to Darryl and said, "I'm sorry God did that to you."

"Did what?" Dawkins replied.

"Gave you a kid like that, that you've got to take care of all your life."

"No," Darryl said, "I feel sorry for you, because you never learned how to love people unconditionally."

A great many things can be said about Darryl Dawkins, but one thing that can never be said is that he doesn't love his fellow man.

He became the first player to make the leap from high school to the NBA when the Sixers drafted him fifth overall in 1975, out of Orlando's Maynard Evans High School. (That came one year after the ABA's Utah Stars chose a Virginia high-schooler named Moses Malone.)

Moses was glowering and single-minded, and never changed. Dawkins was glib and fun-loving; he never changed, either. While his career numbers (12 PPG, 6.1 RPG, 57.2 percent shooting) are okay, he endlessly frustrated coaches and front-office types—in Philadelphia, where he spent seven years, as well as New Jersey, Utah, and Detroit—all of whom took one look at his sculpted 6'11", 250-pound frame (not to mention his skillset) and expected much more.

It never quite happened, but the sideshow was something to behold. He shattered those two backboards on November 13 and December 5, 1979, respectively—in Kansas City, where the Sacramento Kings' forerunner played, and in the Spectrum.

"The first one was an accident," he said. "The second one, I had to see if I could do it again."

Beyond naming his other dunks ("Spine Chiller Supreme," "Yo Mama," etc.) and claiming he hailed from the planet Lovetron, he had a one-liner for every occasion. It has been said that when he was asked if he knew where they signed the Declaration of Independence, his response was, "At the bottom." And it has been said that when he was asked his favorite color, his response was, "Plaid."

"I never take anything serious," he said. "I don't take myself serious. If you hurt my mother, my kids, my wife, my family, I'd go to jail. I'd be sitting in jail, in a lounge chair with a cigar. But you've got to do a lot to make me mad."

Late in Game 2 of the 1977 NBA Finals between the Sixers and Portland Trail Blazers, a scuffle broke out in which Dawkins accidentally hit teammate Doug Collins—Collins, later the Sixers' coach, has a scar near his eye to prove it—and then was sucker-punched (or at least slapped) by Blazers enforcer Maurice Lucas.

Dawkins, enraged that none of his teammates had his back, ripped a toilet out of a wall in the Sixers' locker room—years later he chuckled at the memory of the other players' $300 shoes floating around in the resultant flood—and barricaded the door with several lockers. It turned out to be a turning point in the series, as

Portland rallied from a 0–2 deficit to win the title in six games. But Dawkins said he and Lucas, who died in October 2010, later made their peace.

Dawkins seems at peace in just about every way, in point of fact. After his stint in Italy he spent some time with the Harlem Globetrotters, then served as head coach for Winnipeg of the International Basketball Association, the Pennsylvania Valley Dawgs of the USBL, and at Lehigh Carbon Community College.

He never dwells on the what-ifs of his playing career, saying, "I would have done it over the same way, because that's what made me who I am. And I always believe in [myself]."

Especially now, because he's no longer flyin'. He no longer has his head in the clouds.

62 Iverson Announces His Retirement

Allen Iverson officially announced his retirement from professional basketball at an afternoon press conference at Wells Fargo Center on October 30, 2013. The press conference was held hours before the 76ers hosted the Miami Heat in the opening game of the 2013–14 season.

In front of family and friends and about 300 people seated behind one of the baskets courtside, the guard with the big heart spoke. Sixers icon Julius Erving and Iverson's former Georgetown University coach John Thompson were among those in attendance.

Iverson, who played in Philadelphia from 1996 to 2006 and again in 2009–10, spent most of career as a 76er. The four-time scoring champion remains one of the most prolific scorers in NBA history, despite barely being six feet tall and about 165 pounds.

Iverson ended his 12-year Philadelphia tenure second all-time on the team's points list (19,931).

The only time when he appeared to shed a tear at his retirement press conference was when he talked about former teammate Aaron McKee, who served as big brother to Iverson.

His farewell press conference was very similar to his playing days, featuring bold, brutally honest statements, fearless comments and the kind of quotes that made A.I. one of a kind. Three things stood out: his love for the game, his love for Philadelphia and 76ers fans, and his insistence to live life his way.

Here are excerpts from the retirement announcement, which lasted nearly an hour.

Iverson's Opening Statement

I am formally announcing my retirement from basketball. I thought, once this day would come, that it would be a tragic day. I never imagined the day coming, but I knew it would. I feel proud and happy to say that I'm happy with my decision and I feel great and I'm in a great mind-set.

I have to thank God for giving me the opportunity to, not really, to accomplish all the things that I accomplished in the NBA, but just giving me the opportunity to be drafted.

People, all the time, ask me what was my greatest moment. It was just being drafted, just getting the opportunity, somebody coming from where I came from. I heard all the stories that no one makes it from Newport News [Virginia] to the NBA. They thought I was crazy, out of my mind. I always believed in myself. My mom always told me that I could be anything I wanted to be. I actually believed it. I fought.

I went through a whole lot to get to this point right here. Coach [John] Thompson gave me an opportunity when nobody in the world would and believed in me.

Basically, saved my life and made my dream come true. I have to thank Michael Jordan for just giving me a vision.

Without that vision, I don't think it would have been possible. He made me want to play basketball. He basically showed me the way and gave me the path....

A Sixer for Life?

I'm always gonna be a Sixer, 'til I die. I'm always gonna be a Hoya, 'til I die....

Expectations? Any Regrets?

Trying to live up to expectations. Trying to be perfect, man, when you know you are not. Being in the fish bowl with every move you make and people talk about everything you do. It is just a hard life to live; it is a great one and I wouldn't trade it for nothing. I have no regrets on anything.

People ask me all the time if I have any regrets and I don't have any. If I could go back and do it all over again would I change anything? No. Because if I could go back and change everything then I would be a perfect man. I know there is no perfect man and there is no perfect basketball player.

My career was up and down, at times, and I made a lot of mistakes, lot of things I am not proud of, but it is only for other people to learn from. I took an ass-kicking for me being me. For me looking the way I look and dressing the way I dress. My whole thing was being me.

He Wanted His Coaches to Be Proud of the Player They Created

Basketball has been great for me. It allowed me to take care of my family for their rest of their lives and made me a household name. It taught me a lot in life in relationships

Iverson and Allen

Hours after Allen Iverson officially announced his retirement from basketball, reporters were still angling for comments summing up A.I.'s career. Reporters huddled in the visitors' locker during the pregame at the Wells Fargo Center while the Miami Heat dressed and stretched.

The defending NBA champions were in town for opening night against the 76ers. A large group of journalists crowded around Dwyane Wade, then LeBron James, each fielding a few Iverson questions. What did he mean to the sport? What did he mean to you? Then Chris Bosh and Mario Chambers took similar questions.

Finally, two reporters stood in front of Ray Allen. One asked if Allen looked up to Iverson and what memories he had of Iverson's career.

Allen, who was in the same 1996 draft class as Iverson, offered a unique perspective. The 18-year veteran never had time to admire A.I. In fact, they were rivals. Allen was the anti-Iverson.

The two were opposites. Allen, the UConn standout is clean-cut. Short hair, no ink on his body. He was a military child. Iverson had cornrows, tats, and spent time in jail.

Yet their careers parallel each other at UConn and Georgetown, both Big East schools at the time. Iverson was always a counterpart of Allen's growing up. They had some pretty heated battles over the years, both collegiately and in the professional ranks.

"He was a guy I always wanted to beat," said Allen, who was named USA Basketball's Male Athlete of the Year in 1995. "I didn't have the opportunity or chance to marvel at what he did. What he did was incredible and incomparable, especially for his height and his athleticism. He had this ability to score. We were always trying to find a way to stop him, as opposed to marveling at what he was doing."

One of the most accurate free-throw and three-point shooters in NBA history, Allen won NBA championships with the Celtics and Heat. Yet the 10-time All-Star still believes Iverson, the Sixers, and the NBA took a chance for a championship away from him.

Allen's most successful season with the Bucks was 2000–01. He was the leader of Milwaukee's Big Three, which also included Glenn Robinson and Sam Cassell. The Bucks lost the Eastern Conference Finals to the 76ers in seven games.

"Yeah, and I still say, to this day, that we got robbed," Allen said. "We played Game 7 in Philly. Game 6 we lose in Milwaukee. We lost the game, but Scottie Williams was suspended for an elbow to A.I. He got called for a foul and over the time we traveled from Milwaukee to Philly it was upgraded and he got suspended for the game. [Being suspended for] Game 7 of the Eastern Conference playoffs is unheard of. At the time I said it was a conspiracy, because I liked our chances of possibly winning Game 7, but we were one man short."

Yeah, he still seems a tad bitter about that one.

But there is more. Take for instance college at UConn: the Big East Conference championship in 1996.

History is written in Allen's favor in this one, because he hit a crazy shot to win the game—but A.I. had the ball with 13 seconds left and he missed a shot from the top of the key, and Georgetown's Jerome Williams got the rebound and missed a shot when he had a chance to win it.

"The story could have been written so many different ways," Allen said. "I was fortunate enough to have [had] the favorable outcome in that one.

"To this day I get Georgetown fans at the time who hated me. LeBron will tell you he hated me because we beat Georgetown then and he wanted to go to Georgetown."

It seems wrong. Fans rooting for the bad boy over the good guy. But that's what Allen says he experienced.

Odd, but Iverson, the rebel who disliked discipline and practice, was loved. Allen, the military kid with a strong work ethic, a rule follower, was, well, not a fan favorite.

It was one of those things. A.I., at the time, was the guy that people loved rooting for. He was a smaller guy, who had so much talent, so much heart and people rooted for him to always win, Allen said.

They were opposites. They were competitors. But they were similar, too. Though they did it differently, they are two of the game's great scorers. They both came through in the clutch to win big games. And neither cared about their public image.

"I just played basketball," Allen said. "I didn't try to put on anything other than who I was. We all carry whatever baggage from how we grew up into the game. I came from a military background so I was always real disciplined and focused at the task at hand. With [Iverson], he had so much swag with him, playing the game, and people loved that. It was great for the game because kids realize that you can be an individual in this game and you can go out and score and you can play your own way and you can win that way. He definitely grew up a generation of kids."

with teammates and the competitiveness of everything. It is real life, but it is a game that teaches you about sacrifice and what it takes to win, in basketball and in life.

How Much Did Philadelphia Mean to You?

It's home. I've been apart of this community for so many years. They grew on me, just like I grew on them. I don't have too many words that I can use to describe Philadelphia fans and their connection to me.

When you have somebody like Dr. J being a Sixer and the way the fans embraced him, the way they do still today, that's what I think about. I always want them to treat me the same way they treat him when he comes back. It is the same way all the time.

When people tell me it's Doctor and A.I. when they talk Philly basketball, and that's like one of the biggest compliments that someone can give you. Doctor and A.I. You put my name in the same sentence as Doc. That's why this day is so special, because of days like that.

When Did He Come to the Decision to Retire?

I'm mentally tired of it all. The passion to play wasn't there. The passion for the sport will always be there. I'd just say it was time.

Favorite Career Moment

Just being on the court jumping up and down when we went to Finals and feeling like we had a chance to win a title.

On Stories About His Personal Life

I hear those stories just like everyone else. I have gotten to a place in life where when you hear those things, yes, it bothers you. It would basically be saying that you are not human, that I don't have a heart.

Sometimes I wish it didn't bother me. My ex-wife Tawanna said you don't have to explain yourself all the time. People don't want to talk about the good things I do. Just the negative Allen Iverson stories.

Do You Regret Anything? The "Practice" Comments?

Nothin'. Not one thing. Not one thing. It is easy to say I wish I would have done this thing, but I can't go back and do over. It taught me a lot.

[The] "Practice" situation, I'm not going to explain what that whole situation [was about]. But it was more than just about that I didn't like practice or things like that.

If I could go back and do it all over again I would never have done the interview, but as far as how I expressed "practice, practice, practice" over and over again, I wouldn't take it back. That sound bite was great for the media, great for the fans.

But they had no idea that my best friend had just got killed. They had no idea that press conference was not about practice. The press conference was supposed to be about me not being traded from Philadelphia, that's what I thought I was sitting down to talk at the podium about. But everybody talked about that [practice]. But you never knew anything about the reason why I was upset and what the press conference was about.

I don't regret anything. If I could take back all the mistakes I made I would have had a perfect career. I would miss no shots. I would have made no turnovers, I would have gone right instead of left when I was supposed to. Everything. I would have got on [Route] 76 at 4:00 instead of five. I can't take any of it back. I don't regret it. It was a blessing to get to this point.

But I've won scoring titles, MVPs, First-Team All-NBA. I've done a lot in this league. Being 160 pounds soaking wet, coming from Newport News, Virginia, what more can you ask for? And my family is taken care of for the rest of their lives.

What do you mean "regrets"? I don't have none.

63 World B. Free

World B. Free has gone from shameless gunner to tireless do-gooder. From all that was wrong about the NBA to all that is right. From the guy the Sixers couldn't wait to ship out of town, to the guy they can't wait to push to the forefront.

He has been back with the team for more than a decade in a nonplaying capacity, working in community relations and as the team's "Ambassador of Basketball." He surfaces each game night, wearing a gaudy suit and making a presentation to a local person who has made a particularly meaningful contribution to the Delaware Valley.

He has been known to work camps and clinics. To venture into neighborhoods where even the cops don't go anymore. To talk to kids about dreams and possibilities. About going to school and staying off drugs. "You can't save the world," he said in a 1998 interview, "but you can help someone."

So yeah, it really is a new World.

Free—then Lloyd—is remembered as a brash young guard, as a guy who never met a shot he didn't like. As being part of a team of me-firsters that had to be stripped down to the chassis before it was rebuilt as the 1983 championship club.

He drove coaches crazy, but just about everybody else tended to like World, and they tend to like him now. He has a certain roguish charm about him, and whatever edge there once might have been has been eroded by time. By personal crises. By spending the vast majority of his 13-year career playing for bad teams in nice places (San Diego, Golden State) and a bad team in a not-so-nice place (Cleveland), after the Sixers shipped him out of town.

He grew up poor in the Brownsville section of Brooklyn, one of 11 children. His father, Charles, was a longshoreman. His mom, Earlene, would try to keep the family clothed and bathed and happy—especially the last. When Lloyd was cut from the Canarsie High basketball team his sophomore year, for instance, he was so disconsolate that he "needed a rubber band to keep [his] head up."

So she told him to keep working at it, and he kept going back to 66 Park, sometimes to play, sometimes to shoot by himself. Before long he had built up a sizable reputation. Somebody saw him play—either saw him soar or uncork that rainbow jumper of his—and labeled him "All-World," right on the spot. It stuck, and years later, while with the Warriors, he had his name legally changed to World.

He made varsity as a junior, won a city title as a senior, and was going to go to the University of Arkansas. But that fell through at the last minute, and he wound up at Guilford, then an NAIA school. He won a national championship there in his freshman year while playing with a friend from the 'hood, a guard named Greg Jackson, and future pro M.L. Carr.

Two years later, the Sixers took him in the second round of the draft, and he became part of a "traveling road show," as then–general manager Pat Williams called it, with George McGinnis, Darryl Dawkins, Joe Bryant, and, a year later, Julius Erving.

Free was largely unhappy coming off the bench behind Doug Collins, and he didn't hesitate to let people know about it. But he did have his moments, like the time he rained 27 on Boston in Game 7 of the 1977 Eastern Conference Finals. "I was still a little kid," he said, "but looking at these guys I'm like, *I'm going to make a name for myself.*"

He did: the Boston Strangler.

"Nobody remembers that," Free said. "All the time they'll be like, 'Andrew Toney, the original Boston Strangler.' But the people that played with me, they know who the original Boston Strangler was."

Gifted as he was, the team tired of him. Billy Cunningham had succeeded Gene Shue as coach early in 1977–78, after the we-owe-you-one flameout against Portland in the 1977 Finals. Cunningham wanted to reshape the team, to make it more cohesive, more defensive-minded, more Erving-oriented. Williams shopped World around prior to the 1978–79 season, but he didn't find a taker until the day before the opener, when the Clippers offered a No. 1 pick for him. A No. 1 pick in 1984. The Sixers accepted, and used that selection on Charles Barkley.

And World was, well, free. He finished second in the league in scoring in the next two years, behind George Gervin, and was among the top 15 in each of the next eight seasons. By the time he finished his career—with an out-of-shape cameo in Philadelphia in 1986–87 and another with Houston a year later—he had piled up 17,955 points, then 40th all-time.

"I did what I said I could do, as far as being out there," he said. "I knew I belonged and deserved to be out there on that basketball court with those players."

He won his share of supporters along the way. There are those in Cleveland, for instance, who said he saved the franchise in the days after bumbling owner Ted Stepien departed, that without World, there really was no reason to watch those Cavaliers.

But the prevailing notion is that Free was out for himself. That he didn't make a team better. That nobody ever won with him in their backcourt. World, naturally, has an answer for such criticism. "You have to know your personnel," he said, not a bit perturbed. "Why throw the ball to somebody who couldn't shoot the ball rather than take that shot yourself?"

He doesn't mind talking about how he got bilked out of a pile of money early in his career by his agent, money he claims he later recovered through legal action.

Or about how when he asked John Lucas, then the Sixers' coach/general manager, about a job with the team in the late '90s, Lucas didn't recognize him at first. World had ballooned from the 190 pounds he weighed as a rookie, past what he calls his "mature weight" of 215, all the way to 260. "Lose some weight," Lucas told him, and "we'll talk."

Thirty pounds later, there was a new World. And once again, he made a name for himself.

Game Night: The Flight Squad

They hustle onto the court in the gap between the third and fourth quarters of each Sixers home game, their time in the spotlight limited to no more than two minutes. And then the 13 members of the Flight Squad make the most of it, engaging in something called acro-dunking—acrobatic dunking—in which they sprint downcourt, launch themselves off trampolines, and reach ridiculous heights before jamming, while performing all sorts of midair gyrations.

Their act is usually well executed and well received, and Christian Crosby, the troupe's 25-year-old captain, made one thing abundantly clear during a conversation in March 2013: it's not as easy as it looks. It takes core strength, coordination, preparation. Also, no small amount of courage, given the heights he and the others achieve.

"It's very, very easy to get injured jumping off the trampoline and doing slam dunks—especially when you incorporate flipping into the mix," he said. "It's just a very dangerous thing."

Certainly they make it look easy, more often than not—so much so that when the Flight Squaders do a workshop, they invariably come across an outlier who is certain he can duplicate their moves. More often than not, Crosby said, he finds out otherwise.

"When you jump off the trampoline, you'd be surprised how uncoordinated some of the best athletes are," he said. "It's a completely different type of skill. It's completely different muscles you're using off the trampoline than you would if you were playing football or basketball, or something like that. It's a completely different ballgame, when it comes to doing acro-dunking."

A great vertical leap doesn't necessarily translate off the trampoline. It's a matter of having strong abs and a strong lower back—and the gift of timing. "A lot of guys come in thinking that just because they're good at basketball they'll be good off the trampoline," Crosby said, "and they're unpleasantly surprised when they don't even reach the rim."

The Flight Squaders come from varied backgrounds. Some are gymnasts. Some are breakdancers. Some are martial artists. Crosby, a native of Voorhees, New Jersey, falls into the latter category, having taken up tae kwon do at his dad's martial arts school as a teenager and later achieving a second-degree black belt. He went on to study film at the University of the Arts in Philadelphia but was heavily involved in the performing arts as well.

After he appeared in a commercial touting tourism in the city someone suggested that he pursue a spot on the Hair Raisers, the Flight Squad's predecessor. He made the team, but his ambitions soared higher than the dunkers.

He has written on his website that he had something of an epiphany in Dallas in 2009, while touring as a backup dancer to the singer Raven-Symoné. He saw how she had made a name for herself and decided he wanted to do the same, and more. He has since started his own clothing line—the Nice Brand, he calls it, since he regards himself as an affable guy—and believes that the sky truly is the limit for him.

"I enjoy progressing, and I enjoy doing," he said. "I enjoy working. I enjoy creating and aspiring. I love living. It's something I enjoy, and it's something a lot of people don't do. People are so worried about what they're told they have to do and all they do is stress about it. They stress about school. Then they stress about college. Then they stress about getting a job. Then they stress about getting a spouse. Then they stress about having a family. Then they stress about becoming a millionaire.

"They forget to live and enjoy life. Me, I just enjoy each segment of my life. That's what helps me aspire and to stay positive and optimistic about everything I want to do in my life. I try to enjoy each moment, and I think that's what's brought me to where I am today."

His goal, then, is to keep soaring. That's not as easy as it looks, either. It takes timing and, again, no small amount of courage.

65 Derek Smith

Jim Lynam's relationship with Derek Smith, one the former coach will forever treasure, was bracketed by two phone calls, each to the coach's wife.

The first came in the summer of 1983, from outside a gym in Los Angeles. The second was in the summer of 1996, from a ski resort in Oregon.

The first afforded Lynam an opportunity to comprehend Smith's considerable presence. The second forced him to come to grips with his absence.

He knew something was amiss immediately after he interrupted his ski trip to phone his wife, Kay, that August day in '96, in an era before cell phones were commonplace. Normally the most even-tempered of people, she was upset. And then she broke the news to her husband: Derek Smith had died.

Derek Smith dead? At 34? The guy Lynam had coached with the Clippers (when Smith was on the ascent) and the Sixers (when he was just hanging on)? The guy who at that point was working under Lynam as an assistant in Washington?

It couldn't be. This was the guy whom one of his Clippers teammates, Norm Nixon, had nicknamed "Joe Rock." He was that tough. Tougher than tough. "A man's man," as John Nash, the former general manager in Philadelphia and Washington, would describe him years later.

He had died of a heart attack while on a cruise with his family, as well as Bullets and Washington Capitals season-ticket holders; it would later be determined that he had an allergic reaction to seasickness medication. And it seemed a final, cruel twist. He had grown up poor and fatherless in Georgia. He had seen NBA stardom robbed from him by a knee injury. And he had seen his career cut short as that injury lingered.

Lynam delivered the eulogy at a memorial service at a small church near Louisville (where Derek played his college ball), but has no idea what he said. "You're on remote control," he said. "You're in a form of a trance."

What Lynam did remember is something the preacher said at the beginning of the service: "We come here to celebrate the life of Derek Smith, and celebrate we will."

After all, there was so much to celebrate, so much to salute.

Lynam didn't know Derek before the summer of '83 but grudgingly agreed to give him a look as a favor to a friend, Portland general manager Stu Inman. And Smith, who had been cut after an indifferent rookie year with Golden State, made an immediate impression when he showed up for a workout at Loyola Marymount University. It was yes-sir this, no-sir that. "And he didn't look at me in the eye," Lynam said, "he's looking at me in the brain with this penetrating stare."

The two of them repaired to an auxiliary gym and cleared off a court cluttered with weightlifting equipment and the like. It must have been 110 degrees in there, Lynam recalled, maybe 115. When Derek was asked to execute a few dribble drives he didn't just lay up the ball, he dunked it—hard. It seemed to Lynam that he was bent on tearing the basket down, that he wanted to make a statement about his ability to play in the NBA.

He was less impressive when asked to shoot spot-up jumpers, but Lynam then told him to incorporate a dribble or two before firing. And just like that, Smith began raining in shot after shot. He made something like 100 out of 108, by Lynam's count.

The coach had seen enough. He sent Smith on his way and went looking for a pay phone, so that he might call Kay in

Manhattan Beach. And on a typically cloudless Southern California day, he told her, "I may have been hit in the head by lightning."

By 1984–85, Smith was one of the finest shooting guards in the NBA, averaging 22 points per game for Lynam's Clippers (by then based in Los Angeles) and memorably schooling a rookie named Michael Jordan early in the season. Though Chicago won the game, Smith outscored Jordan 33–20 and threw down a reverse tomahawk jam that can still be found on YouTube.

The next year, he started off even better, averaging 23.5 points through the first 11 games. Then his left knee crumpled, and with it, his career.

He drifted to Sacramento, then the Sixers—there to be reunited with Lynam, who was coaching a team starring Charles Barkley and featuring a stellar supporting cast (Rick Mahorn, Mike Gminski, Johnny Dawkins, et al). Smith served as leader of the second unit, a locker-room counterbalance to loudmouths Barkley and Mahorn and mentor to youngsters Scott Brooks and Hersey Hawkins. Also defensive stopper: OPEN IN CASE OF MICHAEL JORDAN.

"Derek," Hawkins said, "was one of the great guys to ever play this game. A great friend. It was a privilege to play with him."

But it was not the least bit enjoyable to practice against him. "No, he was a junkyard dog," Hawkins said. "He was all into you, physical, and not intimidated by anyone—not even Charles. Most people Charles could intimidate."

But not Derek.

The Sixers breezed to an Atlantic Division championship and won a round in the playoffs. But in a second-round series against Jordan's Bulls, and Chicago took out the Sixers in five.

To this day, there are those who believe it might have turned out differently if Derek had been right. "I don't want to overstate it—you know, 'woulda, coulda, shoulda,'" Lynam said. "But I'll tell you this: Our chances would have been a heck of a lot better had we had him. He was not only respected, but in a certain way, [he was] a feared kind of guy."

Woulda, coulda, shoulda—it was something Derek Smith never said. He dealt with reality, played the hand life dealt him (as unfair as it often was), approached things head-on. It is why everyone still wants to celebrate him all these years later.

66 The Son Also Rises

Nolan Smith was searching. Just where was Kevin Johnson, anyway?

Someone pointed the Portland Trail Blazers' second-year guard in the direction of the 76ers locker room one night in March 2013, before Portland lost to the Sixers in the Wells Fargo Center. "Turn right and go through this door," Smith was told. "The trainer's room is straight ahead."

Smith did as he was instructed, and before he knew it Johnson—K.J., as everybody calls the Sixers' head athletic trainer—was standing before him.

Johnson is a relentlessly pleasant man, always smiling, always ready to dispense a kind word. But the mere sight of Smith made him brighten that much more.

"Lookin' good, man," he said, as the two men hugged.

Their meeting was brief. But their connection is everlasting.

Mr. Kevin—that's what Nolan used to call him, even after he had become a star at Oak Hill Academy and Duke, two storied basketball programs. The nickname harkened back to a day when Nolan was young and he needed some moorings after his father's death.

"K.J.," Nolan said, "was someone who became like a father figure in my life."

Emblazoned on Smith's right arm is a tattoo bearing his father's likeness underneath the words FOREVER WATCHING.

It turns out a great many others have been, too.

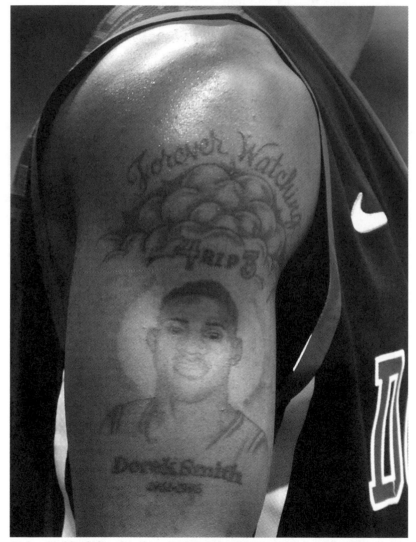

Nolan Smith's father, Derek, is FOREVER WATCHING, as symbolized in the former's tattoo.

His dad, Derek, had been a force of nature—at the University of Louisville (where he won a national championship), all too briefly with the Clippers (where a knee injury cut short his rise to stardom), and with the Sixers' 1989–90 Atlantic Division championship team.

By the end of the 1990–91 season he had resurfaced with the Celtics. His defensive work against Indiana Pacers star Chuck Person caught the attention of Kevin Johnson, by then the Pacers' assistant trainer. Even now Johnson can remember screaming at the refs, calling Derek a hack, wondering how in creation this guy could possibly get away with such mayhem. Gimpy-legged but game, Smith slowed Person just enough. And the Celtics won the series in seven.

Three years later, after Lynam summoned him to be his assistant coach with the Washington Bullets, Smith made the acquaintance of Washington's trainer…Kevin Johnson.

"Man, you're not going to believe this," Johnson told him. "I couldn't stand you when you were with the Celtics. You were hacking all my players up." Smith laughed, and they immediately became friends. K.J. remembers that Derek was "rock solid," teaching the young Bullets—Juwan Howard, Chris Webber, and the rest—about what it took to be a pro. And Johnson remembers Derek always had Nolan in tow, that the younger Smith always tagged along to practices and games. Nolan would ask Johnson to tape his ankles. He would stretch with the players, and go through the layup line.

More than once it has been written that Derek, a no-nonsense dad, put Nolan through his paces on the court, that he was always reminding him that if it was worth doing, it was worth doing to the best of one's ability.

Johnson remembers something else, too. He remembers that Derek had never been on a boat until K.J. took him out on the Chesapeake Bay in his 24-footer, shortly before Smith and his family—wife, Monica, and daughter Sydney, in addition to Nolan—went on an Atlantic cruise with Bullets fans in the summer of 1996.

Derek Smith didn't survive that cruise. He died of an allergic reaction to seasickness medication at age 34.

Nolan was eight at the time. The last day of his dad's life, the younger Smith played a 14-year-old in a game of one-on-one on the ship's deck. The kid was bigger and stronger, and had his way. Nolan would later tell ESPN.com's Tom Friend that he grew so frustrated, he fired the ball into the ocean. But before he knew it, Derek was at his side; he had been looking on from afar, forever watching. And he told his son such tantrums were unacceptable, that nobody was going to want to play with him if he acted like that. From that point forward, Nolan said, he always tried to be the best teammate he could be.

The Bullets extended him the same courtesy, rallying around their tiniest teammate after Derek's death. It was everybody— Webber, Howard, Gheorghe Muresan, Tim Legler. And it was K.J., too. He would pick Nolan up for games, and often give him rides home as well.

And they would talk. "Some of the talks were...I couldn't answer all the questions," Johnson said. "Like, 'I couldn't believe it happened.... How do you think it happened?' We just tried to make it seem like he wasn't going to lose that part of his life."

"There's no telling where I'd be without those guys," Smith said, ticking off the names. "A lot of the guys on that team just stayed in my ear and made sure I stayed on path. They helped me a lot to grow into the man I am today."

His career gained momentum. He became a star at Duke, winning a national championship in 2010, exactly 30 years after his dad won his.

The Blazers took him in the first round in 2011, meaning he again crossed paths with Hersey Hawkins, who had been a teammate of Derek's with the Sixers and was by then Portland's player programs director. Hawkins saw a lot of Derek in Nolan. They looked the same, acted the same, approached the game the same.

"The kid's competitiveness and his work ethic—no question you develop some over the years," Hawkins said, "but you're born with a lot of those things. I can just see his dad in a lot of the stuff that he does."

But Nolan appeared in only 84 games over those two seasons, averaging 3.3 points on 37.1 percent shooting. And toward the end of 2012–13 season he told the *Oregonian*'s Joe Freeman that he understood the frustration of the fans, since Denver had drafted star forward Kenneth Faried immediately after the Blazers chose him.

At the same time Smith sounded frustrated himself, saying he welcomed becoming a free agent in the summer of 2013, so that he could start over. "I'm not one to make excuses," he told Freeman. "I don't point fingers. I don't blame anyone for anything that's going on. This just wasn't the right situation for me. And I think everybody can see that. I'm just going to learn from it and move on."

Oklahoma City, coached by Scott Brooks, was mentioned as a possible destination. Brooks had played alongside Derek Smith in Philadelphia. Derek had been a groomsman at his wedding, Nolan a ring bearer. Brooks was also Nolan's godfather.

But as it turned out, Oklahoma City looked elsewhere for backcourt depth, and Nolan spent the 2013–14 season in Croatia.

67 Family Matters: Harvey Catchings

Harvey Catchings had finally had enough. His daughters, 10-year-old Tauja and nine-year-old Tamika, were playing one-on-one at the basket in the driveway of the family's Deerfield, Illinois, home, in their usual knockdown, drag-out fashion. Insults had been exchanged. Blood had been spilled. It was time to intervene.

"Gimme the ball," the former Sixer said.

Tauja followed him back inside the house; she was quite content to play with her dolls. Not so Tamika. She remained on the court by herself, making imaginary moves, shooting imaginary shots. "It's like you can take the ball, but that's just a symbol; I'm going to do what I want to do," Harvey said, looking back to that day a quarter-century ago.

Tamika would later learn that there was a highfalutin term for what she was doing: visualization. If you can see yourself doing it correctly, in time you surely will. She didn't know anything about that at the time, of course. She was just carrying on as best she could, doing something she loved to do.

It might seem that no one would have been able to envision what was in store for her down the line—how she would become one of the finest female basketball players ever—but that wasn't quite true, either. Just a few years after that seminal moment in the driveway, Tamika, then a seventh-grader, informed her dad she was going to play in the NBA, just as he once did. It turned out to be about the only thing she hasn't done, but no matter; she won a national championship at Tennessee, three Olympic gold medals while representing the U.S., and a WNBA title in 2012 as part of the Indiana Fever, for whom she has played all 11 of her pro seasons stateside.

She has been driven not just by the fact that she was bullied as a kid (she was an easy target, in that she wore glasses and clunky hearing aids), not just because of sibling rivalry (besides Tauja, her brother, Kenyon, two years older, was also a formidable player), and not just because Harvey and his wife, Wanda, divorced when she was in sixth grade. Rather, it was *because* of all those things.

Once she found her niche on the court, the classroom taunts stoked an unquenchable fire. She wanted to beat everyone—"and not just beat them," Harvey said. "She wanted to pretty much embarrass you." That carried over to the driveway. Kenyon and Tauja loved to play, but Tamika? She was "like an addict," her dad said—always wanting to play, always seeking to improve, always hating to lose.

Tamika, who ditched her hearing aids upon learning to lip-read, describes herself as having "the worst attitude" of the three Catchings kids growing up. Seemed like she was forever "working overboard" (her words) to improve. And after the divorce, the court was transformed into something else: a sanctuary. "It allowed me a safe place," she said, "where I could take out my frustrations [to an extent] and get better at something I loved to do."

She had a willing mentor in Harvey, who spent the first four-plus of his 11 NBA seasons with the Sixers and now lives in Spring, Texas, where he works in the mortgage industry. His route to pro basketball was an indirect one, his approach to the game growing up the exact opposite of Tamika's. He played exactly eight games of high school basketball, all in his senior year, then quit the team. He much preferred playing drums in the band.

As luck would have it, he had an aunt in Los Angeles who had been talking up her lanky nephew—Harvey was 6'9" by the time he reached the NBA—to the UCLA coaches. And on a visit out there the summer after he graduated he was granted an audience with Denny Crum, then a Bruins assistant and later a highly successful coach at Louisville. Crum worked Harvey out and saw that he was athletic but raw, and recommended junior college.

Catchings spent a year there, then three at Hardin-Simmons, his skills and passion burgeoning as the seasons passed. The Sixers made him a third-round pick in 1974, and while never a big scorer—he averaged just 3.2 points per game while playing for them, and three others teams—he defended, rebounded, did all the dirty work.

He played one more year, in Italy, where he crossed paths with his former Sixers teammate Joe Bryant and his young son Kobe— "At that time, [Kobe] was big on soccer," Harvey recalled—before settling in the Chicago suburbs. As his kids grew he would tell them to follow their passion. Tamika had no doubt about hers.

She won an Illinois state title while playing alongside Tauja at Adlai Stevenson High, and later a Texas state title at Duncanville High, after Wanda moved there and Tamika elected to accompany her mother. (Tauja remained behind, choosing to stay with her dad. It was, Harvey recalled, "one of the most difficult periods of time for me.")

He would reconnect with Tamika when she landed at Tennessee, where she came under the sway of legendary coach Pat Summitt. Never before had so many demands been placed on the youngest Catchings, especially at the defensive end of the court; she bristled, cried over the phone to her dad, wondered if she would ever be able to stick it out. (She also began wearing hearing aids again—smaller ones this time—at Summitt's urging, the better to hear every bit of instruction.)

"When she came out the other side, being able to channel that energy into being strong defensively and also solid offensively," Harvey said, "she became a totally different player."

After winning a college title as part of an undefeated team her freshman year, she went on to a career that saw her finish with more than 2,000 points and more than 1,000 rebounds. It also ended prematurely because of a shredded knee, which cost her her first WNBA year, but there was more to come. Gold medals in 2004, 2008, and 2012. Seven All-Star berths as a pro. Five selections as the league's Defensive Player of the Year. An MVP in 2011. And, a year later, a championship.

There has been, truly, no slaking her appetite for the game; she has played overseas during each WNBA off-season. In so doing, she has also remained the Catchings family's standard-bearer. Kenyon was forced to give up the game because of a serious intestinal condition, and Tauja walked away after playing at Illinois and a few years overseas; she now sells real estate in Indianapolis, while helping run Tamika's charitable foundation, Catch the Stars. (The two of them no longer play one-on-one, though. No use tempting fate.)

"I would not have dreamed she had the career that she's had," Harvey said, "to be mentioned by historians of the game."

But Tamika? She envisioned it all along.

68 Joe Bryant (aka, Kobe's Dad)

In the 2009 book *The Art of a Beautiful Game, Sports Illustrated* senior writer Chris Ballard uses an anecdote to get to the heart of Los Angeles Lakers star Kobe Bryant, describing how at Lower Merion High School, just outside Philadelphia, Bryant would play a benchwarmer named Rob Schwartz one-on-one after practice every blessed day. The games were to 100, by one. Schwartz told Ballard the most points he ever managed was 12. Bryant would not even concede that, telling Ballard that Schwartz surely never mustered more than five.

In 2012, Ballard wrote in *SI* about Kobe's dad, Joe, who played eight years in the NBA (the first four of them with the Sixers) and seven years overseas, and was by then coaching in Thailand. Ballard, a gifted writer, described how the elder Bryant squared off against one of his players in billiards and was running the table. But with just the eight ball left, Joe set down his cue. "I can't do that to one of my players," he said, according to Ballard's account.

To boil it down even further, a guy nicknamed "Jellybean" sired a son nicknamed "the Black Mamba." Go figure. It is generally agreed that Joe underachieved during the NBA portion of his career—he averaged just 8.7 points per game in those eight seasons—before starring in Europe. It is universally agreed that Kobe is one of the fiercest competitors to ever play the game.

Ballard suggests that the younger Bryant gleaned his killer instinct as much from his mom, Pam, as anyone else. The older sister of Chubby Cox, who played at Villanova and San Francisco (and briefly in the NBA), Pam was the one, Ballard wrote, who leveled Kobe with a forearm when at age 14 he attempted to dunk in a family game. And it was her nephew, Sharif Butler, who schooled Kobe in one-on-one.

"My mom's the feisty one," Bryant told Ballard. "She has that killer in her."

But it would be a mistake to sell Joe short when it comes to Kobe's development. The elder Bryant, who played at Philadelphia's John Bartram High and later LaSalle, was a uniquely skilled player, adept at handling the ball despite standing 6'9". "Joe always had the great line," former Sixers coach Doug Collins, once a teammate of Bryant's in Philadelphia, told reporters in 2010. "He said, 'I did things before Magic Johnson did them. But they called him Magic and they called me Tragic.'"

Bryant was trapped behind Julius Erving and George McGinnis on the depth chart in Philadelphia, and enjoyed only modest success while playing for the Clippers and Rockets during his NBA career, which ended in 1983. In Italy it was different. He put up big numbers. The fans would chant his name. And they would cheer when his young son came out at halftime during games to hoist jumpers.

Kobe would also show up at practices and pester his dad's teammates to play him one-on-one. And when his grandparents mailed videotapes of NBA games, father and son would pore over them—Joe telling Kobe where the ball would go before it went there (and why), and Kobe watching the moves of the game's greatest players and mimicking them when he repaired to the court on his own.

And Joe was far from a pushover when it came to his own one-on-one scrums with his son. "I didn't beat him one-on-one until I was 16," Kobe told *SI*'s Ian Thomsen in 1998. "He was real physical with me. When I was 14 or 15 he started cheating. He'd elbow me in the mouth, rip my lip open. Then my mother would walk out on the court, and the elbows would stop."

But more than anything, Joe gave Kobe vision, imagination, and support. Ballard wrote in 2012 that the elder Bryant "was the anti–Marv Marinovich, empowering rather than dictatorial, encouraging his son to dream grand dreams."

So it was that Jellybean begat the Black Mamba.

Michael Carter-Williams

Upon winning the NBA Rookie of the Year Award in the spring of 2014, Sixers point guard Michael Carter-Williams talked not about what he was, but about what he hoped to become. Not about what he had done, but about what he still needed to do.

He became the only Sixer other than Allen Iverson in 1996–97 to be named Rookie of the Year, and was just the third rookie since 1950–51 to lead all first-year players in scoring, rebounding, and assists. (The others were Cincinnati's Oscar Robertson in 1960–61 and Phoenix's Alvan Adams in 1975–76.)

Carter-Williams was also the third player to average 16 points, six rebounds, and six assists in his first season, joining Robertson and Magic Johnson, who did so in 1979–80. And finally, he was the first player in 26 years drafted 10th or lower to be named the Rookie of the Year, having been chosen 11th the previous summer. (Mark Jackson, taken 18th by the Knicks in 1987, was the last.)

Yet no one was fooled into believing it had been a surpassing rookie season, or a portent of greatness—including Carter-Williams himself. His had been in an unusually weak rookie class, and because he played on such a poor team—the Sixers went 19–63—he had been allotted more minutes and shots than first-year players typically get.

New head coach Brett Brown, while often trumpeting Carter-Williams' cause, also noted his point guard's flaws. He needed to get stronger, Brown said, and needed to improve his mechanically flawed jumper. (MCW shot only 40.5 percent from the floor and 26.4 percent from three-point range.) And there were times when he displayed "a level of entitlement," according to the coach, wanting more calls from referees than rookies usually get, much less those who play on bad clubs.

Finally, there was his defense, something Carter-Williams mentioned at length when addressing reporters after being named Rookie of the Year. He admitted there were times it simply wasn't good enough, and indeed it was notable how often he failed to keep swift point guards in front of him, and how often he got hung up on screens in pick-and-roll situations, a staple of nearly every NBA offense. That often led, in turn, to the complete breakdown of the Sixers' defense, which was the worst in the league.

There were times he and Brown "had it out" about defense and everything else during games, Carter-Williams admitted that day. "I think that made our relationship even closer," the younger man claimed.

Two months earlier, Brown spelled out the challenges facing his point guard. The Sixers were amid a 26-game losing streak, a skid that equaled the longest ever in the four major U.S. sports, and in Brown's mind that only raised the stakes for Carter-Williams. Was he going to tough it out? Was he going to establish himself as a leader going forward? And yes, was he going to defend?

"Those are real questions that we don't shy away from," Brown said. "I think that he has a chance to grow, and has a chance to be a really good player. How good, who knows? It's very early days. But that responsibility is magnified right now tenfold, where you're going to look around, similar to Thaddeus [Young] to a point, and I'm looking at you. I'm looking at my point guard, and how you respond to the end of this year is going to be very telling on what we are going to expect of you moving forward. And I expect big things from him, and I'm going to coach him hard. I owe that to him."

Carter-Williams began the season with a 22-point, 12-assist, nine-steal, seven-rebound performance, as the Sixers stunned the two-time defending champion Miami Heat, part of a 3–0 start. But before long, reality set in, and the Sixers sank in the standings—even more so when they unloaded veterans Evan Turner, Spencer Hawes, and Lavoy Allen at the trade deadline in February.

There were nights Carter-Williams was able to use his wiry 6'6" frame to good effect, nights when he was able to slither to the rim for baskets, scurry downcourt in transition, or even make one or two awkward jumpers. But too often he forced things, turned the ball over or excluded teammates. Too often he would get "broken down" on defense, as he admitted.

He would hear about all of that from Brown, who in his younger years had been a point guard himself. "I have a lot of trust in Coach, just going through this whole year and him really being on my back about every little thing—on the court and off the court. I really look up to him and appreciate what he does, every single day," Carter-Williams said at his Rookie of the Year news conference.

Carter-Williams played some of his best ball in the season's latter stages. His shooting percentage went up and his turnovers went down. "I think he's continued to move up the food chain," Brown said after the season's final home game, a victory over Boston.

But nobody was fooled. There was still much to be done.

70 Luke Jackson

At first blush Luke Jackson's career, which began late because of the ignorance of his time and ended early because of injury, might appear insignificant. One supposed analyst, apparently blessed with neither perspective nor a working search engine, went so far as to include Jackson on a list of all-time Sixers draft busts on a website in 2011, right alongside the likes of Shawn Bradley, Christian Welp, and Sharone Wright.

The sole reason for that appears to be that Jackson, the fourth overall selection in the 1964 draft, averaged 9.9 points and 8.8 rebounds during his eight-year career. There was no consideration of sacrifices he made while playing alongside Wilt Chamberlain, Hal Greer, and several other stars on some strong clubs, including the 1966–67 title team. The examination began and ended with the stat sheet.

Jackson's former teammates paint an entirely different picture. Chamberlain once labeled him "the ultimate power forward," according to Robert Cherry's 2004 book *Wilt: Larger Than Life.* Billy Cunningham, the sixth man on the championship club, told author Terry Pluto that Jackson was his "favorite" on that team, because he spent his time rebounding, defending, and, as Cunningham put it, "setting picks to get Greer and myself open."

And every day Jackson approached his job enthusiastically. "Great guy, great teammate," Matt Guokas Jr., another member of the title team, said in February 2012. "Always had your back. Tough, physical. I don't think it would be fair to call him an enforcer, because he was a more skilled player than the 'enforcers' of that day. He could shoot the ball, he could rebound. Played his man well."

There are those besides Chamberlain who view Jackson as the prototypical power forward, though Guokas struggles to define that. "Is that Kevin McHale, Karl Malone—low post, back to the basket?" he said. "Luke could do that, but with Wilt he didn't do that. He would do that when Wilt was out of the game, which was almost never."

Jackson did it when he played center as a rookie, averaging career highs of 14.8 points and 12.9 rebounds per game and making his lone All-Star appearance. Then Chamberlain arrived and his numbers went down. But as he said in March 2013, "He made my life a lot easier."

Like many others, he marveled at the things Wilt did on the court—as much at the defensive end as anything else. Time and again, Jackson said, Chamberlain negated great centers, guys like Walt Bellamy and Nate Thurmond. "They were big guys, big as Wilt, but they'd put it up, and he'd throw it back at them," he said. "That was amazing to me, because that's what I did in college [at Pan American, an NAIA school in Texas]. Nothing came down the lane that was going to be put up was going to go in the hoop. That was my thing. If you come in here, you've got problems. Even in the NBA, same thing. Wilt was the best I've ever seen at doing that."

Better, he believes, than even Bill Russell.

"Russell was great, don't get me wrong," he said. "Wilt was my man, and everybody from Boston, I'm sure, loves Russell. But I love Wilt. I'll say he was the best center that ever played the game."

It all fell into place in 1966–67, the Sixers winning 68 games—a record to that point—then dispatching Boston in the playoffs before beating San Francisco for the championship. But it fell apart almost as quickly. Boston rallied from a 3–1 deficit to beat the Sixers in the 1967–68 playoffs, then won it all again.

Wilt was traded to the Lakers in 1968, which put Jackson back at center. And he got off to a strong start in 1968–69, averaging 14.4 points and 11.4 boards. Then his left Achilles gave out on a routine move to the basket against Phoenix, and he was never the same. "I came back and tried to play a couple more years," he said. "It just got too tough to do."

Nor were things all that easy after he retired in 1972. Not at first, anyway. "You still have a desire to do something, and something is holding you back," he said. "It will eat you up for a while, and that did for me, for about five or six years."

Jackson, now 72, finally came to grips with himself, working as the coordinator of parks and recreation in Beaumont, Texas, for 22 years before retiring in 2000.

Growing up in another Texas town, San Marcos, a half-century earlier, he had first attended a high school that was integrated, if only to a point; blacks were not permitted to take part in extracurricular activities. But Jackson was spotted in a summer basketball tournament by Texas Southern coach Ed Adams, who told Jackson he could move in with his brother Henry, principal of Morehouse High School in Bastrop, Louisiana, and play there.

Jackson flourished during his three years at Morehouse. And after starting out at Texas Southern out of gratitude to Ed Adams, who had died a year earlier, he moved on to Pan American. Again he became a star, so much so that he made the 1964 Olympic team. "I enjoyed that, because I'm from a little small college," he said, "and everybody's from these mega-universities."

If he had any doubts about whether he could play for the Sixers, they were dispelled very early in training camp. Right away he felt like he could compete. Right away he felt like he could contribute. "And," he said, "I just went out and did what I had to do, and wound up being a major piece of the puzzle."

That never changed, despite what the stat sheet might say.

71 George McGinnis

There are those who believe George McGinnis saved pro basketball in Philadelphia—including McGinnis himself. "I think people who understood the game knew what I did for the 76ers," he told NBA.com in 2011. "I got them from out of the playoffs into the playoffs and helped make us championship contenders."

His argument is not without merit. McGinnis, a muscular forward imported from the ABA's Indiana Pacers in 1975, chased the stench of 9–73 away and made the Sixers relevant again. He also made them an appealing destination for the likes of Julius Erving, which in an odd twist hastened McGinnis' exit; indeed, few players have gone from star to sidekick to the scrap heap more quickly than he.

But he was an important figure in the short term. "Let George Do It" became the team's marketing slogan when he arrived, its rallying cry. And McGinnis, the ABA's MVP and leading scorer the previous year, delivered for the most part—except in practice, which he hated, and in the playoffs, where he all but disappeared.

By 1982, the year he turned 32, he was out of the game. Erving led the Sixers to a title the very next year, at the very same age. Then Dr. J played four more years beyond that. (It's also notable that Michael Jordan began his second threepeat at 32, and that Kareem Abdul-Jabbar still had a decade left in the pro ranks when he reached that age. But McGinnis, by contrast, was toast by then, his career arc having resembled a sprint up the Matterhorn, and a tumble off the summit.)

Maybe his abysmal practice habits finally caught up with him. ("He was a corner-cutter," former Sixers general manager Pat Williams writes in the 1983 book *We Owed You One*.) Maybe he suffered a crisis of confidence, for his considerable skillset eroded quickly. Or maybe it was something else.

"I've always thought that, deep down, George's problem was that he really didn't enjoy basketball all that much," Williams writes. "He had gotten by on his agility and strength and God-given skills, but he wouldn't work to correct his weaknesses, and over the summer he hardly touched a basketball. He was just not immersed, absorbed, in the game. It was an attitude the Sixers could not afford any longer. So George left, and it was a sad ending to what could have been a beautiful story."

The beginning had promised so much. The Sixers had shrewdly drafted him in 1973, the first year he was eligible to be chosen by NBA clubs, even though he was putting up huge numbers for the Pacers by then. (He would ultimately be a three-time All-Star and two-time champion in his four years in Indiana.) The Sixers were unable to sign him at first. The Knicks did so, in May 1975, in contravention of league rules. The Sixers howled, and new commissioner Larry O'Brien moved quickly to negate the contract.

It was left to the Sixers to hammer out a six-year deal, for something close to $3 million—big money in those days. And that first year in Philadelphia, George did in fact do it, averaging 23 points and a shade under 13 rebounds, making the All-Star team and leading the Sixers to the playoffs for the first time in five years. "George was the turnaround factor in pro basketball in this town," Williams told *Sports Illustrated* in 1982. "Julius put up the walls and a roof, but it was George who built the foundation."

In deference to all McGinnis had done, Williams sought his blessing before moving forward on the Erving deal, on the eve of the 1976–77 season. He has since acknowledged that he put McGinnis in a bad spot. "What was he going to say: no?" Williams asked *SI.*

And while McGinnis and Erving were friends—a friendship that stayed intact, despite reporters' attempts to draw them into a he-said, he-said war of wills—the on-court mesh between them was not a good one. Both needed the ball. So too did a half dozen other guys. The Sixers were nonetheless good enough to reach the 1977 Finals, good enough to take a 2–0 lead over Portland. Then the Blazers swept the next four games to take the title. McGinnis, struggling with a pulled groin, played miserably. His average of 14.2 points was seven fewer than in the regular season, he shot just 37.4 percent and missed a potential game-tying jumper in the closing seconds of the sixth game.

Coach Gene Shue made it known that he wanted McGinnis gone. Shue's successor, Billy Cunningham, reached the same conclusion after the 1977–78 season. And never mind that McGinnis averaged more than 20 points and 10 rebounds per game for a third straight season that year. He again struggled in the playoffs, this time against Washington's Elvin Hayes. It was time to go.

Williams got on the phone with Indiana, which owned the top pick in the draft: Would the Pacers take McGinnis in return for that choice? It nearly happened, and if it had, the Sixers would have chosen North Carolina point guard Phil Ford. But the Pacers wanted the Sixers to pick up part of McGinnis' contract extension. Owner Fitz Dixon drew the line there, and the deal died.

What about Kansas City, which owned the draft's second pick? The Kings wanted any deal with the Sixers to include Joe Bryant. The Sixers balked, as Bryant had shown real promise in the postseason, and that trade went by the boards, too. (And the Kings took Ford, who played brilliantly early in his career, then fizzled out.)

Then Denver general manager Carl Scheer called, offering Bobby Jones. It was a deal similar to one Scheer had turned down when it was proposed by Williams the summer before, but now he was ready to talk. And before long, the trade became a reality.

The transaction came at great personal cost to Cunningham, who was close to McGinnis. He once told this author that McGinnis didn't talk to him for a decade after leaving town.

McGinnis has said it was more like three years. Whatever the case, there were scars. "I didn't like the way it ended," McGinnis told NBA.com. "I was bitter. I was young and immature and that's when you say and do stupid things. I didn't think I deserved to be traded. I felt like I was used. The place was [terrible] when I got there, 3,000 to 4,000 people a game, and we had them selling out."

McGinnis made his last All-Star team with Denver in 1978–79, but things went south for him after that. By 1981–82 he was a bit player for the Pacers, just seven years after he had been their biggest star. "Being the type of sensitive person I am," he told *SI* in 1982, "if I don't feel good vibes from the people I'm playing for, I don't shoot well, I don't pass well, I don't do nothing well. If I'd had the inner strength, there's no telling what I would have done.... It hasn't been easy for me."

He and his wife, Lynda, now live in Indianapolis, where in 1992 he founded GM Supply Co., which provides abrasives-cutting tools to automotive and pharmaceutical manufacturers.

72 Caldwell Jones

Some of the details have been lost in time, but this much is clear: no sooner did the 76ers fly back from Los Angeles on June 1, 1983—having completed a sweep of the Lakers to win the title the night before—than four team members felt a need to tend to one last matter.

Maurice Cheeks, Andrew Toney, Franklin Edwards, and Earl Cureton all made their way to the home former teammate Caldwell Jones maintained in town, despite being traded to the woeful Houston Rockets before the 1982–83 season. The deal, which also included a first-round draft pick, brought Moses Malone in return, and he proved to be the final piece to a championship puzzle. But it also brought great anguish, since Jones was beloved by his teammates and coaches.

Coach Billy Cunningham admired the way Jones sacrificed scoring in favor of dirty work like rebounding and defense. Cunningham thought of him as "a warrior," a guy who would play through injuries, and a guy who would do whatever it took to win. If that meant wrestling with Kareem Abdul-Jabbar in the low post, so be it. If that meant chasing Larry Bird around the perimeter, fine. No task was too menial for Caldwell.

His teammates took note of that: Caldwell, it seemed, never cared about how many points he scored, only whether the Sixers won or lost. And they revered him because he was a soothing presence in the locker room, a guy who treated everyone with respect. Nobody was cooler. Nobody was classier. Nobody reached out so much to his teammates, no matter where they stood in the pecking order.

Malone had once played with Jones in the ABA, with the Spirits of St. Louis, and also thought a great deal of him—so much so that according to former Sixers owner Harold Katz, Malone balked at signing a six-year, $13.2 million contract with the team when he learned that Caldwell was no longer on the roster. It took all of Katz's powers of persuasion to convince Malone to stay the course.

So while the Sixers breezed to 65 victories and won 12 of 13 postseason games, they never forgot about Caldwell. Which is why Cheeks, Toney, Cureton, and Edwards paid their visit immediately after the title was won. In some versions of the story, they cracked open cans of beer; in others, someone brought along a bottle of champagne. In some versions, they all stood in Caldwell's kitchen; in others they remained in his driveway.

What is certain is that they all raised a toast. "Now it's official," someone (likely Cureton) said.

Jones hailed from a family that was large in number and sheer size. He was one of eight children born to Caldwell Sr. and Cecilia in McGehee, Arkansas. The shortest was the lone daughter, Clovis, who stood 6'3". Caldwell Jr., a skinny 6'11", was one of five Joneses to play center at Albany (Georgia) State, where he averaged more than 21 points and 21 rebounds per game in his four years. He was also one of four to play in the NBA; the others were Wil, Major, and Charles.

Caldwell broke into pro ball with the ABA's San Diego Conquistadors, coached by Wilt Chamberlain. One day, according to a 1975 story by Joe Hamelin of the *San Diego Union*, the 37-year-old Chamberlain decided to suit up and show his players a thing or two. He demanded that they drive the lane and challenge him, one by one, and when they did, he would reject their shots with disdain.

All except Caldwell's. He drove in and rose up and up, throwing down on Wilt.

He averaged double figures in points and rebounds each of the three years he spent in the ABA, playing not only for the Conquistadors and Spirits but also the Kentucky Colonels. Then he landed with the Sixers when the ABA dissolved in 1976, becoming the ultimate teammate. Never again in his career (which lasted 14 more seasons) did he average more than 10 points a game; his NBA best was 9.9, with Houston in 1983–84. And only twice in the NBA portion of his career did he average more than 10 boards a game, both times in Philadelphia (11.9 in 1979–80 and 10.0 in 1980–81).

He was content to cede the spotlight to others during his six seasons with the Sixers, unbothered by the fact that other guys—guys like Julius Erving, George McGinnis, Doug Collins, and later Toney—put up big offensive numbers while he was left scrounging for scraps. "I enjoy winning," Jones said. "If I could score less and win, I was happy. Playing basketball's a lot more fun when you're winning."

Cunningham came to regard him as the team's most important player, because he always sacrificed so much. "Nobody notices him because he's quiet," Cunningham told *Sports Illustrated* in November 1979. "But he amazes me. He plays forward, he plays center. As long as I'm coaching and he's healthy, I want him with me."

That season ended with the Sixers losing in the Finals to the Lakers. Before Game 6, Jones found himself jumping center not against Abdul-Jabbar, who was injured, but rookie guard Magic Johnson. Caldwell won the tip. "It was," he later said, "about the only thing we got that night." Magic, in the first signature moment of his brilliant pro career, went for 42 points, 15 rebounds, and seven assists, as the Lakers clinched the series.

The Sixers lost again to the Lakers in the 1982 Finals, and the decision was made to shake things up. Darryl Dawkins, who throughout his seven years in Philadelphia had either joined Jones up front or alternated with him at center, was traded to New Jersey. And the Sixers signed Malone, the ultimate hard hat, to an offer sheet.

The Rockets had two weeks to either match the offer, let Malone walk, or arrange some other compensation. In time a deal was struck, much to Cunningham's chagrin. John Nash, the Sixers' assistant general manager at the time, said Katz agreed to send Jones and the first-rounder to Houston because he didn't want to pay Jones starter's money to back up Malone. Katz has said he wanted to keep Caldwell, but Houston was "adamant" about his inclusion in a package. Del Harris, who coached the Rockets at the time, has said Charlie Thomas, the team's owner, was going to let Malone walk. Thomas had paid less than $10 million to acquire the team; no way did he want to shell out $13 million for his best player.

"He was appalled and shocked," Harris said. "He determined to let him go."

So Caldwell wound up playing for a 14–68 team. "That one year felt like four years," he said. "Any time you're losing, it takes five to 10 years off your life."

After a while, the Rockets were counting down the quarters until season's end. And Jones' former team was storming toward a long-awaited title. He was genuinely happy for his friends, but he was sorely missed. "If there is an unfairness in life, it's that I have a ring from Philadelphia and Caldwell doesn't," Edwards said. "I remember telling Caldwell that, because he deserved to be there."

Cunningham went so far as to offer Jones his championship ring early in the 1983–84 season. Caldwell, true to his nature, turned it down.

Jones spent two years in Houston before going on to Chicago, Portland, and finally San Antonio. While his playing time may have decreased as the years passed, he was always regarded as the consummate professional, a guy who would practice hard and show the younger guys the ropes; he notably did that for a rookie named David Robinson in his final stop.

By then Caldwell was, at age 39, the oldest player in the league. "I guess that means I did something right," he told the *Los Angeles Times*' Thomas Bonk in May 1990. "Or else I'm very lucky. Or else someone is watching out for me."

Mostly, it meant the first of those things. And everyone was willing to drink to that.

73 Andrew Toney

Andrew Toney's career has been reduced to a series of snapshots, and faded ones at that.

Here's Andrew as a rookie guard with the Sixers in 1980, facing veteran Henry Bibby in a training-camp drill—and blowing past him, again and again. (No surprise, either; Toney was the rookie assigned to Bibby, meaning he had to perform all sorts of menial tasks for his more experienced teammate. Toney hated that, and exacted his revenge on the court.) Bibby was cut before the season started; Toney was on his way.

And here's Andrew trying to find his way to the visitors' locker room within Boston Garden for the first time. "Where the gym at?" he asked. Right, it was just a gym. Not the gritty cathedral made famous by Russell, Cousy, Bird, and company. Not the house of horrors where the hopes and dreams of so many teams (the Sixers foremost among them) had gone to die. To Andrew Toney it was just another gym, just another proving ground. Which explains in part why he played so well against the Celtics; he would quickly come to be known as "the Boston Strangler," a nickname previously held by former Sixer World B. Free.

And here's Toney, the ball in his hands, crouching before Lakers defensive stopper Michael Cooper on a Wednesday night in January 1983 and ignoring Coach Billy Cunningham, who had angrily sprung from his seat: *What was Andrew doing?* Moments before Cunningham had painstakingly drawn up a play for the closing seconds of overtime. And Toney had instead elected to freelance, certain that even on a team featuring Moses Malone and Julius Erving, he was the best option at that moment. And he was; he banked in the game-winning 12-foot jumper over a tangle of hands to win it.

Those who knew him, watched him, or played alongside him remember him as relentless, fearless. As a guy wholly unimpressed by lofty reputations, seemingly impossible circumstances, and, at times, authority figures. Had fate (and poor feet) not intervened, he would have been an all-time great, a Hall of Famer. As it stands, he was a comet, flashing through the NBA firmament for just eight

Toney (22), "the Boston Strangler," takes off.

seasons before his injuries ultimately did him in. He was forced to retire in 1988, at the age of 30.

Which led to one more snapshot: Andrew Toney, dressed in a green Philadelphia Eagles jersey (the No. 81 of Terrell Owens, who then played for the Birds) and carrying a beer while making his way to his seat in the Georgia Dome's lower stands, just behind the Eagles' bench, before a game against the Atlanta Falcons in September 2005. He was living in that area with his wife (and still does), and working as a middle school health teacher—a job he no longer holds. He had said then that he golfed but could no longer run very far before his feet gave out; his paunch confirmed as much.

He had become an afterthought—"the John F. Kennedy or the James Dean of Philadelphia sports," as Tim Malloy, the Sixers' former assistant group sales director, once described him. "He's frozen in time," Malloy said, "and still carries the Boston Strangler image. No one sees him or can get to him, so he remains forever raining jump shots on the Celtics' heads."

In reality Toney was an equal-opportunity assassin, shooting down one opponent after another; Cooper once called him "one of the most fearless scorers" and a guy who "could have easily led the league" in that department, had the Sixers not had such a star-studded roster. But the games against the archrival Celtics were so intense, so fraught with meaning, that his heroics were magnified. He lit them up for 35 points during a game his rookie year, poured in 25 in a single quarter in a game his second season, and had games of 39 and 34 in the 1982 Eastern Conference Finals—the latter in a memorable Game 7 victory by the Sixers, after they coughed up a 3–1 lead in the best-of-seven set.

The Celtics tried one defender after another against him over the years: M.L. Carr (whom the other Sixers dubbed "Lunchbox," since Andrew so often ate his lunch)...Chris Ford...Gerald Henderson...Quinn Buckner...Danny Ainge. They even tried Larry Bird on him at times. Nothing really worked until they acquired the late Dennis Johnson, one of the finest perimeter defenders of his era, before the 1983–84 season.

Years after his retirement Ainge would admit that Toney "struck fear into [him] like no one else." While Ainge regarded Michael Jordan, Magic Johnson, and Isiah Thomas as the greatest players he faced, Toney was "not far off." To put it in an updated context, he was a bigger, stronger, more efficient version of Allen Iverson. Like Iverson, Toney could score inside and outside, but he took better shots and made a higher percentage of them. Also like Iverson, he had a disdain for defenders.

"He was mean," former teammate Franklin Edwards once said of Toney. "On the court he had a nasty attitude. He felt if you couldn't guard him, you shouldn't be on him.... I don't think there was such a thing as overconfidence when it came to him. He believed he could make every shot. He's the only guy I ever played with who believed he could make every shot."

Toney summed up his approach perfectly when reporters converged upon him after that January 1983 victory over the Lakers: "I know I can't make 'em all, but I'll never shy away from taking 'em."

While Toney had played at a relatively unknown school (Southwestern Louisiana), he was hardly a secret to NBA scouts. Sixers sleuth Jack McMahon went down to look at him in a tournament and didn't bother to stick around for the second night; he had seen quite enough in the opening round. He was certain Toney was going to be a big-time pro, that he would be a handful for any defender.

It was far less certain whether Toney would still be on the board when the Sixers made the eighth overall selection in the 1980 draft. The Nets also liked him, and had the two picks immediately before Philadelphia's. But New Jersey opted for North Carolina forward Mike O'Koren at No. 6 and Duke center Mike Gminski at No. 7, leaving Toney available.

Andrew Toney would be a Sixer after all.

"I want you to know we're giving you an NBA title," Nets general manager Charlie Theokas said over the phone to his Sixers counterpart, Pat Williams. "When you win it, order a ring for me."

The title came in Toney's third season, 1982–83. That was also the first of two straight seasons he made the All-Star team. But after the 1984–85 season his feet began acting up, and the slide toward oblivion commenced. All that remained were the snapshots, and faded ones at that.

74 Hinkie's Rebuild

Sam Hinkie does most of his work underground. His public appearances are few and far between, his interviews infrequent. When the 76ers' general manager finally emerged from his bunker the day after the NBA Draft in June 2014, he said he was "borderline shocked" at how patient the team's fan base had been during the rebuilding process he was directing.

At that point, however, he was asking everyone to wait some more.

The Sixers had gone 19–63 during the 2013–14 season, at one point losing 26 straight games to equal not only the NBA record for consecutive defeats, but a record for the four major American sports. That was hardly an accident, as Hinkie had stripped the club of most of its proven talent (and indeed stripped some more at the trading deadline in February), the idea being that the payoff would come in a draft deep in talent—a draft in which the Sixers held the Nos. 3 and 10 selections.

Instead Hinkie netted two 20-year-olds with those two picks: Kansas center Joel Embiid and Croatian forward Dario Saric, neither of whom figures to play for the team in 2014–15 (and in Saric's case, the 2015–16 season either). The Camaroon-born Embiid already has a repaired right foot, and Saric has a restrictive contract (in Turkey).

If Hinkie believed he was doing the right thing, others weren't so sure.

"Tanks Again?" screamed a back-page headline in the *Philadelphia Daily News* the day after the draft.

The night before, a reporter named Matt Moore assessed the Sixers' draft as follows on CBSSports.com: "GET YOUR SEASON TIX NOW! CAN'T REBUILD FOREVER!" All caps, with exclamation points.

Sports Illustrated's Chris Mannix said on the television program *Olbermann* that NBA general managers were texting him, wondering if Hinkie has a 10-year contract. (He doesn't.) CSNPhilly.com's John Gonzalez and the *Daily News*' Dick Jerardi were yelling at each other on TV the day after the draft, with Gonzalez backing Hinkie and Jerardi arguing that the Sixers might have at least chosen one player—say, Doug McDermott, Creighton's high-scoring forward—capable of taking the court for them in 2014–15.

On that same program, there was a fan poll that showed nearly an even split between those fans who gave the Sixers an A for the draft and those who gave them an F.

Hinkie seemed impervious to the heat. In his news conference the day after the draft, he breezily explained that he was trying to acquire the best players possible, that the team was seeking to become "championship caliber."

"It doesn't happen overnight," he said.

His manner wasn't so much smug as supremely confident; he seemed to *know* that this approach, as unconventional as it is, is going to work.

"He has a plan, and he's going to work the plan through," said Houston Rockets assistant coach Chris Finch, who worked alongside Hinkie during his eight years with that organization. "And the plan is about winning a championship.... I'm not sure Sam concerns himself with winning 33 or 36 games [a year]. What matters is laying the foundation for a championship team."

Embiid is a curious case. While he had only begun playing basketball in 2011, his stock soared during the 2013–14 season, the only one he played at Kansas, to the point that he came to be regarded as a more promising pro than even his teammate, forward Andrew Wiggins, and Duke forward Jabari Parker. The week before the draft Cleveland, holding the top pick, was said to be leaning heavily toward Embiid.

Then it was revealed that Embiid had suffered a stress fracture in his right foot that would require surgery. The Cavaliers' thinking changed. So too did Hinkie's. "I sniffed opportunity the moment it happened," he said.

So who is Sam Hinkie? A product of Marlow, Oklahoma, a town of 5,000 in the southern part of the state, and Oklahoma University, where as a senior *USA Today* named him one of the nation's top 60 undergrads.

He earned his MBA at Stanford, interned with the San Francisco 49ers and Houston Texans, and then landed with the Rockets, rising to the position of assistant general manager. In a profile of Hinkie that appeared in the *Oklahoman* in March 2014, writer Berry Tramel spoke with a man named Duane Lovett, who had been one of Hinkie's best friends growing up.

"There's lots of smart people," Lovett told Tramel. "But he thinks outside the box. That's kind of him in a nutshell. [He] doesn't do things the way everybody else does."

Now he is doing it again. It remains to be seen if it is the proper course.

75 Leon Wood

Leon Wood will forever be remembered as one of many wasted first-round draft picks made by the Sixers. He'll forever be the point guard they chose when they could have taken John Stockton. The guy who played for six teams in six NBA seasons before flaming out.

But he will also be remembered as the guy who successfully reinvented himself, for while his playing career did not amount to much, he found his niche in the NBA as a referee in 1995 and has served in that capacity ever since. And making it in the league, he told the *Los Angeles Times* that year, was always his "No. 1 priority."

"Even though I didn't become an All-Star," he told the *Times*, "I did get to the main show."

His selection by the Sixers in 1984, which appears ridiculous now, is defensible. He had assembled a glittering résumé, averaging a California-prep-record 33.7 points per game at Santa Monica's St. Monica High (41.5 as a senior) and setting school records for points (1,876) and assists (744) at Cal State Fullerton before making the 1984 Olympic team, on which he won a gold medal alongside Michael Jordan.

The Sixers, an aging team at that point in their history, had the Nos. 5 and 10 picks in the 1984 draft, both the result of adroit trades they had pulled off six years earlier. The first came from the Clippers in exchange for World B. Free, the second from Denver (along with Bobby Jones) for George McGinnis.

Charles Barkley was chosen at No. 5, and Wood was the pick at No. 10. (Stockton, a future Hall of Famer, went 16th, to Utah.) But the Sixers had a very crowded backcourt, veterans Maurice Cheeks, Andrew Toney, and Clint Richardson having been joined a year earlier by Sedale Threatt. In 1991 Wood told the *Los Angeles Times* he felt he had been "picked by the wrong team," and because of that had been "playing catch-up ever since."

Sixers general manager Pat Williams cut to the heart of the matter when Wood was traded to Washington in January 1986, having appeared in 67 games during a season-plus in Philadelphia: "Defense will always be an area of question in his game. He'll never be known as a great defensive player. Someday, maybe he could be adequate."

Wood's NBA career also included stops in New Jersey, San Antonio, Atlanta, and Sacramento; in all he averaged 6.4 points in 274 games. He also spent time overseas, and in the Continental Basketball Association. But by 1994 he was finished as a player. Coaching was an option, but a friend suggested officiating instead, and he began working rec leagues, high school games, pro-am leagues, whatever.

According to the *Los Angeles Times*, the NBA spotted him at a referee camp in Texas. Wood worked 24 games as a replacement ref when the regular officials were on strike early in the 1995–96 season and was the only replacement official retained the following year. He became the third ex-player to make such a transition, joining Stan Stutz, who did so in the '50s, and Bernie Fryer, who did so in the '80s. (Haywoode Workman would later follow them.)

There was, of course, an adjustment. Wood told the *Times* in 2009 that at first he sensed some paranoia from the coaches who had cut him during his playing career. "They were thinking they weren't going to get the calls," he said, "and I said, 'It's not like that.'"

Others, like Washington forward Harvey Grant, thought Wood might be giving former teammates a break. Grant told *Sports Illustrated* in April 1997 that the previous season Wood worked a game between the Bullets and Jordan's Chicago Bulls. And, Grant said, "Michael committed a foul right in front of him, and he didn't call it. I said, 'Oh, you and Michael played in the Olympics, so you're not going to call that, huh?' He got a big charge out of that."

Jordan getting away with one? Not exactly a novelty.

But Wood's path to the "main show" assuredly was.

76 Johnny Dawkins

The ovation welled up around Maurice Cheeks as he was introduced in the Spectrum the night of November 17, 1989. And Cheeks, looking odd in the silver and black of the San Antonio Spurs, stood on the court and studied his shoe tops.

Surely he was thinking one thing, and one thing only: *Please stop.*

The fans, having risen to their feet, would not. He gave the smallest of waves, and still they roared. They went on for more than a minute, wrapping up only when the public-address announcer continued on with pregame introductions.

Little Mo was back. Back where he belonged. Back where he had served loyally and well for 11 years, before being banished in the clumsiest of trades.

Such was his appeal that Johnny Dawkins, the man who replaced him at point guard with the Sixers (having come the other way in that deal with the Spurs just a few months earlier), was left to battle a ghost during his five years in town. Not that night, though. That night he lined up against the flesh-and-blood Cheeks and outplayed him, collecting 20 points and 11 assists in a Sixers victory, to Cheeks' 15 and seven.

But for a sizable portion of his Sixers tenure, Dawkins fought the perception that he could never be the guy the fans had grown to know and love. The guy who had been there during the glory days. The guy who had pranced downcourt to begin the celebration of the 1982–83 title.

Eventually the talk quieted, partly because Dawkins proved to be a capable player, helping the Sixers win an Atlantic Division title in his first year with the team, partly because of other circumstances. He injured a knee four games into the 1990–91 season, sat out the rest of the year, and was never the same. The team crumbled. Guys were sent packing—Charles Barkley and the rest. Before anybody knew it, Dawkins was the third guard on a team that was coached, allegedly, by Doug Moe.

He spent the 1994–95 season with Detroit before packing it in, the consensus being that he never quite lived up to the promise he had shown at Duke. And he sure as heck didn't make anyone forget Maurice Cheeks, who remains a beloved figure in Philadelphia to this day.

Outwardly, Dawkins always handled the whole matter with aplomb. The night of Cheeks' homecoming he showed the proper amount of respect and expressed relief when it was over. "I'm glad he only comes once a year," Dawkins said, "just like Christmas."

And late that season, he told Jere Longman, then of the *Philadelphia Inquirer*, "Everyone likes Mo, but I think they have respect for me because I've shown I play hard and I'll play hurt. If I continue to do that, I may not win 'em all over, but I'll win enough over."

Which is pretty much how it went. He was never embraced, but neither did he warrant Shawn Bradley–level derision.

In time Dawkins returned to Duke as an assistant coach, spending a decade working under Mike Krzyzewski and helping the Blue Devils win a national championship in 2000. There were other moments to cherish, as on February 19, 2006, when guard J.J. Redick stood poised to break the school's scoring career record, which was held by Dawkins.

Twenty years earlier, with Dawkins about to surpass the mark held by Mike Gminski—later a teammate in Philadelphia—Gminski, then early in his NBA career, sent Dawkins a handwritten letter.

"And," Gminski said in January 2013, "I've probably written two or three of those in my life."

Gminski, now an accomplished broadcaster, was in Cameron Indoor Stadium to call the Duke-Miami game the night Redick stood on the precipice. Beforehand Gminski and Dawkins crossed paths in a hallway beneath the stands.

Dawkins reached into his pocket and produced the letter the older man had written him, all those years before. Then he reached into another pocket and pulled out another envelope.

"This," he said, "is the letter I've written to J.J., when he breaks my record tonight."

Gminski remembers that his broadcast position was behind the Duke bench. When Redick put up the shot that would give him the record, Dawkins rose out of his seat. So too did Gminski. "All three of us were dead on-line, looking at what was going on," Gminski said. "It was just a surreal moment."

Dawkins left in 2008 to take the job as Stanford head coach, where he has experienced tough sledding. The Cardinal won 26 games and an NIT championship in 2011–12, and made an NCAA Tournament appearance in his sixth season on the job in 2013–14—something they did three times in four years under Dawkins' predecessor, Trent Johnson.

Once again, Johnny Dawkins has a tough act to follow. But it's not as if he hasn't been in that position before.

77 Rick Mahorn

Before 1989, all of Mike Gminski's meetings with Rick Mahorn had been on the court, none of them pleasant. "I hated him so bad for eight years, it wasn't even funny," Gminski recalled in 2013. "If he were drowning, I would have stomped on his head and put him underwater."

Mahorn was one of the most feared men in the NBA, a wide-bodied forward who tested the limits of the rulebook, and his opponents' patience. He pushed and shoved, elbowed and kneed, clutched and grabbed. He had been, with burly running mate Jeff Ruland, one-half of the McFilthy/McNasty combination in Washington (a designation dreamed up by Johnny Most, the Celtics' craggy broadcaster), and one of many Bad Boys in Detroit, where the Pistons made intimidation an art form.

But right before the 1989–90 season he became a Sixer. The Pistons, fresh off a championship, exposed him to the expansion draft and the Minnesota Timberwolves took him, only to balk at his salary demands and trade him. Once he was in Philadelphia, attitudes toward him immediately changed: sure, Mahorn might be an SOB, but now he was *their* SOB.

Still, bridges needed to be built, and Mahorn knew it. So early in the 1989–90 season he had lunch with Gminski, the Sixers center, and told him to forget about the past, that they were now teammates and he would always have his back. "From that day forward," Gminski said, "he became one of my best friends in the world. He was an unbelievable teammate."

The star of that team, Charles Barkley, had always been friendly with Mahorn, and others besides Gminski quickly warmed to him. "Hated him before he got there, loved him while he was there," guard Hersey Hawkins said. "Great teammate. As physically intimidating as he was on the court, he was just as nice off the court."

The team meshed beautifully, en route to an Atlantic Division championship. The defense made the kind of improvement that might be expected with a guy like Mahorn around, but was better at the other end of the court, too. Suddenly opponents, presented with a front line of Barkley, Gminski, and Mahorn, were forced to defend Gminski with a small forward, knowing that a center or power forward would have to play Barkley, who stood a shade under 6'5" but played much bigger. And Hawkins, a gifted shooter, would spend each game night running his defender off Mahorn's screens. "He took pride in the fact that he would get you open," Hawkins said.

Barkley and Mahorn were given a cute nickname—"Thump and Bump"—but they were close with Gminski as well, so much so that Barkley came up with the idea that all three of them should get their ears pierced, should the club win 10 in a row. They reeled off 12 straight victories, and Mahorn and Gminski kept their vow. But Barkley put it off while he was in Miami for the All-Star Game, and only made good when his two teammates dragged him to some kiosk in some mall in New Jersey.

What they didn't know was that they had to leave the studs in for a time in order to maintain the piercings. The problem was, NBA rules prohibited players from wearing jewelry during games, so they had to remove their earrings beforehand, and trainer Tony Harris had to jam them back in their ears afterward. "He had to do that the whole rest of the year," Gminski said. "There was a price to be paid for that bet."

Mahorn was ejected from four games that year, fewer than usual for a player whose reputation for thuggery had been cemented on December 18, 1982, when as a Washington Bullet he wiped out the Sixers' top three guards with blind screens. According to the account by Phil Jasner, the *Philadelphia Daily News'* late beat writer, Andrew Toney suffered a bruised shoulder, Maurice Cheeks was knocked woozy, and Clint Richardson was left with a welt on his head.

The Sixers, early in their run to the championship, were outraged. "This is vicious, the way he's doing it," general manager Pat Williams told Jasner. "It makes my blood boil, it's so wrong.… He's established himself as a dirty player."

Coach Billy Cunningham thought it likely that Mahorn was going to end someone's career, and was bothered by the fact that he seemed to derive such pleasure from seeing opponents sprawled on the floor. "Someday," Cunningham told Jasner, "someone is going to get him."

And before the teams met the following month, Jack McMahon, the grandfatherly assistant coach, said Mahorn's antics had made him "the angriest I've been in 10 years."

"If I was younger, I'd have been out on the court," he told Jasner. "There's just something about the guy's manner that really bothers me. It's as if he enjoys it. There's something wrong with that."

There were other years, other incidents. In his final year with the Pistons Mahorn dropped Mark Price, Cleveland's star guard, well off the ball, prompting howls of protest. And there were times he embraced his reputation as an enforcer, other times when he emphasized that there was much more to him than that.

In a 1989 piece that appeared in the *Los Angeles Times*, he bragged about the night he took out the Sixers' backcourt, but then dismissed his reputation as "media hype."

"When I leave the court, I'll pet your dog, I'll kiss your daughter," he said. "I won't sit and call everybody names."

That 1989–90 season, one of two he spent in Philadelphia, he was a finalist for the J. Walter Kennedy Citizenship Award, for his work with the Special Olympics in Philadelphia. It was also noted that he had outfitted a youth basketball league in Detroit and that he had continued to provide underprivileged kids with tickets to

Pistons games. (A few years later Sam Smith, then of the *Chicago Tribune*, wrote that Mahorn would collect the gift certificates he received for appearing on pre- or postgame shows and then buy coats and anonymously donate them to the Salvation Army.)

So there was more to Rick Mahorn than met the eye. And late in the 1989–90 season, there was blessedly less. The Sixers secured the Atlantic Division championship with a victory over the Pistons at the Palace of Auburn Hills, a game marred in the closing seconds by a wild brawl notably featuring Barkley and Detroit center Bill Laimbeer.

And not featuring Rick Mahorn.

78 Rick Mahorn on the 1989–90 Team

Rick Mahorn doesn't remember much about the prank he participated in playing on Manute Bol after he joined the team for the 1990–91 season, but he remembers having fun on those Sixers teams from 1989 to 1991.

In fact, the 1989–90 team, which won the Atlantic Division title, was his most enjoyable season in basketball. And that's saying something, considering he won an NBA title in 1989 with the Detroit Pistons.

"It was more fun playing with Charles Barkley and the boys," said Mahorn in January 2014. "I'm telling you, I get the biggest smile on my face because that was a brotherhood. I can name everybody on that team and tell you where they are right now. We stayed that close."

Teams could only protect eight players in the '89 expansion draft, and Detroit left Mahorn unprotected and Minnesota selected him. The Timberwolves refused to pay his salary demands and Philadelphia traded for him.

Much like the 1993 Phillies, which no one expected to do well but who made it to the World Series before losing to Toronto, there were no expectations for the 1989–90 76ers. They were a unique collection of talent. There was Ron Anderson, Scott Brooks, Johnny Dawkins, Mike Gminski, Hersey Hawkins, Derek Smith, Bob Thornton, and, of course, Charles Barkley.

Anderson, whom Mahorn called "the Quiet Assassin," came to the team in a trade from Indiana. Brooks was a tenacious little backup point guard. Smith, much like Anderson, was tough as nails and believed he should be starting, would not back down from anyone. Dawkins, who replaced fan favorite Maurice Cheeks at point guard, formed a dynamic young backcourt known as Dawkins and Hawkins with Hersey Hawkins,. Thornton was a seldom-used backup center known as "Vanilla Thunder."

"I remember times when we'd go on the road and we'd all go to each other's room," said Mahorn, now a radio announcer for the Detroit Pistons. "The guards would come to my room. They'd knock on my door. They'd fight. We'd wrestle. They'd try to push the door open. I'd push the door. It was Hersey Hawkins, Johnny Dawkins, and Scottie Brooks. They'd charge room service on my room, or we'd order movies, or meet down in the restaurant, and every time, it was always Hawk who had to pay. Whose time is it to pay? It was always Hawk's turn. Oh, gosh, that was just fun."

Mahorn seemed to get the best out of Barkley, serving as sort of a big brother, often motivating and challenging the Hall of Fame forward. Barkley averaged 25.2 points, 11.9 rebounds, 3.9 assists, and 1.9 steals per game during the 1989–90 season. Mahorn believes the league MVP in 1989–90 should have gone to Barkley, not Magic Johnson.

Barkley had Moses Malone, but he often said Moses was like a father to him. He had Julius Erving, but Dr. J was more of an elder statesman—not to mention he conducted himself differently on and off the court compared to Sir Charles. What he had in Mahorn was someone close to his age (Barkley was 26 and Mahorn 31) who was an equal and had a track record as a winner.

"It was more of a mutual respect, because I had to check Charles Barkley. And if you are checking Charles, it was like playing my alter ego, who's a very talented guy," Mahorn said about his relationship with Barkley. "He could flat out play basketball. He was special. Oh, Lord, glad I had a chance to play with that dude. That dude was badass."

But Barkley needed to be motivated, and Mahorn knew exactly how to light a fire under the superstar. They communicated well. But the talks were normally more about challenging Barkley to be great. "He'd do some things like say, 'I'm so tired tonight.' I'd be like, 'Boy, I did the same shit you did last night. What do you mean you're tired?'" Mahorn said. "'All right, I can do it,' he'd say."

Mahorn used teammates who were not as talented as Barkley to challenge him. He would have Thornton bust on Barkley, which got the superstar mad and caused him to practice with the team.

"Charles didn't want to practice and I'd say, 'B.T. [Thornton], get 'im,' and he'd say, 'Charles, you ain't shit. I'll bust your ass, Charles Barkley,'" Mahorn said. "Next thing you know, Charles would go in and put his practice stuff on and we'd be going to war. I mean, our practices were warlike.

"Then one game we played the Knicks, up at the Garden. We wanted to see how many dunks we could do on Pat Ewing. I told him I could get three on him. He said, 'I'm gonna get four.' You watch that game, man, we were trying to kill Ewing. I got him from the free-throw line, then Charles got him from the free-throw line, off a free throw.

"One day, he was just cussing me out. We were at the free-throw line and he says, 'I'm bored.' I said, 'Fuck you, you're bored.' We started cursing each other out. We were across from each other during free throws and he was like, 'Fuck you.' 'No, fuck you.' People thought we were mad at each other, but it was more like getting your mind right. It made it fun. It wasn't a game. It was the fun of playing the game."

And that 1989–90 team had a lot of fun playing the game. The Sixers finished with a 53–29 record and at one point won 12 straight games and advanced to the second round of the playoffs.

The success was unexpected. The previous year the team had a respectable 46–36 record. They finished second in the Atlantic, but were swept 3–0 by the Knicks in the first round of the playoffs.

In both 1990 and '91 the Sixers faced the Michael Jordan–led Chicago Bulls in the second round of the playoffs and lost to them, the eventual NBA champions, in both seasons. It would be the first two of six titles Chicago would claim in the 1990s. But losing two years in a row to the Bulls didn't sit well with Mahorn.

"[We lost] because Charles didn't hit his friend [Jordan]," Mahorn said in a matter-of-fact way. "He didn't hit his friend, so we didn't go nowhere. At the time, that's when Charles, as a basketball player—it was more of a friendship. I told him in Detroit I still had friends, but I hit 'em every day. They'd be my friends after the game, not before or during.

"Missing Derek Smith [who was injured] in that 1990 playoff series, that hurt a little bit, because he didn't care about Michael Jordan. His attitude was, *I'm Derek Smith and I can play, too.*"

Mahorn remembers laughing a lot. He's reminded of the bond every time he looks in the mirror. More than 20 years later, he still has an earring, compliments of that 12-game win streak. He said Gminski, known as G-Man, and Barkley also got their left ears pierced.

"Charles said something one night with Gminski and me," Mahorn recalls. "Charles said, [Mahorn changes his voice to imitate Barkley] 'Yeah, if we win 10 games in a row, we are all going to get earrings.' Yeah, right [Mahorn rolls his eyes].

"Next thing you know, we win [12] in a row and it was the All-Star break. Everybody was waiting until the break. We wanted to see who had their earring in their ear. The G-Man had one in his ear. I had one in mine and Charles had one in his. It was that bond. You look and we still have rings in our ears. My mother said, 'You are 30 years old and you are getting an earring in your ear?' I said, 'Yeah.'"

Shawn Bradley

As wrong as the 76ers were proven to be in picking Shawn Bradley second overall in the 1993 draft, they were not alone. A great many personnel men throughout the NBA viewed Bradley as a unique talent, as a 7'6" center who possessed guard skills and would thus revolutionize his position, if not the game itself.

Yes, there were caveats. Everyone seemed to agree that it would take time for Bradley to develop. But few believed he would be the bust he ultimately became. Washington general manager John Nash, the former Sixers assistant GM, told the *Philadelphia Daily News* six weeks before the draft that while Bradley needed work, he might very well become "a player who makes the All-Star Game from 1997 through the year 2003." Shortly before that, Sacramento Kings general manager Jerry Reynolds told the *Philadelphia Inquirer* that within five years he might become "a seven foot six Bill Walton." And Golden State coach/vice president Don Nelson told the *Inquirer* Bradley was "Manute Bol with skills."

"He'd be my No. 1 pick," Celtics scout Rick Weitzman told the *Daily News*.

Sure, there were some dissenting voices, like that of Minnesota Timberwolves coach Sidney Lowe, who told the *Daily News* that

Bradley was "just another player." But the consensus was that in time Bradley was going to be great.

The Sixers were so eager to take him that they made it known they would put the kibosh to a rumored trade between Orlando and Golden State, holders of the first and third picks, respectively—one in which the Magic would choose Bradley and ship him to the Warriors (as Nelson coveted him) for the man who would be taken third, Anfernee Hardaway. But Sixers owner Harold Katz announced that his team would select Hardaway if those two teams attempted to consummate that deal.

As it was, Orlando took Chris Webber (later named Rookie of the Year) and shipped him to Golden State for Hardaway. The Sixers took Bradley, provoking giddiness among their front-office types. Then–general manager Jim Lynam told the *Daily News* on June 30, the night of the draft, that there were "high-fives, the whole bit. Harold [Katz] in the air? Yes."

There were few smiles after that. Bradley averaged 9.7 points, 7.5 rebounds, and 3.2 blocked shots per game in two-plus years with the team, and 8.1, 6.3, and 2.5, respectively, in a 12-year career that also included stops in New Jersey and Dallas.

It is not mere hindsight to note that there were ominous signs even before he was drafted. Bradley, who grew up on a Utah cattle ranch, put up impressive numbers against some of that state's smaller high schools. He did have a decent season at Brigham Young, averaging 14.8 points, 7.7 boards, and 5.3 blocks, and his 177 total rejections broke an NCAA freshman record. But in his lone appearance in Philadelphia that season, he was outplayed by a LaSalle center named Milko Lieverst.

Yes, Milko Lieverst.

Bradley went on a Mormon mission to Australia for the next two years, during which he seldom played basketball. As he told the *Philadelphia Inquirer* shortly before the draft, "I didn't want to get into shape, because that's not what I was there for."

Lynam, in a 2013 interview with *Philadelphia Daily News* columnist John Smallwood, took special note of the latter red flag: "His body of work at BYU was no question that of a top, top prospect. What was very difficult to understand was his two-year hiatus—not that he went on a mission, but that by his own admission during that two-year period he did literally nothing athletically. Zero.

"That gave [Katz] pause. He couldn't understand that. When we asked him what he did to stay in shape, he looked us right in the face and said, 'Nothing.' He said he was doing his mission. [With] the benefit of hindsight now, that was the missing piece of the puzzle."

The Sixers picked him anyway. They picked him ahead of not only Hardaway but also future star Jamal Mashburn. They picked him with the idea that they could make him bigger and stronger. They picked him, and then signed him to an eight-year, $44 million contract.

They pleaded patience at the time, saying it would take Bradley three years to develop, but few people exhibited any. He heard his first boos by the tail end of his rookie year. He was buried by both newspaper columnists (the *Daily News'* Bill Conlin labeled him "the Sixers' $492,000-an-inch mistake") and talk-radio hosts ("The opinion is that he's a wuss," WIP's Al Morganti told the *Sporting News*) by the following summer. By his second season there were reports that the Sixers were trying to trade him, and early in his third, they did peddle him, to New Jersey for Derrick Coleman.

He had played at somewhere between 205 and 210 pounds in his lone year at BYU, and claimed to weigh 248 when he returned from his mission. The Sixers, wanting to bulk him up more, gave him protein shakes and put him on a 7,000-calorie-daily diet; in the September 27, 1993, issue of *Sports Illustrated*, Bradley was photographed alongside piles of food. It made for a good story. It was also fiction. The *Daily News'* Mark Kram wrote in December of that year that Bradley was "not an enthusiastic participant" in that diet, a fact confirmed by Pat Croce, then the Sixers' strength-and-conditioning consultant, in a 2012 interview with this author.

Croce, who a few years later became the team's president, recalled walking into Bradley's house one winter's day, seeing "hundreds" of McDonald's coupons on his kitchen table and informing him in no uncertain terms he needed "to get the steaks and the protein and the things we're telling you [to eat]."

Croce said Bradley countered by saying that the coupons entitled him to various freebies.

"Come on—the guy just made $48 million [actually $44 million] and he's got to worry about free McDonald's coupons?" Croce said. "And they're not even healthy for him. And we've got to put weight on him."

After his rookie season—a season in which he averaged 10.3 points, 6.2 rebounds, and three blocks in 49 games, before dislocating his left kneecap—Bradley declined to remain in Philadelphia to work out, as Katz wanted. The team instead dispatched Lee Haney, an eight-time Mr. Olympia, to supervise Bradley's weightlifting sessions in Utah. And when he returned to Philadelphia, he spent 10 days learning low-post play from Kareem Abdul-Jabbar.

Bradley was routinely booed during his second season, but John Lucas, who succeeded Fred Carter as coach, remained in his corner. "The idea with Shawn was it was going to take three years," Lucas told the *Dallas Morning News*, "and it turned into three months. Let's get back to three years."

Bradley responded with some strong play late in that season. It appeared to be a turning point, a sign that better days were coming. But 12 games into the 1995–96 season he was traded.

In retrospect, Croce said, it's unlikely that Bradley ever could have been a dominant player. "Could it work that he played basketball? Yes," Croce said. "But to be what they thought he could be? To take him over Penny Hardaway? No. He didn't have the killer instinct to use that 7'6" frame to go and dominate. Just imagine if it was Moses [Malone] or Charles [Barkley] in that body. We wouldn't even be talking about Wilt."

80 Derrick Coleman

The *Wall Street Journal* reported in April 2010 that Derrick Coleman, who spent six of his 15 NBA seasons with the Sixers, had filed for Chapter 7 bankruptcy protection. On the face of it, it appeared to be another case of an athlete run amok, of a player too ill-disciplined for his own good. He was, after all, an icon of unmet potential during his playing career, a poster boy for petulance—literally, seeing as he was pictured on the cover of the January 30, 1995, issue of *Sports Illustrated*, and featured prominently in the accompanying story about troubled (and troublesome) NBA players.

As with a great many things about Coleman, the bankruptcy story is not as simple as it seems. While there was ample evidence of extravagance on his part—according to the *Journal* story his assets included three vintage cars, two Sea-Doo watercraft, and two chinchilla fur coats—his financial troubles could also be traced in part to his attempts to revitalize downtrodden parts of his native Detroit. In particular Coleman had sunk money into a strip mall called Coleman's Corner, which included four stores and opened in 2007.

Sports Illustrated's Selena Roberts reported in '08 that Coleman had sunk some $6 million of his own money into the place, and planned to invest much more. She also wrote that the mall represented the first retail center to open on Detroit's Linwood Street since it had been ravaged during rioting in 1967. The mall included a barber shop and a pizza franchise owned by Coleman and managed by one of his childhood friends, John Johnson.

Roberts made particular note of the fact that these businesses were not protected from ne'er-do-wells by steel bars or Plexiglas, as was commonly the case with other stores in inner-city Detroit. "As a kid I got tired of talking to people through glass," Coleman told her. "Why can't I have a conversation with you without talking through glass?"

Ominously, Roberts reported that Johnson expressed concern when Coleman refused to raise prices when food and fuel costs shot up. And that Johnson had seen a 2 percent drop-off in profits at the pizza shop when in the summer of 2007 Coleman decided to offer slices for a dollar apiece from 11:00 AM to 7:00 PM. Coleman nonetheless expressed optimism, saying he hoped to eventually own seven blocks in the area. He was, he said, following in the footsteps of fellow Syracuse alum Dave Bing, once a Hall of Fame guard with the Pistons and a man who was about to become Detroit's mayor.

By 2010, Bing was listed among the creditors to whom Coleman owed some $4.7 million, according to the *Journal*. Coleman, who during his NBA career had earned some $91 million according to basketball-reference.com, listed just $1 million in assets. The *Journal* reported that Coleman owed $1.3 million to Comerica Bank in connection with a lawsuit, $1 million to Thornburg Mortgage Home Loans, and $50,000 to Bing in connection with another loan.

Such a tale—one that began with such promise, only to end so badly. That too sounds much like Coleman's playing career. While he averaged 16.5 points and 9.3 rebounds per game in his 15 seasons, he never played like the top overall pick he had been in 1990. Rather, his time as a pro can best be summed up by something he said early in his career: "Whoop-de-damn-do"—his response after a reporter noted that New Jersey Nets teammate Kenny Anderson set a poor example by missing practice.

Coleman, who spent his first five seasons with the Nets, was also known during that time for refusing to check into a game on at least one occasion, and for handing coach Butch Beard a blank check to cover his fines, since he had no intention of adhering to the team's dress code.

New Jersey foisted him on the Sixers in 1995 in exchange for Shawn Bradley, a deal that benefited neither team. Coleman— seldom in shape, and often absent for extended stretches each season with one injury or another—departed in free agency in 1999, only to return three years later at the insistence of Coach Larry Brown, who remained more intrigued by Coleman's skillset than infuriated by his chronic underachieving.

His only significant stretch with the Sixers came late in the 2002–03 season, when Brown inserted him at center and he played a key role in the team's charge to the playoffs. But he departed Philadelphia after the following season, and was out of the league by January 2005.

So much promise. So little production.

So—whoop-de-damn-do.

 **Todd MacCulloch**

Todd MacCulloch would catch the ball, and finish plays around the basket. Sounds simple, but it really isn't. Not when defenders were lurking, defenders who were usually just as big as the seven-foot MacCulloch, and more athletic. But MacCulloch was remarkably efficient in his days as a 76er, so much so that Marc Zumoff, the team's television play-by-play guy, would marvel at the young center: why, it was as if time stood still when MacCulloch caught the ball in the post.

If only.

Time ran out on MacCulloch's career far sooner than he might have hoped. Forced to retire at age 27 because of a neuropathy in both feet, he played just four seasons in the NBA, three of them with the Sixers. The transition to civilian life was not an easy one; he said he "fell into some depression" and went through a period where he "didn't really want to get out of bed."

He leaned on his family, starting with his wife, Jana, as well his faith. The fans were supportive. And because he did some radio work alongside Sixers broadcaster Tom McGinnis for five years, he didn't have to cut the cord right away. He could still be around the team, still see some familiar faces, still travel to games.

In 2008 he and Jana gravitated back to Washington State, having bought a house on Bainbridge Island, just off the Pacific coast from Seattle, five years earlier. They started a family—the couple has two young children—and Todd was free to indulge his passion for pinball.

It was a game he had taken up as a kid in Winnipeg, Manitoba, and something he began to pursue more seriously as the years passed. He purchased three machines in 2001, after signing a six-year, $34 million free-agent contract with the New Jersey Nets, having been wooed after spending his first two NBA seasons with the Sixers. He returned to Philadelphia via trade one year later, and when his physical condition ended his career—he saw his last action during the 2002–03 season and officially retired in '04—he began to play more.

Ranked 187th in the world as of early 2013 (currently 211th), he competes in five or six big tournaments throughout the country each year. He is also part of leagues in Seattle and Vancouver, and is the owner of 30 machines. "I kind of thought I was alone at first, that there must be something wrong with me that I really enjoy these games," he said. "I've come to find out that there's several hundred of us around the country that really enjoy the game."

The stakes are not usually that high. He once won $18 at a tournament in Seattle, then had to pay $20 for parking. Another time he won $30 at an event, but had to use part of his winnings to get the trophy engraved. "I think that keeps the egos in check," he said.

He finds it interesting that whatever he might have gained from playing basketball—especially in the way of poise, seeing as he played for the Sixers in the '01 NBA Finals and the Nets in the '02 Finals—doesn't necessarily translate, that there were times when he first started playing competitive pinball that he "ended up sort of choking."

He did win a 2011 tournament in Chicago, though, whetting his appetite further. "I strive to have that feeling again," he said. "That was a good pinball feeling, but nothing like winning the Eastern Conference championship or something like that."

Like any kid growing up in Canada, he played hockey as a kid, but at age 12 took up other sports—volleyball and hoops foremost among them. Forced to choose between the two of them as a sophomore in high school, as he had shown an aptitude for both, he decided on basketball, since it was the game favored by his friends.

He wound up starring there, and at the University of Washington. A second-round pick of the Sixers in 1999, he stuck around because, again, he would catch the ball and finish plays around the basket. Even Allen Iverson, who wasn't always inclined to share the ball, would throw it to MacCulloch. (On the team bus one time, MacCulloch remembers Iverson saying that Todd's hands were so soft there surely must not be any bone in them.)

In four seasons, MacCulloch made 54 percent of his field-goal attempts. And while his numbers would not blow anyone away—he averaged six points and four rebounds per game—it was clear his career was on an uptick, that he would be a serviceable player for a long, long time.

It was during pickup games in the summer of 2002 that he first noticed the tingling in the bottom of his feet. It only grew worse as the year went on, and he was diagnosed with the neuropathies. The cause remains a mystery. Doctors' best guess is that they were brought on by Charcot-Marie-Tooth disease, a genetic neuromuscular disorder. But even now, nobody's completely sure.

What is clear is that the diagnosis hit MacCulloch like a ton of bricks. "Part of your identity, you lose it," he said. "Your career's falling apart, and even though I never totally defined myself as a basketball player, I realized once the game was gone that it defined a whole lot more of me than I realized. I tried to be well rounded and have other interests, but I realized pretty quickly that basketball was a huge part of who I was, and who I wanted to be. When it gets taken away for one reason or another and you don't get to end your career on your own terms, it leaves a real empty void of, really, sadness."

All these years later, his feet are only marginally better than they were. He swims and plays water polo. Best of all, he can chase his kids. But the game he played so simply, so efficiently, has been taken away from him for all time. And he must be content with another game, but it's harder than he might have imagined.

Eric Snow

When competing against prototypical NBA point guards, Eric Snow always seemed like a tugboat among jet skis—a bit of an optical illusion, perhaps, considering he was an exceedingly fit 6'3" and 204 pounds, and a fact ultimately proven irrelevant, since he lasted 13 years in pro ball, including six-plus with the Sixers.

And never mind that his jumper was never textbook pretty either. Or that his dribble appeared to be a tad high. He always seemed to make big shots, and he turned over the ball about as frequently as Dr. Oz wolfs down a Cinnabon.

There were times during his tenure in Philadelphia (1998–2004) when Snow was compared to Maurice Cheeks, the patron saint of selfless Sixers. Same position, right? But Cheeks was a borderline Hall of Famer, Snow a plugger—a guy who plugged a square peg (himself) into the round hole of the NBA. And for a very long time there was no dislodging him.

He had made it abundantly clear as to what he was about long before Game 5 of the 2001 Eastern Conference Finals. But that is the touchstone of his time with the Sixers, the night when every-one—most notably his wife, DeShawn—questioned whether he should play on a right ankle so mangled that before the game he was moving around like Fred Sanford. Only slower.

Naturally, Snow shot 7-for-9, nailing two essential jumpers in the final, frantic 1:47. The Sixers beat the Bucks by a point. And when Snow appeared in the interview room afterward he was wearing a protective boot that extended nearly to his knee. Then he explained that he knew he couldn't hurt himself any worse, so why not give it a shot? Besides, he added, "We may not get this opportunity again."

Turns out he was right. While the Sixers eliminated the Bucks, they ended that season by losing in the Finals to the Shaq-Kobe Lakers—no disgrace.

They had begun it some 11 months earlier, in the gym at the Philadelphia College of Osteopathic Medicine. That July day, a motley crew gathered for rookie camp—the usual flotsam and jetsam (though not Les Jepsen). And Eric Snow joined them.

Far from fearing that his ego might be bruised, he plunged right into drills, because that's what captains are supposed to do. And because he wasn't that far removed from being a fringe player himself; he came into the league as Gary Payton's caddy in

Seattle, then arrived in Philadelphia via trade midway through the 1997–98 season.

Snow talked that day at PCOM about setting an example, and setting a tone. "If there's anything I can do to help, I will," he said.

That might as well be his career epitaph. He was the ultimate team guy, manning the point alongside Allen Iverson and usually drawing the defensive assignment against bigger, more explosive shooting guards—and usually holding his own. No less a player than the aforementioned Kobe Bryant said Snow checked him as well as anyone.

Off the court he earned the J. Walter Kennedy Citizenship Award in 2005, founded the Shoot for the Moon Foundation (an organization dedicated to strengthening families and communities in his native northeast Ohio), and in 2012 donated $1 million toward the construction of a new YMCA in his hometown of Canton. All of which cannot erase the fact that two years earlier he divorced DeShawn, the mother of his three sons, shortly after fathering a child with another woman, but it at least offers the total picture.

The younger brother of Percy Snow, a Lombardi and Butkus Award–winning linebacker at Michigan State and member of the College Football Hall of Fame who later played in the NFL, Eric had also been a Pop Warner star. But he turned his back on football when he reached Canton McKinley High School, a perennial power, choosing instead to concentrate on hoops. "I was big into football then, no question," Snow later told *Sports Illustrated*, "but there was so much pressure because of Percy, I think it pushed me to basketball."

He did follow Percy to East Lansing, where he finished second all-time in assists, and was taken by Milwaukee in the second round of the 1995 Draft, then shipped immediately to Seattle. He backed up Payton for three years, then was shipped to the Sixers in January 1998 for a second-round draft pick. Expectations were not high; he had averaged fewer than 10 minutes a game during his time with the SuperSonics.

But it turned out he was the perfect complement to Iverson. As Snow told the *Philadelphia Inquirer* in January 1999, "His strengths are my weakness. He's an offensive player; I'm a defensive player. He's fast and flashy; I'm strong and physical. He's a scorer; I'm a stopper. And we feed off of each other that way."

He had jackhammered out a niche for himself, and he would not be expelled until new coach Jim O'Brien arrived in the summer of '04, bringing with him an offensive philosophy that called for more scoring from the point-guard spot. So Snow was traded to Cleveland, where he played four more seasons before a knee injury forced him to retire—proving once and for all that despite all appearances, he fit perfectly in the NBA.

83 Theo Ratliff

Theo Ratliff is the All-Star who never really was, the champion who might have been. He was injured and then traded during the Sixers' magical run to the 2001 NBA Finals, sacrificed in the deal that brought Dikembe Mutombo from Atlanta. Coach Larry Brown—focal point of Ratliff's momentary ire in the wake of the transaction—often said during the playoffs that Ratliff remained part of the team's success, but it wasn't quite true. Not by then.

Earlier? Absolutely. The Sixers were 36–14 in the games when Ratliff started at center that year, en route to 42–14. He established career highs in points (12.4), rebounds (8.3) and blocks (3.7), with the latter figure leading the league. The Eastern Conference coaches voted him onto the All-Star team, and when Alonzo Mourning was forced to skip the game with a kidney ailment, Brown, who also coached the East team, did not hesitate to name his own guy the starter.

But as Ratliff sat at a table in the ballroom of a Washington, DC, hotel two days before the All-Star Game, he was wearing a cast on his right wrist. All around him, each at his own table, were the other All-Stars, giving interviews to Media Day throng of reporters. There wasn't much traffic coming his way. He wasn't going to play in the game because of a stress fracture in that wrist, and though he didn't know it at that point, wouldn't play again that season. Nor would he ever make another All-Star team, despite playing through the 2010–11 season—16 years in all.

"I'll be positive," he said as he sat there that day, "because that's the only way I know how to be."

But circumstances were already beginning to align that would result in his ouster. Just two days later, in an unusually competitive All-Star Game, the East rallied from a 21-point fourth-quarter deficit to win, with Mutombo serving as backstop for a smallish team, grabbing 22 rebounds to abut the 25 points scored by the Sixers' Allen Iverson. Iverson was named MVP, and Brown began envisioning what it would be like to have a player like Mutombo on his team.

True, Brown was notorious for coveting other team's players, but there were ample reasons to want the 7'2" Mutombo, and they went beyond the health of Ratliff, who as it turned out would need surgery on his wrist two weeks later. There was also the thought that if the Sixers managed to come out of the East, they would face a team featuring a dominant big man (or two), whether it was Sacramento (Vlade Divac, Chris Webber), San Antonio (David Robinson, Tim Duncan), or the Lakers (Shaquille O'Neal).

Ratliff was, at 6'10", more a power forward masquerading as a center. He often made that work to his advantage, as he was long-legged and lithe, a breathtaking athlete who could outrun anyone at his position. In part because of him, the Sixers were the fastest team in the league. And while he was adept at swooping from the opposite side of the court to block some unsuspecting opponent's shot, the question remained as to whether he could stand toe to toe with some thumper in a playoff series.

Word got out that other teams, notably the Knicks, were interested in Mutombo. The Sixers' hand was forced. On February 22, they shipped Ratliff, Toni Kukoc, Nazr Mohammed, and Pepe Sanchez to the Hawks for Mutombo and Roshown MacLeod. It was a gut punch to Ratliff. "It's a dirty business," Ratliff told Phil Jasner, the late *Daily News* beat writer. "Sometimes I guess they have to do dirty things to make things happen like they want it to happen. Sometimes you just have to do dirty things in business."

While Ratliff mended the rest of that season (and much of the following one in Atlanta, when he was beset by hip and abdominal problems), the Sixers moved on, going 15–12 in the regular season with Mutombo (and 56–26 in all), then getting past Indiana, Toronto, and Milwaukee before losing to the Lakers in the Finals. And Shaq was dominant, despite Mutombo's presence.

Ratliff left behind whatever anger he might have felt and attended two Sixers home playoff games. The rest he watched on TV, telling the *Inquirer* it was an agonizing exercise. "My palms start sweating," he said.

Ratliff, who began his career in 1995 with Detroit, played with six other teams besides the Pistons, Sixers, and Hawks: Boston, Minnesota, San Antonio, Charlotte, Portland, and the Lakers. (He actually had a second tour of duty with the Sixers, too, in 2008–09.) He led the league in shot-blocking twice more, and since retiring in 2011 has set up an outfit called Future Phenom, which makes posters from athletes' photos.

According to the company's website, Ratliff was Defensive Player of the Year in 2003–04. That's not true, though that was one of the years he led the league in blocks, while playing for Atlanta and Portland. What is true is that he was a valuable player and a valued teammate for a long, long time. Not to mention a great fit in Philadelphia. Until it was decided that he wasn't.

84 George Lynch

"Play the right way" was the mantra George Lynch heard from his coach at North Carolina, the legendary Dean Smith, and again when he played for Larry Brown (UNC '63) in Philadelphia. There is a hint of hauteur to it—the Carolina Way is the only way?—but more than a little truth, since playing the right way involves playing hard, playing unselfishly, playing smart (and guarding your guy, of course).

"I wish I could have heard it every year I was playing," Lynch said.

That he did not is something of a regret, and indicative of the fact that he thought the wrong way, however briefly. Disgruntled with his contract, he asked the Sixers to trade him after the 2000–01 season—the year they lost to the Lakers in the Finals— and Brown reluctantly obliged him on the eve of the following campaign, sending him to the Hornets as part of a three-team deal.

Lynch lasted four more seasons (12 in all) before he had to retire due to foot problems, and it wasn't until 2012 that he was reintroduced to the play-the-right-way philosophy, when Brown, the newly hired coach at SMU, added him to his staff as the assistant strength-and-conditioning coach.

Looking back, Lynch wishes he had a mulligan, wishes he hadn't "let people get into [his] inner circle" before requesting a trade. "I let some people get in my ear that shouldn't have," he said, "so it was just a situation where I lost touch with what was really important—playing the game, playing for a great coach like Coach Brown."

After playing for the veteran's minimum of $550,000 in 1998–99, his first year with the Sixers, he re-signed with the team for $15 million over six years. The problems began when the team acquired Toni Kukoc from the Bulls during the 1999–2000 season. Kukoc, while more talented than Lynch offensively, did not turn out to be a threat to his job at small forward, since Kukoc's defense was lacking (*he didn't play the right way*). But he did make substantially more money than Lynch, something that did not escape the notice of Steve Kauffman, who had replaced Lee Fentress as Lynch's agent.

"I had signed a contract," Lynch said. "I should have just honored it." Instead, he asked out.

Three years earlier, he had made it quite clear he had wanted in. He was a free agent that summer—the summer of '98—having just completed his second year with Vancouver, after three with the Lakers. That also happened to be the year of the NBA lockout, so Lynch found his way back to Chapel Hill for the school's alumni game. There, he crossed paths with Larry Brown. Lynch had never met the man before, but he obviously knew his reputation and résumé. One of Brown's daughters, a UNC undergrad when Lynch was on campus, had years before raised the possibility of him playing for her dad.

So when Lynch found himself seated alongside Brown that day, he brought that up himself. "Save a spot on your roster for me," he said.

Brown did. Lynch, never a big scorer, became a key defender for the coach during his three years in town, one of the many blue-collar guys Brown arrayed around Allen Iverson. And it worked. Iverson scored big, everybody else took care of the grunt work, and the team won, attracting legions of admirers along the way. George

Karl, then coach of a Milwaukee club that would lose to the Sixers in the '01 Eastern Finals, called them "a proud team." The fans responded as never before, often threatening to blow the roof off the home arena during the run to the Finals.

Such a workmanlike approach took its toll, though. Lynch broke his left foot in the fourth game of the 2001 Eastern Semifinals, against Toronto, and didn't return until Game Four of the Finals, and then only in a limited role. The series had already begun to slip away from the Sixers by then, and they would fall in five games. That was due in no small part to the play of Los Angeles stars Kobe Bryant and Shaquille O'Neal, but also because guys like Rick Fox and Robert Horry made significant contributions—and the latter were guys Lynch would normally guard. It led him to wonder if things might have been different (a little different, anyway), had he been healthy.

"If I was able to play, I'm not sure if we would have won it [all], but we would have won more than one game," he said.

That was the end for him in Philly. His career came to a halt in 2005, because of plantar fasciitis in both feet. "I was out there playing some games, and I couldn't feel my feet," he said. "I couldn't feel myself walking. I knew I was moving, but you couldn't feel the bottom of your feet."

There were rumors he would be reunited with Brown, who had moved on to coach the Knicks, but that never panned out. Lynch instead became a personal trainer in Dallas. He founded a youth basketball program. Then he went to Cal-Irvine as the strength-and-conditioning coach before hearing his old coach's siren song once again.

As always, it was irresistible.

85 Aaron McKie

More than once in his life Aaron McKie has wondered where he fit in. It was true when he was a teenager and he found his North Philadelphia home padlocked, his family having been evicted. It was true in 1997 when McKie, four years into his NBA career, was traded from the Pistons to the Sixers, his hometown team.

Not there, he thought at the time. *Not to a sorry outfit featuring known troublemakers like Allen Iverson and Derrick Coleman.* "I'm just like, *It's over. You're going to a bad team. You could get lost*," he recalled in March 2013, at which point he was in his sixth (and last) season as a Sixers assistant coach.

Instead of being lost, McKie found himself. He became an invaluable contributor to a team on the rise, a friend to Coleman and Iverson (especially Iverson), and a favorite of coach Larry Brown. It was Brown who called him "a pro's pro" and "everything I believe in."

"I love Aaron," the exacting coach told Stephen A. Smith, then of the *Philadelphia Inquirer*, in 2000. "He plays hurt. He's unselfish. He's got unbelievable character, and he's an underrated player."

The guy who often had trouble fitting in suddenly fit in everywhere. He was able to play off Iverson at the offensive end (no easy task), find his shots on those rare occasions when the ball found its way to him. He became a defensive presence, often taking on the opponents' best perimeter threat, emerged as a team spokesman as well as someone who mediated the skirmishes between Brown and Iverson.

McKie could sense during his first season in town that the Sixers were building something, that Brown was assembling the necessary blue-collar pieces around Iverson. That year, he said,

"We made a pact with each other: 'Look, we're going to come out and play hard, and we want to be spoilers. All these teams that are jockeying for position in the playoffs, we're going to come in and, excuse my language, bust their asses. And we're going to let them know, y'all are going to have a problem on your hands next year.'"

They were better the following year, and better still the year after that. And in 2000–01 they rode the crest all the way to the Finals. Brown was named Coach of the Year. Iverson was the MVP. And McKie, quite deservingly, was named the Sixth Man of the Year.

Every night the team battled, capturing the imagination of the city. For once the Sixers weren't at the bottom of the city's pecking order; fans gravitated to the arena to watch Iverson and his hard hats. "It was fun," McKie said. "There was just electricity in the building every night.... We were going to play hard no matter what."

The Sixers petered out against the Lakers in the Finals, losing in five games. McKie in particular struggled, and while he insisted he still had something left in the tank—"It might not have appeared that way, but at least I thought I did"—he also admitted he was playing with a sprained ankle and a torn labrum in his right shoulder, the latter an injury that would require off-season surgery.

The team slipped back to the middle of the pack after that. Brown left after the 2002–03 season. Players were scattered to the winds. McKie stuck around until 2005, after playing seven-plus seasons for a team he had hoped never to play for to begin with, and was finished as a player two years later.

That he even had a career is something of a minor miracle. His dad, Woodrow, died of heart failure when Aaron was nine. His mom, Pearl, left home when he was 14. Some strong male role models, including community coach John Hardnett and Simon Gratz High School coach Bill Ellerbee (and later Temple coach

John Chaney), came into McKie's life. So too did his aunt, Rose Key, who took him in when he came home to find that padlock on the family home.

"I didn't really know what I was doing," Key, who died in 2006 at age 72, told the *Inquirer*'s Mike Jensen in 2001. "I didn't have any kids of my own. I just did the best I could. He and I were two good buddies. He never gave me any trouble."

Rose made sure Aaron was home at a certain time, made sure he wasn't hanging out on the corner, made sure he made his bed each day. "I wouldn't be here today without her," McKie said. "Gave me discipline. Taught me values and morals. Not that I was a bad kid. You could be the best child, but you do need guidance. You need to be put on the right track. She was that for me. She was somebody I trusted.... She was my rock."

He starred for Ellerbee at Gratz, and Chaney at Temple. Portland took him 17th overall in the 1994 draft, and later shipped him to Detroit. And before long he found himself in a place he didn't want to be, wondering where he might fit in.

Turned out it was only everywhere.

86 Elton Brand

If the Sixers did not get the best of Elton Brand, at least they got the best he had to offer. If they did not get what he had been, at least they got all he had left.

He spent four years with the team, alternately serving as elder statesman, elbow jump shooter, and enforcer. He would later admit that his tenure "wasn't a full success," and that was inarguable, since he averaged 20 points and 10 rebounds a game in the nine years he had spent elsewhere, and just 13.3 and 7.4 with the Sixers. But neither was it a complete failure.

After he was gone—after he was cut loose in the summer of 2012 via the amnesty provision of the NBA's collective bargaining agreement with its players, and scooped up by the Dallas Mavericks—Doug Collins, the coach at the time, would talk about Brand's "soul." About how he was "all about winning." Even accounting for Collins' capacity for overstatement, there was a great deal of truth in that, for Brand offered leadership and stability to an otherwise young team.

Brand was the one who always remained at his locker after every game—every blessed game—and addressed reporters, understanding that giving interviews was part of the responsibility of being a professional. He was the one Sixers teammate Thaddeus Young said had been "like a big brother" to his less experienced teammates. And on the court, there were repeated instances when he let opponents know the Sixers were not going to be trifled with.

An example: One night late in the 2011–12 season, New Jersey Nets guard Deron Williams drove hard to the glass, intent on dunking. Brand, remembering that Williams had slammed early in the teams' previous meeting (and that it had propelled Williams to a 34-point night, and the Nets to a victory), delivered a hard foul before Williams could ever get to the rim.

The upshot was that Williams went to the line, made one of two free throws, and settled for 14 points—and the Sixers won going away.

"Same kind of play [as the first game]," Brand said after that one, "and I said, 'Not this time.'… He was trying to go for the big dunk to kind of energize himself, the crowd, the team.… I wasn't going to let him get that momentum play going. I wasn't going to let him get a nice dunk and get excited and juiced."

Days before that Brand had given the Sixers a lift in a different way, scoring a season-high 25 points and collecting 10 rebounds in a victory over Atlanta, right after a loss to the lowly Wizards had dropped the team out of first place for the first time in three months. Such a performance had been routine when he played for Chicago, which had chosen him first overall in the 1999 draft, and the Clippers, where he had twice been an All-Star in seven seasons.

That he was no longer capable of putting up such numbers on a consistent basis rankled some fans, since Brand had signed a lucrative five-year, $80 million contract with the Sixers in the summer of 2008. But others seemed to appreciate that his value to the team exceeded mere points and rebounds.

"He's a pro's pro," Sixers president Rod Thorn told the *New York Times* late in the 2011–12 season.

At that point he was playing despite a dislocated pinkie finger and a fracture of his left hand. The following year (his last with the team), he dislocated his right thumb, then injured his neck and shoulder in Game 1 of a first-round playoff series against Chicago.

The most telling injury of all (though no one knew it at the time) had been the torn left Achilles he suffered in the summer of 2007, while in the off-season with the Clippers. He missed all but the final eight games that season, and while he opted out of the final season of his contract told ESPN.com that it was his "intention to stay." His agent, David Falk, told the same outlet that Brand was interested in "finishing his career with the Clippers" if the team added more pieces. ESPN.com reported that Brand particularly wanted the Clips to sign guard Baron Davis away from the Warriors.

The Clippers did just that. And Brand left anyway.

He would sign for what he called "the Philly Max." And as the deal was being finalized, he heard from then–Eagles quarterback Donovan McNabb, whom he had first met years earlier, when Brand, a native of Peekskill, New York, made a recruiting trip to McNabb's alma mater, Syracuse. Brand had been impressed by what a big deal McNabb was on campus, and they had connected to some degree. But Brand went to Duke anyway.

When they crossed paths again, McNabb's message was simple: *I'll lead the championship parade, and you can bring up the rear.* And in truth, there was a great deal of optimism at that point—if not for the Eagles (for McNabb had long been a polarizing figure in town), then certainly for the Sixers, which had made the playoffs the year before and had a crying need for a big man of Brand's pedigree.

But there would be no parades for either team. The Eagles fell a game short of the Super Bowl in 2008, then jettisoned McNabb after another season; he would be out of football by 2011. Brand suffered a shoulder injury his first year with the Sixers, limiting him to 29 games, and he struggled in his second, under coach Eddie Jordan. But Collins, who had always specialized in reclamation projects, reached out to Brand when he was hired in 2010. He made it clear he would lean on the veteran, that he would make him a focal point.

That's how it turned out. Brand made mid-range jumpers, rebounded, patrolled the paint. In 2010–11 he delivered hard fouls to Washington's JaVale McGee and Clippers rookie sensation Blake Griffin. And in a first-round playoff series against Miami, his block of LeBron James' shot late in Game 4 helped preserve the Sixers' only victory over the Heat.

The next season, shortened to 66 games because of the lockout, Brand wasn't quite as good, and the writing was on the wall: surely he would be the one "amnestied."

"I want to be here, absolutely—be here with this young team," he said the day after the season ended with a loss in Game 7 of an Eastern Conference Semifinals series against Boston. "But it's whatever's best for the organization for me. Whatever happens, so be it."

The notoriously hard-bitten Sixers fans, long before having realized what Brand brought to the table, cheered him when he returned to the Wells Fargo Center in November 2012 with the Mavs. He said he was happy to be back, that he harbored no ill will toward his former team. Then he put up 17 points and eight rebounds, his best game to that point in the season (albeit in a loss).

Elton Brand had, as always, performed like a pro's pro. That would never change.

87 Hotel Lures Sixers

During the 76ers' greatest era of basketball, the team trained in Lancaster, Pennsylvania, and the man responsible for bringing the team to Amish Country, nearly two hours away from Philadelphia, was Philly real estate developer Steve Solms.

Solms, who Philly GM Pat Williams called the Sixers' No. 1 fan, traveled with the team for away games and had eight to 10 courtside seats. Such a big fan of the team was Solms that when Julius Erving played his first game with the Sixers in 1976, the team's No. 1 fan presented Dr. J with a doctor's bag.

The developer owned the Treadway Inn hotel in Lancaster with business partner Ted Ginsberg. Sixers coach Billy Cunningham and Solms were good friends. In 1978 Cunningham wanted to get the team out of Philadelphia, away from the media. Solms suggested the team stay at his hotel and train at Franklin & Marshall College. Training camp in Lancaster became an annual event from 1978 to 1994. The following year, John Lucas, in his second year as coach, moved camp to the University of Delaware.

In Lancaster, fans experienced close interactions with the players at practice, which usually included a free open session for the public in the afternoon and a time for autographs after practice. Players mingled with fans at the hotel as well. Because of the closer interactions with players, it was easy to become a fan of the team.

Drew R. Anthon, who grew up in western Pennsylvania and attended Mount Lebanon High School, was a Pittsburgh Steelers and Pirates fan in football and baseball, respectively. With no pro basketball team in the Steel City, he and his family quickly adopted the 76ers as their team. His three children grew up with the Sixers as part of their childhood, interacting often with the players.

Anthon, who became a partner in the hotel in 1977 and later bought out Solms and Ginsberg in 1983, bought his first season tickets with the team in 1978 and has had seats ever since.

His original five seats were by the tunnel leading to the locker rooms. It was great for his children to see professional players from both teams emerging through the tunnel, he said. In 1996, when the team moved to the First Union Center (now called Wells Fargo Center), he changed the location of his seats. Two are at center court and three others are in row four, opposite the home team's bench.

His three children all played basketball in high school at Conestoga Valley in Lancaster, but his daughter Dionne had the most success. She was a four-year starter on the University of Pennsylvania's women's basketball team, and she became only the second Penn player (male or female) to score more than 1,200 points, grab 600 rebounds, and dish out 250 assists (she had 1,293 points, 609 rebounds, and 294 assists).

A member of the University of Pennsylvania Hall of Fame since 2005, she wore No. 10 in high school and college in honor of her favorite player, Maurice Cheeks. She liked that he wasn't flashy, but a quiet leader, Drew Anthon said.

Being around the pro players likely had an influence on his children. "It surely didn't hurt," Anthon said. "They were basketball fans, but I'm sure that involvement and that association only fueled their desires to enjoy basketball as their favorite sport."

The players on those great Sixers teams of the late 1970s and early 1980s had almost a rock star status. Anthon said he tried to group them in an area of the hotel with ample security and a special room for team breakfasts. "We would provide them one or two special dinners that would be our way of saying thanks for coming up," he said. "It would just be the players, the coaches, Steve Solms, Ted Ginsberg, and [me]. No press."

Ever wanted to be the fly on the wall when basketball minds were talking hoops? Anthon had the opportunity on several occasions. In 1983, the championship year, he was sitting in a room with Solms, Cunningham, assistant coaches Matt Guokas and Jack McMahon, and trainer Al Domenico. They were going over scouting reports of the Los Angles Lakers. "It was a very fascinating experience from a non-coach standpoint to understand the level of sophistication, even back in the early '80s, of what the scouting was like," Anthon said.

He had many conversations about basketball with Cunningham and assistant coach Chuck Daly, and Anthon would not mention the player but recalled Cunningham putting a stop to a Sixer who was trading autographs with young fans who agreed to wash the player's car.

He said most of the players were nice and, with the exception of one player, conducted themselves the same on the court as off. Mo Checks was very quiet, almost introverted. Julius was articulate and pleasant. Moses was Moses; "his command of the English language wasn't great, but he was very nice," Anthon said. Charles, as in Barkley, was friendly and very gracious, often posing for photos. Andrew Toney was very similar to how he was on the court—like he had a chip on his shoulder, Anthon said. "I'm not saying it as a negative, but I'm just saying he was no different on the court or off the court," he said. "Toney was Toney. He was like, 'Give me the ball. I want to score at the end.' That's how he was walking around."

The one exception was Bobby Jones. He was the most soft-spoken, nicest, most down-to-earth guy out of all the 76ers, Anthon said. The total antithesis to who he was when he played.

"He was an animal on the court," he said. "He was aggressive, but when he wasn't on the court, he was really, really nice."

Looking back, Anthon said his hotel (now renamed the Best Western Eden Resort Inn) was busy without the 76ers' business, and in some respects it was more of a hassle having the team stay. It wasn't that he needed the business or that it brought in an extra revenue, he said. But local residents thought it was neat having the Sixers practicing and staying in Lancaster, and there were no negatives to the experience.

"As a sports fan—of all sports, but specifically basketball—it was a nice experience," he said. "It was a fun time. How else can a fan get that close an association with a team and not come away with a positive experience?"

Steve Mix

The night of March 29, 1982, the Sixers arrived in Milwaukee for a game the following night against the Bucks. Julius Erving and his longtime road roommate, Steve Mix, settled in their hotel room to watch the NCAA Championship Game between North Carolina and Georgetown, a game ultimately decided on a jumper made by a Tar Heels freshman named Michael Jordan. They were joined by George Shirk, the *Philadelphia Inquirer*'s beat writer.

Before tipoff Erving had a craving for hot fudge sundaes, and called room service.

The game began. No sundaes.

Halftime arrived. Still nothing.

Erving rose to use the restroom. Mix, always of a mischievous bent, dialed room service himself. And in his best Erving voice he wondered just who in creation these people thought they were, taking forever and a day to bring Dr. J his hot fudge sundae.

No sooner did Erving emerge from the restroom than the sundaes arrived. "He doesn't have to know about this," Mix whispered to Shirk.

"I used to do that a lot," Mix recalled. "I think sometimes he kept me as a roommate so that I could answer the phone. He would get calls all the time from various people. I would use that, 'Hello, this is Julius Erving.'"

In 2012–13 Mix found himself playing a new role—that of women's basketball coach at Division III Trine University, in Angola, Indiana. He led the Thunder to a 14–12 record in his first (and only) season on the job, the first time Trine finished above .500 since it went 18–13 a decade earlier, its last season in the NAIA ranks.

"This has been fun," he said a few days before his team closed out its season with a loss to Calvin in the Michigan Intercollegiate Athletic Association tournament. "The kids have been extremely enjoyable. They work hard, and they do everything I ask of them."

He asked a lot of them at the defensive end of the court, since the Thunder was, he said, "offensively challenged." And during games it was more a demand than a request. He was "very, very intense" then, said senior forward Sydney Spragg, a captain and the team's leading scorer. Also "quite animated," she added. "Sometimes it was fun to deal with, and sometimes it wasn't," she said. "He made sure to tell you when you did good. He was on you when you messed up."

And yes, there were times he trotted out stories of his days as a Sixers forward, usually during practice. He would talk to his players about the way in which he would try to challenge guys like Erving every day, and how that would bring the best out in each of them.

Everybody seemed to grasp that, and tried to put their best foot forward. And on Senior Night he hugged Spragg and the other two seniors, thanking them for all they had done. "That was definitely the best part of the season to me—him saying thank you for playing for me," Spragg said.

In an inadvertent bit of symbolism, one player's sister also produced a bubble gum card from Mix's playing days that night, and asked him to sign it.

Same guy, different guise.

The position at Trine was not one the then-65-year-old Mix actively sought, but he was recommended by the parent of a girl he had coached in AAU ball, back in his hometown of Toledo. School officials reached out to Mix in the spring of 2012, and he visited the campus in Angola—a rural town of some 8,600 souls in the northeast corner of Indiana—for a sit-down with the university president.

Mix was concerned as to whether the school was truly interested in winning—"because," he said, "there's a lot of times the ADs, with women's sports anyway, where it's just a matter of filling a spot." He received assurances that the administration was all in, which is all he needed to hear.

During the subsequent interview process, he met with Spragg and 10 other returning players. She said his background in pro hoops was "definitely intriguing" to all of them.

"Then again," she said, "the NBA's different than D-III girls' basketball."

"Coaching's coaching," he insisted. "It's just a matter of finding out what the players can do and can't do, and then putting in a system based on their strengths and not their weaknesses. I was able to do that."

He told the players that he would want them to be in shape before the season began. That he would want them to practice and play fast. That he would hope to press and run. And for the most part, Spragg said, he stuck to his plan.

After a 13-year NBA career he spent 22 years as a part- or full-time color analyst on Sixers telecasts, then five years doing games in the Mid-American Conference. Sprinkled in were various coaching stints: 20 years of AAU girls' ball...five years as an assistant with the Canadian men's national team...four with his son's high school team in summer ball.

He also ran his own basketball academy, and worked with the Sixers' big men one summer, when former teammate Maurice Cheeks was the coach. He interviewed for a post on Doug Collins' staff in 2010, and yearned to get back with the Sixers in some capacity, believing that their big men could always use more polish.

His attachment to the franchise runs deep. Drafted out of the University of Toledo by Detroit in 1969, he spent two-plus years with the Pistons before going to camp in 1972 with the Sixers, only to be cut—cut by a team destined to go 9–73, the worst 82-game season record in NBA history. He has often said it was the best thing that ever happened to him, in that it allowed him to return to his hometown and work out that year with fellow Toledo native Howard Komives, whose 10-year pro career was winding down.

Always a rugged rebounder and low-post defender, Mix knew he needed to hone his outside touch, and he did so, in long, sweaty sessions with Komives. He made time for those while working at a wine and beer distributorship at night.

And on weekends he and his wife would drive to Grand Rapids, Michigan, so that he could play for a team called the Pickers, of the Continental League. There were times, he said, when the team traveled by camper to road games—10 guys were crammed into one vehicle, driven by the coach. And the pay was paltry—$105 for a win, $85 for a loss.

But he tore it up in that league, and his team won the title. And the next year, he made the Sixers. The season after that—1974–75—he made his one and only All-Star team. He became so proficient at knocking down jumpers from the right baseline that broadcaster Bill Campbell took to calling that area of the court "Mixville."

"Then Doc came [in 1976]," Mix said with a laugh, "and I was relegated to the bench. I was a little upset with Doc. I thought he should be playing behind me."

Mix remained with the Sixers until 1982, playing in three Finals. He was also part of a Lakers team that lost to the Sixers in the 1983 Finals, having been signed away from Milwaukee late in the season, after James Worthy broke a leg.

In other words, the Sixers celebrated a championship on his last night in uniform—May 31, 1983—but he happened to be wearing the wrong one. "I think I got the most out of my ability I could," he said. "There was nothing left in the tank when I retired."

There was plenty of time for other guises, though. Plenty of time to fill roles even he might not have envisioned.

Jerry Stackhouse

Jerry Stackhouse first came to Philadelphia as the third overall pick by the Sixers in the 1995 draft. And one of the first things they did was hand him a hard hat.

He was given a tour of the arena now known as the Wells Fargo Center, which was still under construction. It would be "Stack's House," everyone decided at that point.

"I was telling someone about that the other day," Stackhouse said after a Brooklyn Nets game-day shootaround in the arena late in the 2012–13 season—his 18th (and last) in the NBA, and hours before the Nets lost to the Sixers there. "I was here, with a hard hat on, [wearing a] three-piece suit."

Stackhouse, who played his rookie year in the Spectrum and a little more than a year in the new place, was evicted early in the

1997–98 campaign. The Sixers decided to hitch their wagon to Allen Iverson, taken first overall in the '96 draft, and despite all the ups and downs of his 10-plus years in town, you'd have to say they made the right choice.

Stackhouse, now 39, was left to build something on his own, and he did so. Unlike Iverson, he will not make the Hall of Fame, but his was a very, very good career, one in which he has averaged 17 points while playing for eight teams. More significant is the fact that he became one of the league's most respected players, revered by coaches and teammates, friends and foes.

To last as long as he did, you have to be talented and tough. Canny and competitive. Also willing to adapt to changing circumstances. At various points in his career Stackhouse has been the Guy (he averaged 29.8 points, second-most in the league, for Detroit in 2000–01), the Sidekick (he was sixth man on a Dallas club that reached the Finals in 2005–06), and at the end, the Sage Veteran.

He appeared in just 37 games for Brooklyn in 2012–13, averaging 4.9 points per game. But coach P.J. Carlesimo said he planned to use Stackhouse in the playoffs, knowing that the veteran had "the ability to contribute to us—perhaps even more so later on, because of his experience." (Stackhouse wound up playing 28 minutes over four postseason games. He missed 9 of the 10 shots he attempted.)

To stay ready, Stackhouse put in the extra time. After the shootaround that day in March 2013, he worked on post moves with and against fellow reserves Tornike Shengelia and Mirza Teletovic. It was no gentle exercise; they took turns banging and bumping each other for several minutes, and after being thwarted by Stackhouse on one move, Teletovic walked away rubbing his eye, apparently having been poked.

Stackhouse looked on impassively.

Some 90 minutes before the game Stackhouse was again on the court, firing up shots—wing jumpers, wing three-pointers, pull-ups from each elbow. Anything to stay ready.

And he tried to prepare himself for life after basketball as well. He was elected a vice president of the National Basketball Players Association during the 2012–13 season, and will no doubt remain active in that organization. He mentioned broadcasting and coaching as possible options as well—and he would appear to be particularly well suited for the latter, given the various roles he has filled during his playing career.

"My perfect route would be something like Mark Jackson," he said, referring to the former player who at that moment had moved from broadcasting into coaching. (Jackson, who lost his job as Golden State's head man after the 2013–14 season, then returned to the booth.)

Then–Sixers boss Doug Collins, who coached Stackhouse for part of the 1997–98 season in Detroit and the entire 2002–03 campaign in Washington, called him "one of the smartest players I've ever coached." Collins said a high basketball IQ is typical of guys who hang around a long time—guys like Stackhouse, Jason Kidd, Kurt Thomas, and Derek Fisher.

The other common denominator, Collins said, is that such players are "incredibly competitive and…get to a point in their career where they understand the best role they can play."

Maybe they won't play for the better part of a week, he added, and then be forced to play 20 minutes. "And when they do," Collins said, "they're very, very effective. That's a real coach's dream."

During the 2012–13 season Stackhouse discussed with Jonathan Abrams of Grantland.com how important it is to be adaptable, and how that contributed to his longevity. "I look at a guy like Allen Iverson," Stackhouse told Abrams. "There's no way, from a talent level or what he's done for the game of basketball, he shouldn't be on somebody's team right now. But we know why. We know why."

Iverson, seven months younger than Stackhouse, did not play in the NBA after his 25-game cameo with the Sixers, likely because he was unwilling to accept a role as anything other than a center-piece. Which is why he is unlikely to get another job in the league, even though he is seven months younger than Stackhouse.

Consider, Stackhouse said, Iverson's three-game stay with Memphis, early in that 2009–10 season. "He still came in with the mind-set of, 'I want to compete for a position,' and probably could have won the position," Stackhouse said.

But that wasn't really the point anymore.

"I think teams make decisions for their future," Stackhouse said, "where they want to go and as far as developing younger guys. And you have to kind of accept that.... Whether it was pride or ego or whatever—I think he still felt like he was the best player on the court. A lot of teams were turned off by that. It's unfortunate, for a guy who had that type of career, what most would think is a Hall of Fame career, not to be able to go out the way he would like to go out, now to be sitting around, hoping and wishing for something that in all likelihood is not going to happen."

Stackhouse considers Iverson, whom he sees on occasion, a friend. "That was my guy," he said. "Still is."

It could have turned out very differently between them, since both were young bucks with the Sixers in 1996–97, both potential franchise cornerstones. And they did have their disagreements. While it has never been confirmed that friends of both players once fought outside the team's practice facility, Stackhouse and Iverson did get into a dust-up at a shootaround in 1997, about which Stackhouse was famously quoted as saying, "It was a fight between one guy who didn't know how to fight and another guy who didn't want to fight."

There is little doubt Stackhouse was the latter party, as he has never been hesitant to mix it up, if he felt that was required. Besides Iverson he scrapped with Utah's Jeff Hornacek (an ex-Sixer) during a game in 1995–96, Pistons teammate Christian Laettner during a card game in '99, and Utah rookie Kirk Snyder after a game in 2005.

Stackhouse has mixed feelings about all this. While he wants to be a good example to the three kids he has by his wife, Ramirra, he also said this: "I feel like I'm a guy that never started much, but I don't have a problem bringing some closure to some things," he said. "It's not the proudest moment, to have that stuff out there, but at the same time, I'm always going to protect myself, protect my teammates. And I live by that code."

He's not sure he and Iverson could have ever thrived together in Philadelphia—not so much because of the egos involved but the fact that Stackhouse was a shooting guard, while, in his view, Iverson was "a shooting guard in a point guard's body."

"Could we have made it work?" Stackhouse wondered. "Possibly."

In the end it worked out well for all concerned. Stackhouse was sent to Detroit with Eric Montross, for Aaron McKie and Theo Ratliff—two vital pieces in the Sixers' rebirth. Iverson led the club to the Finals in 2001, and Stackhouse was free to build something big, something substantial.

No hard hat required.

90 Scapegoating Scott Brooks

The Oklahoma City Thunder, a favorite to reach the NBA Finals for a second straight season in 2012–13, instead fell to Memphis in the Western Conference semifinals. And after they did so—after they fell in five tough games to a worthy opponent—everyone came looking for scalps. More than anything, they came looking for the one belonging to Scott Brooks, the coach.

Never mind that circumstances aligned against them—that the front office had traded their third-best player, James Harden, to Houston before the season, or that Russell Westbrook, their second-best player (at worst), had been kayoed for the rest of the playoffs when he suffered a knee injury in a first-round series. Never mind that even short-handed, the Thunder gave the Grizzlies everything they wanted.

Never mind any of that. The Thunder had lost, and the coach surely had to be the reason, according to his critics. They noted that the team became too dependent on Kevin Durant, its lone remaining star. (Even Turner Sports analyst Charles Barkley, Brooks' former Sixers teammate, jumped on that one.) They complained that Brooks gave too much time to center Kendrick Perkins, who looked shot according to advanced analytics (his minus-0.7 Player Efficiency Rating was the worst ever) and the naked eye (he couldn't make a layup).

Clearly, the thinking went, the Thunder was being held back by its head coach. Clearly he needed to be replaced.

Then again, it was not the first time Scott Brooks had been underestimated.

Jim Lynam first saw him in 1987, playing with a ragtag bunch of summer league All-Stars against an unlikely amalgamation—a team combining the Atlanta Hawks and the Soviet national team, in the run-up to that year's Goodwill Games. Which meant Brooks, a 5'11" point guard from Cal-Irvine, was going against Hawks point guard Doc Rivers and guys like Sarunas Marciulionis, who later played in the NBA for the Warriors.

Lynam usually preferred penetrating point guards. But Brooks' shooting touch caught his eye. So too did his competitiveness. He reminded Lynam a little of himself in that regard.

Lynam called UNLV coach Jerry Tarkanian, since Vegas was in the same league as Irvine. "Do I know Scotty Brooks?" Tarkanian barked into the phone. "The little [bleep]. We could never guard him."

Nobody could. In his last year with the Anteaters, Brooks scored 24 points a night. He took particular delight in torturing the University of Pacific, a school near his home in Lathrop, California. He had always dreamed of playing there, but the Tigers showed little interest in him coming out of high school—there was the height thing, after all—and were no more enamored of him after he spent a year at Texas Christian and another at San Joaquin Delta Community College.

So the last time he faced UOP as a senior, he went for 41. "I don't want to admit it," he told reporters afterward, "but I did want to take it to these guys."

Lynam, armed with Tarkanian's endorsement of Brooks, convinced the Sixers to invite him to training camp in the fall of 1987. And every day, Lynam recalled, Brooks "played his brains out" while going head to head with no less a point guard than Maurice Cheeks (later his assistant coach with the Thunder).

But Brooks somehow failed to make the team. It's not a happy memory for Lynam, who said that it came down to the fact that others in the hierarchy didn't like Brooks' game nearly as much as he did.

One other thing, too. "When it's your guy," Lynam said, "you've got to be careful what battles you're going to fight."

Brooks went to the CBA, and lit it up for Albany (the Patroons, if you must know). In fact, that club went 48–6 under Bill Musselman, a remarkable record in any league.

Lynam, who succeeded Matt Guokas as the Sixers' head coach midway through the 1987–88 season, assumed Brooks would return to Sixers camp the next fall. But Brooks' agent, Frank Catapano, informed him one day that that wasn't the case. And not only that, but Brooks was flying to Detroit at that very moment, with the intention of going to the Pistons' camp.

"I went nuts, and I've never done that," Lynam said as he stood in the bowels of the Wells Fargo Center one night in February 2012.

Lynam, who by then was doing some TV work for Comcast SportsNet, grew animated in the retelling of his years-old exchange with Catapano. "I said, 'Frank, lemme tell you, and I'm gonna tell the little [bleep bleep]—that ain't right. He belongs here,'" he said.

Catapano said it was too late, that Brooks was already en route to Detroit. But he did have to change planes, so the agent expected to hear from him.

"Good," Lynam said. "Have him call me."

Brooks did, and got an earful.

"I'm gonna tell you this," Lynam yelled into the phone. "I know [Detroit general manager] Jack McCloskey. He's a friend. You ready? You're cannon fodder. There's no spot for you there."

Brooks changed his ticket on the spot and came to camp with the Sixers. And this time he made the team, spending two years with the Sixers before making stops in Minnesota, Houston, Dallas, New York, and Cleveland.

"Jim Lynam? I wouldn't be coaching, wouldn't have my career if it wasn't for him," Brooks said in 2012. "He's the only guy, outside of my family, who thought I had a chance to make the NBA. I owe him everything."

That might be true. But as Lynam pointed out, Brooks also made the most of his opportunity.

"He never was outclassed," he said. "The other guy might be a little taller, a little quicker, a little this, a little that, but he always knew how to do his job. If you approach it that way, you might be a little surprised with the results."

The same thing applies in coaching. He spent some time in the minor league ABA, then as an NBA assistant in Denver, Sacramento, and Seattle, Oklahoma City's predecessor. And early in the 2008–09 season, he succeeded P.J. Carlesimo. But four years later, everything came full circle: Scott Brooks was again being underestimated. And once more he would have to try to prove everyone wrong.

Pat Williams

Pat Williams felt like the luckiest man in the room. And not without reason, either. The night of May 21, 2013, the Orlando Magic's senior vice president represented his team at the NBA Draft Lottery in New York City.

He was a veteran of the lottery, for better or worse, having been on hand when his team earned the first overall selection on no fewer than four occasions—three times with the Magic, the other time as the Sixers' general manager in 1986. (It turned out badly that time, as the Sixers traded the choice to Cleveland for forward Roy Hinson, and the Cavaliers snapped up center Brad Daugherty.)

On Williams' latest visit, there was talk of him bringing a Ping-Pong ball sprinkled with pixie dust from Disney's Magic Kingdom. More pertinent was the fact that the Magic had the best odds of earning the top pick, having finished with a league-worst 20–62 record. But as it turned out, Cleveland earned the top pick. Orlando would have to settle for second.

Yet Williams still felt like the luckiest man in the room. Any room.

The pain began in his back, just a few days after running the Disney Marathon in Orlando, in January 2011. He guessed he had slipped a disc or something. He was, after all, a 70-year-old man, far removed from the time in the late '80s when he cofounded the Magic, and even further removed from his stint as the Sixers' GM (1974–86).

As the years passed he had settled into his administrative post with the Magic, while also serving as a motivational speaker (he made dozens of appearances each year), authoring books (he had written more than 70 by 2012), and taking care of his kids (he and his wife, Ruth, raised 19, including 14 adopted from foreign countries). And running marathons, too. The Disney Marathon was his 58th.

It was also his last.

After doctors found no evidence of a back problem, Williams was advised to get some blood work done. And that revealed he had multiple myeloma, a cancer that begins in the plasma cells in the bone marrow and, if unchecked, leads to tumors in the bones themselves.

It is treatable, but not curable. And Williams, true to form, responded with a grandiose gesture. At a news conference in February 2011 during which he discussed with reporters the nature of his diagnosis, he removed his suit jacket and revealed the blue T-shirt he was wearing underneath, emblazoned with a slogan: THE MISSION IS REMISSION.

By the following year, the mission was accomplished. After undergoing chemotherapy for some 18 months, the disease had been put on hold. He resumed his full speaking schedule. He continued to write. And while his marathon career was over, he still worked out regularly. "A lot of people just give up," he said in September 2012. "I can't do that."

Indeed, quitting has never been in his DNA. This is a man who dispenses motivational quotes at the drop of a cliché, to the point of mentioning them on his voice mail, right before advising callers to "make it a great day." This is a man who turned to his faith more than ever in the wake of his diagnosis, someone who maintained an optimistic outlook. And if he might have been tempted to slip, he received a note of encouragement from golfer Arnold Palmer, who maintains a Florida home and had had a bout with prostate cancer years earlier. In the letter, which Williams framed, Palmer urged him to keep his chin up, and listen to his doctors. "This is not something I volunteered for," Williams said, "but the Lord had it on my agenda."

His agenda had always been crowded. After graduating from Wake Forest, he was a catcher in the Phillies' minor-league system, working with, among others, future Hall of Famer Ferguson Jenkins. In time he migrated to the front office, and out of the blue he received a call in July 1968 from Jack Ramsay, who said he was taking over as coach and general manager of the Sixers; would Williams be interested in coming aboard as the team's business manager?

Williams was. He signed a three-year contract for the princely sum of $20,000 a year.

A year later he left to become the Chicago Bulls' general manager, with a promise to Ramsay that he would consummate the trade of Jim Washington to the Sixers for Chet Walker—a coup for the Bulls, as it turned out.

Later Williams served as the Atlanta Hawks' GM, but in 1974 he returned to the Sixers. When he accepted the John W. Bunn Lifetime Achievement Award from the National Basketball Hall of Fame in September 2012, he joked with the crowd that he had to leave Atlanta after trading "Pistol" Pete Maravich to the New Orleans Jazz.

His second stint in Philadelphia lasted until 1986. And in that time he became known for his offbeat promotions—he was the one behind the infamous "We Owe You One" advertising campaign, for instance—as well as his astute decisions. The biggest, no doubt was when he approached then-owner Fitz Dixon in the fall of 1976 and convinced him it would be a good idea to send $3 million to the Nets for the rights to Julius Erving.

A decade later, Williams departed for Orlando; his last act in Philadelphia was to get Cleveland to send $800,000 to the Sixers, in addition to forward Roy Hinson, for the first overall pick in the NBA Draft. That, coupled with the trade of Moses Malone to Washington for Jeff Ruland and Cliff Robinson, qualifies as one of the darkest days in franchise history.

The Magic happened in Orlando, and Williams was at the same time able to engage in his own pursuits—in things that "bring me joy, bring me pleasure, bring me fulfillment," as he said during that February 2011 news conference.

But as he said later that day, "I've always felt there was another chapter in my life, maybe a grand finale to all my years in baseball and basketball, and all the years of speaking and writing. I wasn't quite sure how it was going to play out, but perhaps we're seeing that now."

By the following year, it was clear the chapter was going to last a while longer. It was just as clear that Pat Williams would continue to feel like the luckiest man in the room. Any room.

92 Doug Collins

To no one's great surprise, Doug Collins announced he was stepping down as the Sixers' coach the day after the 2012–13 season ended. He stood before reporters in a corner of the team's practice facility and insisted it was his call, that he had not been pushed out—despite published reports indicating the ownership group would be only too happy to see him go.

Retained as an advisor to majority owner Josh Harris, Collins said he would have vacated his job on the bench even if the season had been a success, as opposed to the 34–48 clunker it was with center Andrew Bynum sidelined all year by knee problems. Collins had decided to resign at the end of the season by "about Christmas," and informed team officials of his intentions roughly two months later.

Certainly he sounded like he had one foot out the door when he ripped his team after a February 26 loss to Orlando—he preferred to look at it as "being honest"—and there were signs weeks earlier of just how much the job was wearing on him.

Seated in his Wells Fargo Center office before a game against Memphis in late January, he produced a laminated 3x5 card from his travel bag. On it were listed the names of several legendary NBA coaches, alongside the worst seasons each of them endured. It was a veritable who's who—everyone from Jack Ramsay to Doc Rivers, Larry Brown to Lenny Wilkens.

"How 'bout Pat Riley?" Collins asked, mentioning the name at the very top of the list. "Loses Dwyane Wade and goes 15–67. Loses 15 in a row, wins one, loses 11 in a row. One-and-26. Pat Riley." Collins had scrawled those particulars on the card, in felt-tipped pen, right next to Riley's record in 2007–08, his final season on the bench. Wade had been slowed by a knee injury for much of that season, and Shaquille O'Neal, nearing the end of the line, was traded midseason.

Then there was Collins, without Bynum and without much of a team. As he sat in his office that night, the Sixers were 18–25, and hours away from falling to 18–26. He would tell reporters a few days later he had expected them to win 60 percent of their games when they acquired Bynum from the Lakers in a four-team trade the previous summer, almost the exact opposite of what it was.

He insisted he was not one to dwell on what-ifs, though he would frequently mention how keenly Bynum's absence was felt. He did so after the Orlando game, and he did so again when he stepped down.

Certainly that laminated card offered one more reminder of the realities of his profession, of how a coach could only do so much. Collins had repeatedly changed lineups. He had buried guys on the bench, then reinserted them in the rotation. He had at times praised his players, and at times chided them. He was normally patient with reporters (and incredibly blunt in off-the-record sessions), but at times he turned prickly, as when one of them asked after a game if the players might be tuning out their coach.

But in the quiet of his office he seemed happier, more reflective. At age 61 he was coaching his fourth NBA team, and the one for which he had played all eight of his injury-marred pro seasons. "They always say live your dream; I've outlived mine," he said.

And never mind the overarching what-ifs of his career. As an Olympian in 1972, he had wobbled to the free-throw line after getting knocked woozy and made the foul shots that appeared to give the U.S. the gold medal…only to see the Soviets win in controversial fashion. As a Sixer he was named to four All-Star teams… only to see foot and knee injuries force him to retire at the age of 29. As a first-year coach in Chicago, he inherited no less a talent than Michael Jordan, in 1986…only to see Jordan reach his greatest heights under another man, Phil Jackson.

Yet Collins seemed comfortable with his life and career. "A lot of people find misery when there's a lot of joy," he said. "I'm not going to do that and deprive myself. You can say all the things that didn't happen, and I can say, 'Well, let's talk about the things that did.' My résumé ain't bad in 40 years."

He has always prided himself on the relationships he has built in coaching, knowing that in his younger years he thrived because of the men for whom he played. Growing up in Benton, Illinois, there was his high school coach, Rich Herrin. At Illinois State University there was Will Robinson, the first African American coach in Division I history. Collins viewed them both as surrogate parents, as he did Illinois State athletic director Milt Weisbecker, since his own parents divorced just as he was heading off to college.

"I never really had a close relationship with my father," he said. "At that point in time, I don't know that fathers got real close to their sons. I knew how much he loved me."

But he cherished the bonds he developed with his coaches. He would go on scouting trips with Herrin. He would sit in Robinson's office and soak up life lessons. And during a game one night, Collins' nose was bloodied.

"I'm going to find out if you can play now," Robinson told him as he was receiving treatment on the sideline. Collins had no idea what he was talking about. "A man finds out who he is when he sees his own blood," Robinson said. "Now, show me what you got."

Years later, a statue depicting the two men was erected outside Illinois State's arena. Collins treasures that, and what it represents—two men from very different backgrounds (Robinson, who died in 2008, was a longtime coach in the Detroit Public League, while Collins hailed from a lily-white hometown of some 6,000 souls) coming together and making each other better in every way.

"That's why the term 'coach' to me is like being a doctor or lawyer or something like that," he said that night in his office. "Coach, to me, is something that's far deeper than that."

He was the first overall pick in 1973 but was limited to 25 games as a rookie because of a broken foot, a harbinger of things to come. His career gained momentum the following year, and in time he found himself on "the first rock star team," as he called it, featuring Julius Erving and George McGinnis. But those Sixers lost in the '77 Finals—Collins recalled having to get a pain-killing injection in his groin to suit up—and by the time they made it back there, in 1980, he was all but done.

He went into broadcasting before the Bulls hired him, then returned to the microphone before he landed another head coaching gig, in Detroit. Then the cycle repeated itself—he called games for a time, then was in charge during Jordan's two-year swan song in Washington (2001–03)—and again when the Sixers hired him in 2010, he had been out of coaching for seven years.

As with his other stops, there was progress for two years, followed by stagnation. There was a seven-foot asterisk in this case, though, which explained the laminated card. And it explains why three months later, he spent a half hour spelling out for reporters the reasons for his departure—family being at the top of the list.

He said he was "a Sixer for life," and that he didn't plan to coach ever again. He also said, oddly, that he didn't bother to inform his players of his intentions, either individually or in a group setting.

After a while the questions ran out. A publicist asked Collins if he wanted to say anything in closing. He did. "I hope that I've been a man in every way," he began, his voice catching, "and that I've done my job the best way I can do it, that I put my heart and soul in it, that I love this city and I want them to win a championship and that I'll miss you."

Not the job, though. Not after a season like that.

 **Sixers Fans**

Known for always being dapper and wearing Versace before the clothing line became chic, Bryan Abrams of Wilmington, Delaware, is best remembered as one of the team's ultimate 76ers fans.

In fact he and the late Steve Solms, who former Sixers general manager Pat Williams called the team's No. 1 fan, often debated who was the bigger supporter. Solms said it was Abrams; Abrams gave the nod to Solms.

In 36 years, Abrams only missed five home games. From November until June, he told people not to plan anything for him to attend.

He sold his business during the 2011–12 season and lost his season-ticket seats at the end of the season. He hasn't been to a game since, but when he's in Philly he's still recognized.

"I was walking with a friend the other day and he finally said, 'What's your story?' This is the fourth time someone has stopped you to talk about the 76ers,'" said Abrams, who bought a partial season-ticket plan in 1976 and later upgraded to a full plan that had two seats next to the Sixers bench in the Spectrum. "When I had tickets everyone knew I had 41 home games. I didn't come to weddings, parties, or do dates. I'd be at the game."

From the time he was very young, his favorite athlete of all time was Wilt Chamberlain. When the 76ers traded him to the Lakers, Abrams couldn't root for the Sixers.

Once Chamberlain retired after the 1972–73 season, Abrams started rooting for the home team again—intense rooting, to be exact. During warm-ups, forget about talking to him. He wasn't very social, unless the topic was basketball. He was there for the game. And he never booed, even if the team was down 40 points.

His passion did not go unnoticed. In 1996, *Philadelphia* magazine named him "Best Philly Fan in Philadelphia"—that's in any sport. "It's a tremendous honor, and I took it to heart," he said. In the 2011 playoffs Abrams said the *Philadelphia Daily News* did a feature story on him.

He knew all the referees by name. He'd let them know if they missed a call or if he saw an illegal defense, calling for the illegal D throughout the game. In the fourth quarter a ref would call the illegal D and turn toward him and say, "That one is for you."

At the end of one recent season, referee Scott Foster came over to Abrams after the game and said, "You are the most knowledgeable NBA fan"—and even gave Abrams his official referee jacket.

A few months ago Abrams saw referee Joey Crawford at an event. Having worked in the NBA since 1977, Crawford knew the Ultimate Sixers Fan well. Crawford walked over to Abrams and said, "I'll talk to you, but no yelling or screaming at me."

He had relationships with former owners—Ed Snider used to sit beside him at games and valued his opinion about the team—and announcers—he has Bill Walton's phone number and is friends with TNT reporter Craig Sager. Allen Iverson nicknamed Abrams "Day One," because Abrams was in A.I.'s corner from the very beginning.

In fact, ownership and Iverson gave Abrams tickets for away games. He was in Iverson's seats for the playoffs in 2001 at Milwaukee—seats that happened to be near Ray Allen's mother. The two exchanged good-natured banter and a friendship ensued. When Allen later played for the Boston Celtics, the good-natured ribbing continued with his mother at games in Philly.

His favorite team was the 1989–90 Sixers. He sat at the end of the bench and joked with Rick Mahorn and Charles Barkley. The two would say, "Bryan, go get us hot dogs." At the end of the season the squad gave him Barkley's warm-up jacket, signed by every member of the team.

"I still say if Derek Smith doesn't get hurt, we would have beaten the Bulls in the second round of the playoffs that year," said Abrams, who traveled to 10 to 12 road games a year. "I loved that team. Smith knew how to guard Michael Jordan and Jordan didn't like the physical contact."

He developed running, good-natured feuds with certain opponents. Gary Payton liked to talk trash. Antoine Walker hit a winning shot for the Celtics and ran over to stare at Abrams at his seat, which by 2006 was in the second row across from the visitors' bench. Shaquille O'Neal asked him what he was wearing, and Dwight Howard was a friend.

There was also the funny exchange between Abrams and Vince Carter, who was playing for the Toronto Raptors. Carter couldn't hit a shot. Every time he had the ball Abrams yelled for him to shoot. Carter finally made a basket and yelled to Abrams, "What do you have to say now?"

Abrams replied: "Shoot again. You'll miss."

Abrams is just one of many die-hard Sixers fans who became known for their enthusiasm and antics during home games.

Mike Worrall says his loyalty as a 76ers fan goes beyond the days of the Sixers. He was a Philadelphia Warriors fan first. In fact, he says, as a 14-year-old, he saw Wilt Chamberlain score 100 points in Hershey Arena in Hershey, Pennsylvania.

Of course, about 20,000 people claim to have been at that March 2, 1962, game against the New York Knicks, which had an attendance of 4,124 souls. Worrall says he not only was one of them, but it was his first pro basketball game. From this experience, the Ephrata, Pennsylvania, native's love for Philly basketball began.

He bought 76ers season tickets starting with the 1982–83 season, sharing seats with Ken Good of Ephrata. Eventually, Worrall bought out Good, so he could get the first pick of games.

But it was not until the 1995–96 season that Worrall, 65, became known for more than just being a basketball fan. This is when the NBA announced its 50 Greatest Players. A book was published with photos and stories on the players. He bought a copy and came up with an idea.

Always a bit of an autograph hound, Worrall decided to try to collect autographs from all 50 greats. Charles Barkley, then playing for the Phoenix Suns, was the first to sign, doing so by the visitors' tunnel prior to his game against the Sixers.

Worrall said he collected many of his autographs at the All-Star Game in Cleveland, at which the 50 greatest players were in attendance and honored at halftime. He also carried a bag with him to Sixers games, tracking down the greats when they visited Philly.

With his four seats just off the court in the third row across from the visitors' bench, he often spotted celebrities at games. Worrall decided to expand his collection of signatures to not just the NBA's 50 greatest players, but others of note. He'd have them sign by their favorite players in the book. If a notable figure was at a 76ers game from 1995 through about 2009, Worrall likely found them and asked if they wanted to sign his book.

The story behind getting the autographs was almost as important to Worrall as getting the signature. Actor Jimmy Smits, a Lakers fan, was at a Sixers game, his wife sitting across from the Sixers bench in the same row as Worrall.

Smits, wearing a Lakers baseball cap, appeared on the video screen on the scoreboard. Fans booed when they saw him with the cap. He was one of Worrall's favorite actors, dating back to his days starring in *L.A. Law*. Worrall waited for a stoppage in play and approached the actor, asking him to sign the book by his favorite Laker; he obliged, and picked Magic Johnson.

Smits' *L.A. Law* costar Corbin Bernsen was at a different Philly game in seats several rows behind Worrall, who spotted him in the crowd, grabbed his book, and worked his way up through rows of fans to meet Bernsen, who paged through the book, impressed with all the signatures. He signed near Smits.

Worrall spotted actress Kim Delaney, a Philly native, in the Lexus Club, the popular restaurant inside the Wells Fargo Center that's reserved for season-ticket holders and VIP types. She had her son, Jack, pick a player. He chose Allen Iverson. During the 2001 NBA playoffs, late NBC *Meet the Press* host Tim Russert, was at a game with his 10-year-old son. Russert, a Buffalo native, picked Bob McAdoo.

Tracking down players wasn't easy—and sometimes cost him money. He got Moses Malone on "Moses Malone Day." The team retired his number and had a meet and greet event. Worrall paid about $85 to go to a reception with about 100 people. He got his signature.

Julius Erving was in the Lexus Club for a playoff game. Worrall walked by and saw Erving sitting at a table eating. "I went up to him and said, 'I don't want to interrupt your meal, but when you are through will you sign my book?'" Worrall later said. "He was quite willing. I made sure to get a place to sit like 10 feet away so he wouldn't get away. I waited until he was clearly finished and asked if this was a good time now."

Billy Cunningham was a challenging signature to get. He doesn't sign for pay and he turned Worrall down at a Sixers alumni session at Cherry Hill racetrack in New Jersey. Hal Greer, who signed for him at the event, was there with Cunningham, who does not like to sign autographs and was avoiding signing. "I thought I would get him because I paid to be there," Worrall said. "A lot of older Sixers were there, but he wouldn't do it."

Worrall tried at events and games, but Cunningham said no. Finally, Worrall talked to someone in public relations for the 76ers. The PR person talked to Cunningham and he agreed. Not surprisingly, he signed the book by his photo.

Chamberlain was another that was hard to get. Indeed, it was a rarity to get Chamberlain in Philly for an area event. Worrall paid about $50 to wait in line for the Big Dipper, who Worrall believes was at the Cherry Hill racetrack with other Philly alumni that day. Tom Gola signed prior to a LaSalle game. Explorer standout Lionel Simmons, who played for the Kings in the NBA, was at the game and he too signed the book.

Some former players he got when they came in to announce games for TV. Magic Johnson and Bill Walton, on separate occasions, were set up courtside, near Worrall's seats, to announce a game. He got Boston great Bob Cousy prior to a Celtics pregame show; Cousy was announcing on TV, but he didn't do every game. Worrall talked to someone in Boston's front office and got a friend in the Sixers' front office to approach Cousy, who enjoyed paging through the book before signing.

On several instances when Patrick Ewing was playing and, later, coaching, Worrall asked him to sign, but Ewing said no. Eventually, Worrall went to Ewing's former college coach, John Thompson at Georgetown, for help. Ewing signed with Thompson's encouragement, Worrall said.

He's missing three or four players of the 50 greatest, though he does not recall which players he's missing.

Bad health has limited Worrall's attendance at games in the last five years. His nephew, Anthony Worrall, is now in charge of the seats. Of the 50 greatest players, only Pete Maravich was dead when he started collecting signatures. Worrall had a friend who had Pistol Pete's signature and gave it to Worrall to put in his book, which has become a labor of love.

"It just represents the whole great experience of the NBA," he said. "My whole life I've been a fan. The effort to do it and the experience with many individual players makes it special. For the most part, it was a good experience. Some were brush-offs, but most people enjoyed looking through the book. Their joy and my joy coexisted."

Another passionate Sixers fan is Alan Horwitz, who received media attention for his death stare and exchange with Kobe Bryant in 2012. Most would agree he is the team's current super fan. The white hair and goatee of Horwitz, chairman of Campus Apartments, which develops student housing in 26 states, makes him recognizable, as do his antics. Horwitz, who normally wears 76ers retro clothing, rarely sits in his seat.

His trademark poses include kneeling on the hardwood, pleading for the team to play well and standing and making crazy gestures. Horwitz has had season tickets for about 35 years. He's sat next to the scorer's table since the seats became available five seasons ago. Now he's 10 seats from the 76ers bench.

"Now I'm so close, it's like I'm the sixth man on the team," said Horwitz, who grew up sitting in the rafters watching Wilt Chamberlain at Convention Hall.

He's developed friendships with the current players, taking them to Phillies and Eagles games and out to eat. The hustle and effort of the very young players on the 2013–14 roster is worthy of his support, he said, and being friends with the players makes it more interesting, giving him more of a rooting interest.

His encouragement is almost like having another coach on the bench. "In fact, with Doug Collins [in 2012–13], he even let me get into the huddle," Horwitz said. "It makes it fun. You feel like you are in the game."

94 Where to Buy a Jersey

If you want a sports jersey, Philadelphia-based Mitchell & Ness Nostalgia Co. is the place to go.

You can purchase online or at several locations, including a small store with Philadelphia merchandise at Xfinity Live! near the Wells Fargo Center. The flagship store is located at 1201 Chestnut Street, Philadelphia. The Center City, 2,800-square-foot store has hardwood basketball court flooring and features historic memorabilia and images. Even if you just window shop, taking in the atmosphere is an enjoyable experience.

Established as a golf and tennis equipment company in 1904, Mitchell & Ness began providing authentic and throwback jerseys in the 1980s. Be it NFL, MLB, NHL or NBA, this place has jerseys, hats, socks, and more for your favorite team.

The merchandise isn't cheap, though. A Moses Malone red road jersey from 1983 costs $260. A Dominque Wilkins Atlanta Hawks road jersey from 1987 goes for $300. The company has sold sports merchandise for more than 100 years, but the jersey market—especially throwback uniforms—did not become a mainstream part of pop culture until the late 1990s. That's when you saw hip-hop artists wearing jerseys and hats in music videos and celebrities making fashion statements.

If you attended a home Sixers game from 2001 to 2006 you likely saw many fans wearing throwback jerseys. Star Allen Iverson's wardrobe consisted of jerseys like the powder blue of Lance Alworth and the San Diego Chargers.

A man who played a part in the jersey craze is Reuben "Big Rube" Harley. A frequent spectator at games, Harley often wore a throwback jersey in various sports and a hat to match the outfit. "I'm the reason why people know their name," said Harley, who held titles as vice president of marketing and brand development. "I made sure everyone knew their name."

Not bad for a former customer at the retail outlet. He struck up a relationship with management, because he "knew cool jerseys" and saw the reaction when he wore them himself. During his run with the company, which saw him go from customer to an executive, Harley—who was with Mitchell & Ness from 2001 to 2006—became a very popular man at games, and there were often underground transactions taking place.

Before or after games, he gave merchandise to players or delivered their orders. Iverson, LeBron James, Shaquille O'Neal, Jermaine O'Neal, Chauncey Billups, and Carmelo Anthony are just a few of the names who shopped with Harley. Once he gave them a taste, they came back for more.

"When the Sixers had a home game I gave product away, and then players started coming in and buying it," he said, often waiting for Iverson's press conference to end after a game so he could hand him a package. "The whole sports world had my personal cell number, and guys paid a lot to get it. I know of a guy who paid $5,000 to get my cell number."

Supply and demand helps to raise the price of the jerseys, and having celebrities wearing the apparel helps, too.

Over the years, the company gained national acclaim. Harley said people wanted to know the engine behind the throwback apparel craze. The microphone was always in his face. His first interview was on *MTV News* in September 2001. Harley, who turned 40 in February 2014, liked the attention. It was good for business.

Being African American and part of the hip-hop generation, Harley was aware of what was popular, he said. He crashed a lot of parties and video shoots. He maneuvered his way in, wearing sports apparel and giving out samples. "I knew I had a cool product," he said.

Harley said he introduced the Drew Bledsoe 1994 throwback jersey with an NFL 75th anniversary patch on it. The jersey became a big seller and the New England Patriots have worn it in recent seasons. It has also appeared in at least two dozen music videos, he said.

Harley believes that one of the reasons for the popularity of sports apparel is that throwback uniforms transcended race and the color of a person's skin.

"A black kid doesn't worry about the race of the player," he said. "I was a fan of Bledsoe growing up. Bledsoe was white. It [color] doesn't come into play with the sports realm or sports fashion. How many kids got an Iverson jersey? It became a cultural phenomenon."

One that had its roots at 76ers home games.

95 Thaddeus Young

There is an explanation as to why Thaddeus Young is the way he is—why the Sixers forward seems older than his 26 years, why his play seldom deviates on the court and why he's never involved in any drama off it. He provided it himself three years ago, when he returned to his alma mater, Memphis' Mitchell High School, for his jersey number retirement.

As he addressed the teenagers in attendance (kids not all that much younger than he was at the time), he talked about how he would not allow inner-city distractions to get in the way of who he was and where he wanted to go. "I just made sure," he told them, "that I did me."

He had help, of course. His mom, Lula Hall, was in his words "a tough lady" who did not spare the rod. His dad, Felton Young, was once an accomplished player himself, and he gave his son's basketball career direction. But ultimately Thaddeus was responsible for doing himself, and still is.

Even as the Sixers went 19–63 in 2013–14, he played with his usual consistency and verve. Forced to play power forward when the roster was stripped to the chassis, he put on a few pounds but was still undersized at 6'8" and 230 pounds. He did what he could against bigger guys in the post, while continuing to run the court tirelessly—Chicago coach Tom Thibodeau once said that an instructional video could be made of Young's ceaseless rim-running—and score in a multitude of ways.

His scoring average (17.9) was the best of his seven-year career, as were his steal and assist totals. First-year coach Brett Brown appreciated his professionalism (as had each of Young's four previous coaches with the Sixers), saying that the veteran forward was, among other things, "a gentleman."

Doug Collins, the team's previous boss, had gone so far as to say Young was his favorite player. Certainly he was unique. As former Sacramento coach Keith Smart once observed, "He's not a position player; he's a basketball player. He has been a steady pro. Any time he's on the floor, he's productive.... Maybe there's a game where he's not playing well, and then some way he finds a way to have an impact on the game.... He's always lurking."

And never wavering, which is not always easy to do, given the grind of the season and the struggles of the team. As Young put it, "You've got to go into each and every game saying, 'I'm going to go out there and play to the best of my abilities. I'm going to give my team and myself a chance to win each and every night.'"

Henry Baskin, the principal at Mitchell when Young attended (as well as Thad's pastor), called him "probably one of the most focused young men I've ever seen," and a better person than player—even "an icon" in south Memphis. Everybody wanted to come see him play when he was in high school, it seemed. And when he was drafted by the Sixers in 2008, it was as if the whole neighborhood had been selected.

Thad had moved with his mom from New Orleans to Memphis when he was in fourth grade. Four years later, his dad joined them. Felton and Lula never married, but they were unified in raising their son. As Baskin said, "His mom taught him to be humble. His dad taught him to be focused."

On that point there is some disagreement from Jerry Johnson, who coached Thad in high school. "I just think the roots that he came from and the surroundings that he lived in motivated him to excel," Johnson said.

There were drugs and gangs in the neighborhood, Baskin said, but Lula made sure Thad steered clear of trouble. "My mother, she was always on my case," he said. There was this one time, when he

Thaddeus Young led the 76ers in scoring in 2013–14.

was 12 or 13, that things did go haywire. He happened to be standing outside a house that was undergoing renovations, talking with a woman in the neighborhood. Unbeknownst to him, his buddies were inside, trashing the place.

The cops showed up, and the woman accused him of being the lookout. He would have faced charges had his friends not vouched for him. He also would have faced a beating from his mom had she been the one to pick him up at the police station. But Felton came for him instead.

"She would have killed me," Thad said. "I knew once my dad came and picked me up, he understood the guy stuff. But my mom, there was no understanding. She was coming with the belt, ready to beat you down."

His dad, who stands 6'11", played center at Jacksonville University and was an eighth-round draft pick of the Buffalo Braves in 1978, but never played in the NBA. He and Thad did play one-on-one all the time, at a roll-up hoop out in front of their house on Calvin Road. But one day when he was 13, Thad dunked on his dad, a watershed moment for both. "He never played me again after that," Thad said. "He actually stopped playing basketball completely."

Thad's career was picking up steam by then. He had a coach in Johnson who made his players produce their report cards before he let them try out for the team. Because of that (and because of Lula and her belt), Thad took care of business in the classroom, posting a gaudy 4.3 grade-point average.

By his senior year, he was the Tennessee Player of the Year, and a McDonald's All-American. His dad had taken to coaching him in AAU ball, and there were those who wondered if Felton was merely hitching a ride on the gravy train. Johnson insists that wasn't the case.

"In Memphis you've got all the shady dudes that look for a rising star, so they can latch onto him," he said. "Well, Thad's dad shielded Thad away from all those shady-type people.... Basketball players need more fathers like Felton Young."

Thad spent a year at Georgia Tech before the Sixers made him the 12ᵗʰ overall pick in 2008. And very little has changed since then. He's still the same guy, still doing himself.

In August 2014, Thad was traded to the Minnesota Timberwolves as part of the deal that sent Kevin Love to the Cleveland Cavaliers.

96 The Practices of Legends

In the fall of 1971, Glenn Robinson took over as head coach of Franklin & Marshall College's men's basketball program in Lancaster, Pennsylvania. When he entered the 2014–15 season he had 870 victories, 12ᵗʰ all-time among all divisions of college basketball.

But the all-time wins leader in Division III men's basketball history didn't have success early on. In fact, his early coaching career paralleled the rise of the 76ers in the 1970s in many ways. Remember the 1972–73 Sixers and their 9–73 record? By 1977 the Sixers made the first of four appearances in the NBA Finals in seven years.

Robinson led F&M to a 13–11 mark in 1974, the program's best record since 1959. By 1976 his squad broke the school's win total with a 17–8 record; then it reset the mark the following season with 22 wins. By 1979, the Diplomats soared to 27 victories and Robinson's first of five Division III Final Four appearances.

Meanwhile, in 1978 the Sixers began holding training camp at Mayser Center on the campus of F&M. The team came to Lancaster every year until John Lucas took over as coach in 1995. So the F&M coach had a front row seat for the greatest era in 76ers history. The Sixers experienced tremendous success from 1976 to 1995, only missing the playoffs five times while assembling a roster full of All-Stars and future Hall of Famers.

Maurice Cheeks, Dr. J, Moses Malone, Bobby Jones, Andrew Toney, and Charles Barkley practiced on the court at the same time in 1984. The team also used the gym, which was built in 1961 with a capacity of about 3,500, for mini training camps in the spring, prior to the playoffs at least three times.

Robinson coordinated the camps. He was at every minute of every practice. The team usually had two-a-days—the morning practice closed and the late afternoon session, which normally included a scrimmage, open and free to the public. F&M basketball players served as security and ushers at the public practices. It was a great experience for fans, who could get up close to players and get autographs after practice.

There were likely untold things Robinson picked up from observing those NBA practices, but there were a few sets he admits stealing from coaches Billy Cunningham and Jimmy Lynam that the Diplomats still run in games today. There's what Robinson calls the quick-hit play, the way of running off an offensive screen by pinning down, that is virtually unstoppable because of the way the screener aligns himself on the screen.

"It's very effective for us to beat an expiring shot clock," he said. "Even with time on the shot clock, the last 10 seconds is still the last 10 seconds."

He won't name the coaches who he saw run literally no defensive drills. There were other coaches who stressed defense. And then some who started with no defensive structure and the very next year added defense, he said.

"It was fascinating to see [the coaches] learn from their mistakes and fascinating to see how they dealt with NBA talent," said Robinson, who in 2008–09 became only the second Division III coach to reach 1,000 games coached.

As a college coach, there are things he can do to his team that he couldn't with an NBA squad. For instance, NBA players are not good at accepting criticism, he observed. No matter how wrong a player had been, as soon as the whistle blew the player would argue. Some players were hypersensitive—even by professional prima donna standards.

Most 76ers coaches were good at giving out instructions without calling out specific players. But there were exceptions. There was that morning practice in 1993 when a rookie coach called a team meeting. Robinson did not want to reveal the identity of the coach, but a reporter in the gym confirmed it was former player and longtime assistant coach Fred Carter, who was in his first year as head coach with the team. He stopped practice and had the players sit on the court at Mayser gym in front of about 12 members of the media who were sitting in the bleachers. Carter called players out, Robinson said. The players, being strong-willed, started resisting and talking back to the coach. The verbal exchange went on for several minutes.

"It was a huge mistake for a coach," Robinson said. "I felt bad for him. I stood in front of the press so they would not hear or see as well. I think it caught [Carter] by surprise. I think he had the best intentions. It was so agonizing to watch. Not that you don't correct a problem, but not in public."

Besides feeling bad for the coach, Robinson was impressed with how the media handled the contentious exchange. Granted, this was well before the age of social media, where a tweet or blog post is common. As it was, there were no big headlines and stories about the incident, but the press had an inside story that they could use in a broader context. They knew how the players and coaches felt and had depth for subsequent stories. They had knowledge and at the same time built respect and trust with the organization.

Andrew Toney and Darryl Dawkins were among the sensitive players. Straight out of high school, Dawkins wasn't used to being coached or criticized, Robinson observed.

"The first 20 times a coach tried to call him out he argued," Robinson said. "Then assistant coach Chuck Daly said, 'Darryl, if you look at as much film as we did, you'd see this stuff.' They had to figure a way for Darryl to accept that he needed coaching."

Dawkins remembers those training camps in Lancaster well, recalling staying at the then–Treadway Inn and the F&M players getting a free look at practice. "Those college kids got to come in and watch the practice of legends," he said. "George McGinnis, Doug Collins, Dr. J, World B. Free, myself. Now they pay to go practice. Andrew Toney, Mo Cheeks. It was just a great time."

What was like playing on those teams? "It was entertainment, man. It was entertainment," Dawkins said. "If you couldn't entertain, stay on the porch because the big dogs were getting on. I had a lot of fun, man. If I wasn't having fun I stayed home."

Robinson said Toney was sensitive, strong-willed, and tough as nails. Toney the competitor is what the coach remembers the most. There was the simple drill in which the ball is rolled out and teammates go for it. Whoever gets the ball drives to the basket while the other player defends. Henry Bibby made the mistake of getting in front of the rookie Toney and having to guard him. Toney ball-faked and dunked on him.

Then Bibby made mistake number two, Robinson said, by going against Toney again. Equally impressive was the ball fake from the other side and an equally easy layup. Bibby would never go against him again.

"As rookie, a wily veteran couldn't handle him," the coach said. "It was amusing. I could go on for weeks. No one knew how good Toney was."

Before a Pistons-Sixers game in January 2014, Bibby, now a Detroit Pistons assistant coach, smiled when asked about guarding

Toney in the drill. "It shows how good he was," Bibby said. "He was like a [football] lineman. It's a guy that's 6'3" playing against a lineman—solid, strong, hard and just a great basketball player. He could do whatever he wanted to do on the floor as well."

As a veteran, were you frustrated? "Of course you are," he said. "You say, 'This rookie can't do this consistently,' but he did."

Sixers training camp started with a mile run. Toney ran the best time every year he attended. "To me, [there's] no question he had a stress fracture in his feet [which ultimately cut his career short]," Robinson said. "He was a very proud and fit athlete."

Other observations from camps included the Shawn Bradley experience. Bradley was tall, 7'6", but he was not NBA ready with strength or physicality. Teammates would throw the ball to him and Bradley could hold the ball with one hand in a way Robinson only saw one other player do effectively: Kareem Abdul-Jabbar.

But that's where the comparison stops. Put Bradley in the left block and he was easily moved. His teammates got frustrated with throwing the ball to Bradley in the paint and having him travel or get jolted off the block. The idea of drafting someone to make good, instead of having a proven, good player doesn't sit well with the old coach. "Because you draft him you insert him in situations trying to make him good," Robinson said. "I don't know why veteran players wouldn't be alienated with this. Now you change your game to fit *his* game."

He said stats cannot be the only way to evaluate a player. Stats can be deceiving. He sites McGinnis as an example. McGinnis led the league in steals one year, but that didn't mean he was a great defender. Robinson said the forward took too many chances and gambled for steals.

Later he was traded for Bobby Jones, who was a tremendous defensive player.

"I was at [Jones'] first practice as a 76er and at the first break I talked with him. He went out a door and told him I was glad he was here. He's a humble guy. The point is, he played defense and played a role. Basketball is a team sport. It is hard not to make a sacrifice when playing with a player like that. He kind of sets a tone. When you play with a guy like that, who plays so hard, it is sure to rub off. Guys like that instill values."

"We did a lot of work up there," Jones said about training at F&M. "I remember it was so hot in that gym. After practice Julius and I would sit out on the back stoop and we'd watch sweat go down every step. It was about 10 minutes before it got to the very bottom. It paid off. The chemistry was there. When you have the chemistry it really makes it easier."

Robinson said having the Sixers at F&M was first class, terrific. He saw the finest talent in the world. He learned that sheer talent will win, and if you don't have it, you won't.

General manager Pat Williams shared ideas with Robinson, who enjoyed listening to the former Sixers GM talk trades and evaluate players. The first year the NBA limited rosters to 12 active players Robinson knew Williams had difficult decisions to make. "How are you going to decide who to keep?" he asked the 76ers exec. The coach remembers Williams saying it wasn't difficult; they just play themselves off the team. And "as the days went by it became really obvious," Robinson said.

97 The Prodigal Coach...Hovers

Some three weeks after Doug Collins stepped aside as the 76ers' coach in 2013, Larry Brown agreed to interviews with two Philadelphia media outlets. First he told the *Daily News'* Bob Cooney that while he was "comfortable" in his job as Southern

Methodist University's head coach, a position he had held for one year, he wouldn't mind serving as "a resource" to the Sixers. He also reminded Cooney and his readers that he maintained a home in Philadelphia, and that when he coached the team years earlier he had done a successful rebuilding job despite "a pretty bad roster with bad financial situations."

In a radio interview a few days later, Brown said that while advanced statistical analysis—a tool employed by Sam Hinkie, a man about to be named the Sixers' general manager—is something that can help a team, he "wasn't one of those guys" who leaned on such number-crunching. "Basketball is not like baseball," Brown told WIP hosts Anthony Gargano and Glen Macnow.

All of this was classic Larry. The ultimate basketball vagabond (and a guy whose favorite job always seems to be his next job), he didn't campaign outright for the position with the Sixers. But he made it clear he wouldn't mind being considered. (He was not, and the job went to former San Antonio Spurs Assistant Brett Brown.)

As a champion of "playing the right way," Larry Brown saw some merit in Hinkie's thinking. It just wasn't the approach he favored. Rather, he would do it as he had always done it at all 14 of his coaching stops. He would build up his roster with guys would play hard, play cohesively, and play defense. That was the bedrock of his coaching philosophy, the very definition of playing the right way.

Nobody could argue that yielded results, no matter where he coached. The man knows horseflesh, knows how to build a team. Even SMU's 15–17 finish in 2012–13 was regarded as something of a triumph, given its threadbare roster. There was talk at season's end of a promising recruiting class, of better things in the years ahead. But would the 74-year-old Brown stick around long enough to see it through? That was always the question with him.

His impatience manifested itself in smaller ways, too. In the NBA, if his team lost three straight, he wanted to trade everybody.

If somebody set a screen the wrong way, he wouldn't play for a week. "He's a basketball savant, a basketball genius," said Mike Gminski, who played for Brown when he was with the Nets (1981–83). "I've never been around a coach that was more of a genius with regard to the sport, but he just was really tough on players."

Gminski, who later played for the Sixers (though not for Brown), said Brown is particularly tough on point guards and general managers—that because he once played the point he asks more of those who man that position than anyone else, and because of his demanding ways he always wants his GM to tinker with the roster. "He was the best coach after the trade deadline," Gminski said, "because he couldn't move anybody then, and he had to coach that team. But up to that time, he would watch a game somewhere and he'd say, 'We've got to get that guy. We've got to trade for him.' That was how he was, from the start of training camp to the trade deadline. He'd fall in love with everybody else's players and hate his [own] guys."

For all these reasons, it must be regarded as something of a miracle that Brown lasted six years with the Sixers, his longest tenure anywhere. Also because his philosophy ran headlong into that of Allen Iverson, who was about as far from a play-the-right-way guy as you can get. As former Sixers president Pat Croce, often the mediator in their disputes, said one day in the fall of 2012, "Larry knew the world of basketball; Allen knew the streets of basketball. Larry was doo-wop; Allen was hip-hop. They were just different, but they had a common goal and I knew that. They were very much alike in their headstrong ways."

There was, at best, an uneasy peace—and at worst, outright combat. In his press briefings Brown would often refer to Iverson as "the little kid." ("Allen didn't like that," Croce said.) When Iverson was subbed out of a game—as was typically the case twice a night—he would call Brown something far less complimentary, a four-syllable word beginning with "mother."

In 2000–01 they achieved success despite themselves, advancing all the way to the Finals before losing to the Lakers of Kobe Bryant and Shaquille O'Neal. But things often bubbled over, as when Brown complained about Iverson's practice habits and Iverson responded with his rant on that topic after the Sixers were eliminated from the playoffs in the spring of 2002.

Brown departed for Detroit after the following season. Iverson lasted until early in the 2006–07 season, when he was traded to Denver. The surprising postscript came on the eve of the 2012–13 season, when Brown told those who had gathered at a coaches' clinic at SMU, "God put me here to coach Allen Iverson," according to Andy Friedlander's story in the *Daily News*.

"At the time I was doing it, I wasn't so sure," Brown said, adding that while Iverson "was not easy to play with," his will to win and toughness could never be questioned.

"I benefited so much from being around him and at the time I wasn't really aware of it.… Even though people on the outside might have thought it was like that," Brown told Friedlander, as he knocked his fists together, "we were attached. Since I've been away from him, we've gotten closer at a distance."

His relationship with Iverson gave Brown, 72 and out of college ball since 1988 when he took the job, instant credibility with recruits. "People are not sure who I am," he told the *Contra Costa Times* early that season, "but they know I coached Allen."

He took the position with the Sixers in 1997, having been wooed by Croce after stepping down as coach of the Indiana Pacers. Croce, for his part, knew he needed a strong hand after seeing the team, Iverson in particular, walk all over Johnny Davis the year before.

Brown, who had played for the legendary Dean Smith at North Carolina, "wasn't afraid to call out his superstars," according to forward George Lynch, who arrived in Philadelphia in 1999. "Every time Allen made a mistake, he called him on it, just like he called the role players."

As Brown explained a few years later to his friend Charley Rosen, then writing for ESPN.com, Iverson was as deprived on the basketball court while growing up in Newport News, Virginia, as he had been off it. "Coming up," Brown told Rosen, "he never had good coaching. I mean, the kid was so talented that his coaches just let him do whatever he wanted to do. None of his coaches held him accountable for his selfish attitude." Then Brown added, as he seemingly always would (and has) that Iverson always played hard, always competed.

Brown unquestionably made allowances for Iverson. He reshaped the roster, importing guys like Lynch, Eric Snow, Aaron McKie, and Theo Ratliff to do the dirty work. He moved Iverson from point guard to shooting guard and let Snow—steadier, sturdier, more defensive-minded—run the show. Iverson was unfettered, free to hoist shots to his heart's content. And he did.

This was playing the right way? Not to Brown's way of thinking. By December 1999 things had come to a head. In a meeting that included Croce, Iverson, and general manager Billy King in an office off the team's practice court at the Philadelphia College of Osteopathic Medicine, Brown informed Croce he didn't want to coach the team if Iverson remained part of it. Iverson responded by saying that he wanted to be traded if Brown stayed on.

"It was ugly," Croce said in the fall of 2012. "I had to get in and break it down."

Iverson, he recalled, was slouched in his chair, angry. And Brown, Croce said, was fuming because the team president "put him at the same level of Allen and made him sit there." But Croce made some inroads, pointing out to Iverson how disrespectful it was to swear at Brown every time he was removed from a game, and pointing out to Brown that when he sat down his star, Iverson viewed it as being "no different than his jailer when he was in prison."

Croce believed it to be a good talk, that both principals came away better for it. He went so far as to say it was "the turning point for the success of our team." That might be a reach, seeing as the Sixers attempted to trade Iverson to Detroit before the 2000–01 season, a deal that fell through only because Sixers center Matt Geiger, who was also part of the proposed swap, refused to waive a provision in his contract that would have given him a 15 percent raise if he were included.

The run to the Finals followed. The Sixers have not been back since. Brown won a title in 2003–04, his first in Detroit, making him the only coach to win NCAA and NBA championships. He later coached his hometown team, the Knicks, for one unhappy season, then spent two-plus years with the Charlotte Bobcats. But after he was dismissed in December 2010, he was out of the game for over a year before SMU came calling.

And all those years after the fact, Brown found that he and Allen Iverson were indeed "attached." There was no escaping it.

98 LeBron James Says A.I. Is the Greatest

LeBron James, the reigning 2012–13 NBA MVP, said in October 2013 that his two favorite players growing up were Michael Jordan and Allen Iverson. Seems like two good choices. Nothing too newsworthy in that statement. But King James, arguably the best player in the game today, wasn't finished. "Pound-for-pound, probably the greatest player who ever played," James said of Iverson, who announced his retirement about the same time as James' proclamation.

But is it an accurate statement? Should Iverson be in the conversation of the game's greats?

Harvey Pollack offers a different view. He has worked for Philadelphia pro basketball teams since 1946 (first with the Warriors and then 76ers). In his eyes, Iverson, as great as he was, was not even the greatest player in Sixers history.

"I've seen them all," said Pollack, the 76ers director of statistical information. "To me, the greatest player ever was Wilt. That's No. 1 and Jordan is second. The other one is close. You got Larry Bird and Iverson, Barkley and Erving…. There are a lot of guys that are after those two, but they are definitely one and two, Wilt and Jordan."

The 91-year-old Pollack is the only person still working for the NBA since its inaugural season. He recalls players being able to get the ball at the top of the basket and dunk it, but the league made that offensive goaltending. "They changed the rules for Wilt," he said. "Then Dr. J was the high-flyer. Jordan, they changed the rules to help Jordan. Anything they did for Wilt was to hurt him. That was the difference between those two."

Dr. J brought the game above the rim, Pollack said, adding Barkley, for his size, got a lot of rebounds and was a leader. But Iverson makes the top five, right? "Well, except he never won a title," he said. "He only got to the finals once."

Maybe Heat guard Dwyane Wade had a more realistic take on Iverson's legacy. "He was one of the greatest players to ever wear a uniform," he said.

Sonny Hill, founder of the Sonny Hill Basketball Summer League and man with knowledge of all things about Philadelphia basketball, said James can only go on what he's seen.

"He was talking about it from the point of view of [playing] pound for pound with Allen Iverson," Hill said. "And Allen Iverson is one of the grittiest, toughest players to play in this league. But when you talk Allen Iverson, I can run off twenty basketball players that were as great or greater. Was Allen Iverson greater than Oscar Robertson? Hell no. Was he as great as Elgin Baylor? Hell no.

"People can only talk about what they've seen. Take Dolph Schayes out, because of the era he played, but he can't be greater than Wilt. And he can't be greater than Dr. J."

For his take on James' high praise and where others may rank him, Iverson said he only cares about the critiques from guys that played the game. Their opinions are the ones that matter to him.

If Dr. J mentions his name, or if Michael Jordan mentions his name, or one of the other greats like Larry Bird, Magic Johnson, Isiah Thomas, or Barkley mentions him, then he'll listen.

"Somebody like that mentioned my name and said I wasn't one of the greatest, then all right. But if [a guy] who never laced his sneakers up before in his whole life and has walked around with his shoes untied his whole life doesn't put me on his list, I don't care," said Iverson at his retirement press conference. "I let people who love basketball decide that, because I know. One thing about somebody who knows someone who is great but won't say it, they still know it. They still got to live with it."

99 Where to Watch the Game

On this Friday night, a Wing Bowl preliminary was at a fever pitch, as an announcer updated guests on who was leading. A group of about 75 people huddled around the participants.

A few feet away Joe Purcell stares at a big-screen TV. The 76ers lead the Pistons 29–14 in the first quarter in this January 10, 2014, game.

Purcell, of northeast Philly, is a bartender and bar-back at one of the half dozen bars and restaurants at the 80,000-square-foot venue where the Spectrum, former home of the 76ers and Flyers, used to sit. In fact, the outside bar at Xfinity Live!, located about 300 yards from the Wells Fargo Center, present home of the Sixers, was constructed from bricks from the old Spectrum. Inside, the capacity is 3,000 people. The outside bar can hold another 2,000. There is a 32-foot (not inch) Sony LED screen, as well as several other large screen TVs in the facility for sports fans. And there's a mechanical bull, too.

Purcell, 29, said he's watched the 76ers since 1991, and was a big Allen Iverson fan. He was at the game on March 12, 1997, when Iverson beat Michael Jordan on a crossover. "It was unbelievable," he said. "I was a Jordan fan, but when Iverson did that, I transferred over."

Chuck Moore of Manayunk, Pennsylvania, finishes up his supper before heading over, late, to the Sixers game. Wearing a black and red No. 4 Chris Webber 76ers jersey, Moore said he grew up going to games. His mother was a nurse and received tickets for good seats from pharmaceutical reps. He says Xfinity Live! draws both a younger crowd and families, because it is a hub before games. It is the place to be, he says.

Kim Uporsky, of Queen Village, Pennsylvania, watches the Sixers on a big screen while drinking a glass of wine. She gave her game ticket to her son, Damien, who went with two friends. She said she used to enjoy watching Iverson, but has lost interest in the team in recent years. However, the new ownership and the play of 2013 first-round pick Michael Carter-Williams has piqued her interest again.

Philadelphia fans at Xfinity Live! agree on one thing: there is no one definitive sports bar for Sixers games. Besides Xfinity Live!, fans recommend Chickie's & Pete's Crab House and Sports Bar. What started as a corner bar in 1977, now has about 40 locations (including 14 full-service restaurants in the Philly area and four more at Philadelphia International Airport).

In 2003, the 1526 Packer Avenue venue opened. It is only a short walk (about a mile) from the South Philly sports complex, home of the 76ers, Flyers, Eagles, and Phillies.

Various sports talk shows, both TV and radio, take place here, and many past and present Philly athletes have visited. For several years, Comcast SportsNet Philadelphia shot *Monday Night Live* at the South Philly location. There was always a well-known guest on the show, which focused on local pro and college sports. This show helped give Chickie's & Pete's exposure and make it a destination for die-hard fans.

In fact, in 2011 ESPN declared Chickie's & Pete's the No. 1 sports bar in the United States. Roger Falloon, chief operations officer for the restaurant, said there are several reasons for the popularity. "The experience," he said, "Guests know they will have a great game day, in game experience. We often have a live band. People often get into the game. It is a similar experience to being at the game. We pride ourselves on the experience. The other aspect is the quality of our food...that's what separates us from chain restaurants."

Yes, visitors may have made their first visit Chickie's & Pete's for the in-game experience or to see a live sports talk show, but they come back for the food. The signature items include crabs (blue, Dungeness, and snow; king crab legs; and jumbo lump crab cakes), as well as mussels with red sauce. The pizza is also good, because of the quality of that red sauce.

Not to be forgotten are the crab fries, a Philly favorite, which are sold at small stands throughout the city. Back in 1977, owner Pete Ciarrocchi wanted to do something with the leftover crab seasonings. He decided to put it on French fries and served it to his regulars at the bar, who quickly gobbled them up. Ciarrocchi first served the fries to customers just to hold them over while the crabs were cooking, but the crab fries became so popular that they became a staple on the menu.

Besides food and entertainment, they provide transportation with the "taxi crab," a bus that transports fans from the South Philly location to the sports complex for Sixers, Flyers, Eagles, Phillies and music concerts. For $20, fans can valet park their car and be dropped off and picked up right at the venue.

"Pete thought of that," Falloon said. "He thought it would make it more convenient to go the extra mile as a service to people after a game, and hopefully, celebrating after a win, to eat and have a drink."

With two large bars and plenty of TVs, ESPN is plenty right: this is a good spot to root for the Sixers with fellow fans.

100 List-a-Palooza

All-Sixers Team

First Team

F—Julius Erving. Eleven years, and approximately 11,000 highlights.

F—Charles Barkley: Stood a shade under 6'5", but played much bigger. And talked even bigger than that.

C—Wilt Chamberlain: Many of his greatest individual moments came elsewhere, but he was the hub of the great 1966–67 club.

G—Hal Greer: So reliable was his jumper that he used it on free throws.

G—Allen Iverson: On the, uh, short list of great little men, with Isiah Thomas and Tiny Archibald.

Second Team

F—Billy Cunningham: Great coach, greater player. He owned career averages of 21 points and 10 boards a game.

F—Chet Walker: "Chet the Jet" took the slow route to Springfield. He was finally inducted in 2012.

C—Moses Malone: Announced that it was "still Doc's show" when he came to town. But everybody knew better.

G—Maurice Cheeks: His celebration at the end of Game 4 of the 1983 Finals has had to sustain Sixers fans, all these years later.

G—Andrew Toney: Hall of Fame–bound, until his feet gave out.

Third Team (Centerless, out of necessity)

F—Dolph Schayes: The first in NBA history to surpass 19,000 points.

F—Bobby Jones: A deeply spiritual man, but played as if possessed.

F—George McGinnis: Gave the Sixers credibility in the years after the 9–73 debacle.

G—Hersey Hawkins: Overlooked—that happens when Barkley is a teammate—but one of the finest shooters in franchise history.

G—Wali Jones: Stepped in when Larry Costello was injured during 1966–67 title run.

All-Defensive Team

F—Bobby Jones: Made NBA's All-Defensive first or second team every year he was in Philly but his last.

F—Luke Jackson: Revered by his teammates on the 1966–67 championship team for sacrificing his offense and doing the dirty work.

C—Dikembe Mutombo/Theo Ratliff: Tag team of the 2000–01 Finals squad. Mutombo led the league in rebounding, Ratliff led in blocks.

G—Maurice Cheeks: Still fifth on league's all-time steals list 20 years after his retirement.

G—Andre Iguodala: Often decried for what he was not—i.e., a go-to scorer—rather than celebrated for what he was: a guy who routinely erased big-time scorers from the box score.

Best Draft Picks

1. Allen Iverson (first overall, 1996): Yes, it is possible to screw up the top pick, as the Sixers themselves showed in 1986. And while Iverson caused his share of headaches, there's no denying his on-court greatness.
2. Andrew Toney (eighth, 1980): The Nets had the two picks immediately before the Sixers, and even though they liked Toney, they chose Mike O'Koren and Mike Gminski.
3. Maurice Cheeks in second round (36th overall, 1978).
4. George McGinnis in second round (22nd overall, 1973): He was starring for the ABA's Pacers at the time, but this selection allowed the Sixers to get a leg up on the Knicks when he chose to come to the NBA two years later.
5. Sedale Threatt in sixth round (139th overall, 1983): Captain of the all-name team, and a proud graduate of West Virginia Tech, he turned heads in his very first camp by trying to dunk on Moses Malone. And he wound up playing 14 NBA seasons.

Worst Draft Picks

1. Shawn Bradley, 1993: Yes, they picked him over Penny Hardaway and Jamal Mashburn. No, he didn't quite revolutionize the game.
2. Any first-round pick between 1967 and 1972: Here's the roll call, in order: Craig Raymond, Shaler Halimon, Bud Ogden, Al Henry, Dana Lewis, and Freddie Boyd. Which is how, in part, a team goes 9–73.
3. Larry Hughes, 1998: The Sixers used the eighth overall choice on Hughes. The next two picks? Dirk Nowitzki and Paul Pierce.

4. Leon Wood, 1984: Wood, an Olympian, went 10th overall. Six selections later, the Jazz took some guy named John Stockton.
5. Anything after Thaddeus Young and before Marc Gasol, 2007: It's hard to argue with taking Young at No. 12. But with subsequent maneuverings the Sixers netted Jason Smith, Derrick Byars, and Herbert Hill. All of that occurred before Gasol, now one of the league's best centers, went 48th.

Best Trades

1. Wilt Chamberlain from the San Francisco Warriors for Connie Dierking, Paul Neumann, and Lee Shaffer (January 15, 1965): It was Wilt's homecoming, and two years later he was the centerpiece of one of the greatest teams of all time.
2. Caldwell Jones and a No. 1 pick (Rodney McCray) to Houston for Moses Malone (September 2, 1982): About the only one who wanted to part with Caldwell Jones was Sixers owner Harold Katz, who didn't relish paying him starter's money to back up Moses. And Houston was prepared to let Malone walk as a free agent anyway. But no matter how you slice it, a great deal, as Malone delivered a title.
3. World B. Free for the Clippers' 1984 first-round pick (October 12, 1978): That pick, No. 5 overall, became one Charles Wade Barkley.
4. George McGinnis to Denver for Bobby Jones (August 16, 1978): Jones played eight solid seasons with the Sixers. McGinnis, once a star, was out of the league by 1982.
5. Jerry Stackhouse to Detroit for Aaron McKie and Theo Ratliff (December 18, 1997): Stackhouse had a nice career, but he didn't fit alongside Allen Iverson. McKie and Ratliff were key pieces in the Sixers' rebuilding efforts.

Worst Trades

1. (tie) Moses Malone to Washington for Jeff Ruland and Cliff Robinson; No. 1 overall pick to Cleveland for Roy Hinson (June 16, 1986): This is the day the music died. The Sixers had been an upper-echelon club since Julius Erving arrived a decade earlier. They have seldom been close to that level since.

2. Wilt Chamberlain to the Lakers for Jerry Chambers, Darrall Imhoff, and Archie Clark (July 9, 1968): True, Wilt wanted out and wanted to go to the West Coast. But this was the best offer the Sixers could get?

3. Charles Barkley to Phoenix for Jeff Hornacek, Tim Perry, and Andrew Lang (June 17, 1992): Another case of a superstar muscling his way out of town, and his team getting pennies on the dollar.

4. Andre Iguodala, Nikola Vucevic, and Moe Harkless, dealt in a four-team trade that netted center Andrew Bynum (August 10, 2012): The Sixers took a chance on the injury-riddled seven-footer; Bynum never played a single game with the team.

5. Chet Walker to Chicago for Jim Washington (September 2, 1969): Walker played in four All-Star Games in six seasons with the Bulls, and was later elected to the Hall of Fame. Washington lasted two-plus seasons with the Sixers, the third of five teams to employ him.